Understanding Hinduism

Teaching Religions and Worldviews

Series Editor: James D. Holt
This series explores the beliefs and practices of the different religions and worldviews alongside pedagogically supported approaches of how knowledge of each religion or worldview could be taught within the primary and secondary classroom, and to enhance teaching of those students in the classroom who practice that particular religion or worldview.

Books in the series explore the beliefs and practices of each religion or worldview as a lived experience in the UK. Aspects of each religion or worldview are explored including the concepts that form the central beliefs, and then the expression of these beliefs in worship, daily life, and the ethics of believers in the modern day. Each chapter will utilise the authentic voice of those who identify with the religion or worldview today through the use of vignettes and provide reflective tasks for the reader to consider the concepts and how they can be taught in the classroom.

Also available in the series:
Understanding Sikhism, James D. Holt
Understanding Buddhism, James D. Holt

Understanding Hinduism

A Guide for Teachers

James D. Holt

BLOOMSBURY ACADEMIC
LONDON • NEW YORK • OXFORD • NEW DELHI • SYDNEY

BLOOMSBURY ACADEMIC
Bloomsbury Publishing Plc
50 Bedford Square, London, WC1B 3DP, UK
1385 Broadway, New York, NY 10018, USA
29 Earlsfort Terrace, Dublin 2, Ireland

BLOOMSBURY, BLOOMSBURY ACADEMIC and the Diana logo
are trademarks of Bloomsbury Publishing Plc

First published in Great Britain 2024

Copyright © James D. Holt, 2024

James D. Holt has asserted his right under the Copyright, Designs and
Patents Act, 1988, to be identified as Author of this work.

For legal purposes the Acknowledgements on p. xvi constitute an extension of this copyright page.

Series design by Charlotte James
Cover image © anand purohit / Getty Images

All rights reserved. No part of this publication may be reproduced or transmitted in any form or by any means, electronic or mechanical, including photocopying, recording, or any information storage or retrieval system, without prior permission in writing from the publishers.

Bloomsbury Publishing Plc does not have any control over, or responsibility for, any third-party websites referred to or in this book. All internet addresses given in this book were correct at the time of going to press. The author and publisher regret any inconvenience caused if addresses have changed or sites have ceased to exist, but can accept no responsibility for any such changes.

A catalogue record for this book is available from the British Library.

A catalog record for this book is available from the Library of Congress.

ISBN: HB: 978-1-3504-0702-2
PB: 978-1-3504-0701-5
ePDF: 978-1-3504-0703-9
eBook: 978-1-3504-0704-6

Series: Teaching Religions and Worldviews

Typeset by Deanta Global Publishing Services, Chennai, India
Printed and bound in Great Britain

To find out more about our authors and books visit www.bloomsbury.com and sign up for our newsletters.

Dedication

For Jayshree

The genuine friend, who is affected with the joys and sorrows of another, is a medicinal cordial, the sanctuary of the heart, the delight of the eyes, and worthy of confidence.

Contents

List of Figures	ix
List of Tables	x
Series Editor's Foreword	xi
Acknowledgements	xvi
Note on Texts and Translation	xvii

Introduction   1

Part 1 Key Concepts in Hinduism

1 **Dharma**   31

2 **The Nature of the Divine**   46

3 **Hindu Cosmology**   93

4 **The Nature of Humanity**   104

5 **Sacred Writings**   117

6 **Expressions of Belief**   131

Part 2 Contemporary Issues

7 **The Ethical Dimension**   153

8	**Authority and Diversity in Hinduism**	169
9	**Hinduism and Contemporary Britain**	180
	Glossary	197
	Reference List	202
	Index	213

Figures

0.1	Sriyantra by printcolouring	22
2.1	AUM the unicode consortium	49
2.2	Brahma	59
2.3	Vishnu and his avatars	64
2.4	Shiva Yogiraj	69
2.5	Lakshmi by Raja Ravi Varma	75
2.6	Rama and Sita in Hanuman's heart	79
2.7	Ganesh murti	85
5.1	Ramayana fortune line	130
9.1	BAPS Swaminarayan Mandir in Ashton-u-Lyne	185
9.2	Gita Bhavan Hindu Mandir, Withington	185
9.3	BAPS Swaminarayan Mandir, Neasden	186

Tables

2.1	Sample Top Trumps Card	87
3.1	Avatars of Vishnu and Their Relation to Evolution	96
3.2	The Approximate Dates of the Current Yuga Cycle	99
3.3	Evidence of the Kali Yuga Today	103
5.1	Hindu Scriptures (see Prinja, 2003, 129–130)	118
5.2	The Composition of Each of the Four Vedas	120
6.1	A List of Twenty-Two Festivals	144
9.1	Schedule of School Visit (Shri Swaminarayan Mandir London, 2023)	187

Series Editor's Foreword

The teaching of religion in schools has an interesting history in the UK. It has been through various iterations and paradigm shifts. There is a suggestion, and quite a loud one, at the moment that we are in the midst of a change of paradigm as it moves from a world religions approach to one that is focused on religion and worldviews. Much is made of this shift, suggesting that it is a seismic landscape-altering approach within the classroom. Against this background, it may seem odd to write a series of books that focuses on subject knowledge for teachers of what can be seen as reified religious structures that could be seen as artificial creations.

Although the nomenclature used in the systematization of religions has changed to include worldviews, I am not convinced that the change is as seismic as has been suggested. The religion and worldviews approach to the teaching of religion and beliefs in schools is, in some ways, a rebranding rather than anything substantive. Effective teaching of religion and belief in schools has, in the recent past, always taken account of worldviews, maybe without recognizing that this is what has been happening. The 'change' to religion and worldviews will still rely on essential aspects of religions/structural worldviews and it is for this reason that this series of books is being written. What is meant by the 'essential' aspects? That will differ between religions and worldviews; it is at this point that a discussion of the positive contributions of a religion and worldviews approach will help frame the writing of this, and subsequent, books.

There are many ways to discuss what is entailed in a religion and worldviews approach to the teaching of religion and belief in schools and other settings. I often speak about the 'messiness' of religion and worldviews, and this messiness has to do with the two terms: religions and worldviews.

In exploring the term religion, it becomes evident very quickly that the neat structures that we have in our minds, or that are taught in the classroom, are not reflective of the reality that we find in the world today. The various elements that we use in comparative religion enable us to line religions up next to each other and compare various elements, but in some ways, in trying to get them to conform to a particular structure of religion, we have tried to fit square pegs into round holes. Jonathan Z. Smith noted this:

> 'Religion' is not a native category. It is not a first person term of self-characterization. It is a category imposed from the outside on some aspect of native culture. It is the other, in these instances colonialists, who are solely responsible for the content of the term. (2004, 179–180)

In having religions fit an artificially constructed paradigm, it is possible to see that both the constituent parts and the whole have been made less, and their vibrancy and meaning have been lost. One such example is in the development of the idea of what Buddhism is in relation to Christianity or, at least, to the religious structure of Christianity. This has meant that the person of the Buddha, Siddhartha Gautama, has developed as the central focus of Buddhism in the West, and certainly the Buddhism that is taught in classrooms. Authors such as Tomoko Masuzawa (2005) highlight that original Buddhism was mined and reified in the nineteenth century with reference to texts in India, with little reference to the lived reality of different Buddhisms in other countries. As a result, Donald Lopez (1995) suggests that Buddhism is a 'hypostatised object . . . created by Europe, [which, in turn] could also be controlled by it, and it was against this Buddhism that all the Buddhisms of the modern Orient were to be judged' (7). Further exploration of this can be found below; but it remains true to say that the Enlightenment understanding of religion was reinforced as colonial powers sought to make sense of the beliefs and practices that they found among the peoples of the Empire.

In establishing religion as an observable and static phenomenon, the religions themselves began to reflect the structures and emphases of those who studied and wrote about them. While it is possible to see a continued diversity of expression and understanding, certain principles began to be perceived as normative, and as such an orthodoxy (even if only from the outsider's perspective) began to develop and deviance from the constructed norms began to be seen as peripheral, whereas in the past it was part of a vast panoply of loosely related beliefs and practices. This normalization continues today; in 2021, it was argued, by Kalpana Jain, that Indian Prime Minister Modi was attempting to normalize a particular understanding of the Ramayana, and by association, the celebration of Diwali. Establishing a Hindu canon or orthodoxy could be seen as unifying; yet at the same time eroding the diversity and vibrancy of the Hindu community.

It is this approach that, it is argued, developed a post-Enlightenment view of religion and religions. The history of Sikhism, for example, can also be seen to be a reflection of this process where boundaries were established and norms enforced. The typology of religions, in the Western mind, prior to the nineteenth century tended to reflect a fourfold model: that of Christian, Jewish, Muslim, and Heathen/Pagan. Christianity was the 'norm' while Judaism and Islam were seen to be related (but ultimately wrong), and everything else was put into the equivalent of the 'other' category. During the nineteenth century, religious classifications began to develop further with the first recorded use of terminology such as Buddhism (Boudhism) in 1801, Hinduism (Hindooism) in 1829, Taoism (Taouism) in 1839, Zoroastrianism in 1854 and Confucianism in 1862 (see Josephson, 2012). The nuance of difference within and between religions was not explored in great depth, as is illustrated in the classification of Sikhs as Hindus in the earliest Indian colonial censuses. Up until this point in Sikh history, the self-identification and practice undertaken by Sikhs as followers of the gurus were seen to be fairly diverse, but also not a matter that needed to be delineated. There was evidence of practices more associated with Hinduism being followed by Sikhs alongside what could be seen to be more Sikhlike elements. It was in the classification of such that provided the impetus for some Sikhs to begin to establish an orthodoxy that separated the Panth from Hinduism. The publication of *Ham Hindu Nahin (We are not Hindus)* in 1899 is evidence of Sikhs feeling the need to establish boundaries where previously they were not perceived to be important (greater exploration of this Sikh 'orthodoxy' is explored in the Sikh volume of this series).

To some extent, the development of a focus on worldviews within the classroom can be seen as an effort to counter the colonialization of religions, and return the understanding of them to a richer and more diverse expression that allows for individual expressions of religion. In exploring worldviews, the Commission on Religious Education has suggested what they mean:

> The English word 'worldview' is a translation of the German *weltanschauung*, which literally means a view of the world. A worldview is a person's way of understanding, experiencing and responding to the world. It can be described as a philosophy of life or an approach to life. This includes how a person understands the nature of reality and their own place in the world. A person's worldview is likely to influence and be influenced by their beliefs, values, behaviours, experiences, identities and commitments.
> (Commission on RE, 2018, 4)

The Theos Think Tank (2021) video *No one stands nowhere* suggests that a worldview is a complex amalgam of various influences that is constantly shifting and developing. This means that there are personal and institutional worldviews; and that in these institutional worldviews, there is a wide variety of experiences and interpretations. This can be seen to build on the world of writers such as Kimberlé Crenshaw (1989) and bell hooks, who have explored aspects of intersectionality. Crenshaw explored what it was to be a black woman, and how race and gender intersect. This develops into a discussion of worldviews and how they are held by individuals; Trevor Cooling suggests that people 'inhabit' their worldview (Cooling et al., 2020, 29).

This is an important development in the study of religion, but, as suggested earlier, it is not new. People like Robert Jackson (1997) have long suggested listening to the insider or individual voice as a way to understand the complexity of religion. This ethnographic approach recognizes the rich diversity of lived religion. In the wider academic field of Religious Studies, writers such as McGuire (2008) and Ammerman (2021) have similarly advocated for a focus on the lived experience of religion in the lives of individuals. If this is what is meant by 'worldviews' then it could be argued that teaching about religion in schools has been doing this. The focus on worldviews as a concept is a timely reminder that the religions that we explore are not neatly packaged, but they are messy and a result of the confluence of influences and identities in a person's life.

In trying to understand, I imagine a prism, similar to that found on the cover of Pink Floyd's *Dark Side of the Moon* album. The prism is the receptacle where our backgrounds, cultures, experiences coalesce to help make sense of life and the expressions and interpretations of new experiences, and the development of values and the like form. These form a different spectrum of colours for each individual. This intersectionality recognizes and emphasizes that no two people are alike. Simply speaking, in the context of this book, a Hindu brother and sister in the UK would have different perceptions of Hinduism despite similar upbringings because of their gender as well as other experiences that may have coloured their view.

This approach could be seen to problematize the very concept of religion and worldviews to such an extent that religion could be seen to lose all meaning. It reduces religion to an individual expression of an individual belief system.

The argument and purpose of this series of books is to recognize the messiness, intersectionality and worldviews approach to religions, but in a way that does not dismiss everything that is useful about a world religions paradigm. It will recognize the diversity within each tradition, but will also use what can be commonly termed the 'essential' aspects of a religion or worldview that enables diversity to be recognized. The essential aspects need to frame the discussions that are taking place. Ben Wood (2020) argues:

> Some argue that 'essentialism' narrows and limits understanding and fails to provide a realistic picture of the world and religion and belief. Others, myself included, accept this to a point, arguing that 'essentialism' may be limited, but it is a necessary part of the process of learning about religions in a progressive manner, in that what is learnt in this phase is essential for progress to more sophisticated learning. (Wood, 2020, 14)

The Commission on RE (2018) suggests that:

> We need to move beyond an essentialised presentation of six 'major world faiths' and towards a deeper understanding of the complex, diverse and plural nature of worldviews at both institutional and personal levels. (Commission on RE, 2018, 6)

Although it may be not what they intended, I would suggest that 'moving beyond' essentialism does not mean that we need to dismiss the existence of the central elements of a religion or institutionalized worldview; rather, that we should utilize aspects that are helpful to frame our study. Moving beyond is studying religion in a framework of intersectionality or worldviews that recognize the problems inherent in the world religions paradigm. This means that adopting a categorization of all religions as having set commonalities is out of date and does not reflect the lived reality of many people in the world. Any study of religion in schools must begin with a recognition of the diversity that is found within the world.

I argue elsewhere (Holt, 2022) that this diversity is appropriate at every level of the school experience. At the very youngest of ages, it is possible to use language such as 'many', 'most' and 'some' when speaking of religious belief and practice. As pupils get older, it is possible to introduce the nuances and specifics of diversity. It also serves the purpose of exercising a humility of knowledge when we teach; in the intersectional world of religions, it is impossible to know everything about the beliefs and practices of all aspects of a religion; using qualifiers ensures that we are not unconsciously establishing boundaries and norms in religions that do not exist.

One of the consequences of exploring religion and worldviews as a paradigm is the inclusion of systems of belief that are not seen to be religious. For many years, groups such as Humanists UK have argued for recognition and inclusion of non-religious worldviews within the classroom. Many schools, syllabi and specifications now include non-religious worldviews; the worldviews approach can be seen to have expanded what might be explored in the curriculum. In recognizing that the 'big six' have traditionally been prioritized, it is possible that this shift in paradigm will expand what traditions and worldviews should be studied. I have explored the arguments for the inclusion of religions 'beyond the big six', and also the inclusion of expressions of the big six beyond the mainstream, and that we should expand what we understand and teach (Holt, 2019). It is against this background that this series of books works; while recognizing what can be perceived as the 'normative', it will also recognize and explore aspects of diversity within the religious tradition.

It is at this point I feel it is important for me to recognize my own positionality with respect to the religions and worldviews that will be covered in this series. For most of the religions, I will be coming from the perspective of an outsider. I recognize both the benefits and hindrances this may bring. I cannot fully understand what it is like to live as a Sikh or as a Buddhist. The spirituality of Islam or Hinduism is not something that I have experienced as a believer. This does not mean, however, that I am unsympathetic. When I present the beliefs and practices of the individual religions, I will do so, as best I can, in a way that would be understood by believers. I understand and appreciate the impact that religions and worldviews can have on the lives of individuals and communities. As an outsider, I am also able to recognize debates within the community that may be given short shrift by an insider.

As a teacher, lecturer and professor of religious education over many years, I am also able to understand the nuances of what is needed to teach religion and worldviews in the classroom. I will not be able to cover everything, and the selection of material may leave out things that some people think are important. That is the beauty of intersectionality and worldviews; there are a myriad of ways that religion can be understood and presented. It is my hope that this series of books will provide a basis on which to build in the future. I would encourage you to discuss the contents of this book with fellow professionals, your students, but perhaps most importantly with followers of the religions and worldviews explored. The authentic voice is central to understanding the beliefs and impact of religion. This book should provide you with a good knowledge on which to develop your teaching and those conversations.

Acknowledgements

There are many people who contribute to the writing of a book. At many different points throughout my life, there are people I have met, worked with and become friends with, who have contributed to my understanding of religion and especially, in terms of this book, of Hinduism.

There are many members of the Hindu community who have helped with answering of questions over the years that have assisted in my understanding that enabled this book to be written. I will not be able to name them all, but Jayshree Patel, Chandrika Devarakonda, Lovely Dey and Veronica Voiels have been particularly helpful. Nitya Kaza was incredibly helpful in completing interviews within the Hindu community, and this book is all the better because of her involvement. I take complete responsibility for anything that might not quite be understood within the Hindu community.

Within my teaching community so many people challenge me, and inspire me to be better and understand more. John Rudge, Lesley Wakefield, James Dunne, Diane Kolka and Christine Paul have particularly been helpful in my understanding of Hinduism. Special thanks are also due to colleagues and students at the University of Chester.

The biggest thanks of all are reserved for my wife Ruth, and our children, Eleanor, Abi, Ethan, Gideon and Martha, who know that sometimes I disappear and hibernate for a while as I write. I am so grateful for their love and support.

As with everything I do, all credit goes to God. I am nothing without the influence of God in my life.

Note on Texts and Translation

There are different translations available of some of the texts used throughout this book. Although they are in the public domain, I am grateful to sacred-texts.com for their efforts in making these works available for free and for allowing me to quote freely from them. Where certain texts were not available on sacred-texts, wisdomlib.org was used unless otherwise stated. For the *Bhagavad Gita*, the text available on holy-bhagavad-gita.org was used. Again, I am grateful for the availability of these texts in English.

In transliterating from Sanskrit, there are often different spellings in English. The words have been chosen based on their being one of the most frequent ways of spelling. Many Sanskrit words have been italicized the first time they are used, and for many of these, the meaning will be found alongside usage and in the Glossary. It should also be noted that in translating the words into English, some of the meaning may be lost. There is a tendency to try and translate one word into another, and this does not always get the meaning across. I have tried, as far as possible, to recognize the incompleteness of these translations. Diacritic marks have not been used.

Introduction

What is Hinduism? Who is a Hindu? These are questions that are important in writing a book about Hinduism, but they are also important for teachers and individuals. It has been suggested that there is no such thing as Hinduism, only Hindus. There are questions about whether the term 'Hinduism' should be used in a classroom, or society, that is seeking to be decolonized. Suggestions for its replacement include *Sanatana Dharma* or *Hindu Dharma*. In this chapter, we will explore the history of what today is termed Hinduism, and also the nomenclature to provide a greater understanding of the religion that we are teaching and studying.

When beginning to try and define Hinduism, and to explain who a Hindu is, a teacher is faced with a different background and explanation than with any of the larger religious traditions taught in the classroom. With Buddhism, Christianity, Islam, Judaism and Sikhism, it is possible to recognize the diversity within the tradition, and then trace a linear development of the religion found in the modern world to a shared point in history. It is impossible to do this with Hinduism because it is so multi-faceted, and the 'development' of Hinduism as a single tradition does not exist. The teacher of students of any age may begin their discussion of Hinduism with the recognition that what we call Hinduism today is a colonial construct that brought together a disparate range of traditions under one umbrella. Romila Thapar has suggested that:

> What has survived over the centuries is not a single monolithic religion but a diversity of religious sects which we today have put together under a uniform name. The collation of these religious groups is defined as Hinduism even though the religious reference points of such groups might be quite distinct. 'Hinduism' became a convenient general label for studying the different indigenous religious expressions. This was when it was claimed that anything from atheism to animism could legitimately be regarded as part of 'Hinduism'. (2005, 56)

This diversity is important in studying any religion but is especially so when exploring what is termed Hinduism. Although it has a long history, potentially the longest history of the extant world religions today, it was not until India's encounter with colonialism that it began to be defined as a singular belief system. In the Series Foreword to this book, it was noted that the 'first' use of the word Hinduism was in 1829, this is not uncontested. Brian Pennington (2005) suggests that it was first used 'by Hindu reformer Rammohan

Roy' in 1816 (60). Reviewing Pennington's work, Geoffrey Oddie (2007) moves the date earlier by suggesting that 'Charles Grant used the term "Hinduism" in correspondence as early as 1787' (864). In some ways, the exact dating is unimportant, except to emphasize that the 'construction' of Hinduism was a result of colonialism. It is largely accepted that the process of colonialization brought together a wide range of beliefs, stories and rituals into a systematized religion that was called Hinduism. This highlights that it was a conscious act from the outside as a way to structure Indian religion in a way that was intelligible to the British. Although it may not have been intended as an act of violence and may well have been seen as paternalism and civilization by those involved in the process, Chakravorty (2019) highlights the conscious effort it was:

> That indeed was the very purpose of the colonial project – to create uniformity, to reduce difference and de-emphasize variance. Contemporary observers like ourselves may be aghast at the sheer effrontery and audacity of the project, but we must not lose sight of the intent of the original project managers. Their imperative was to reduce the noise in the cacophonic social and religious reality of the subcontinent and extract from it a melody, a clear signal, that would make the place easier to govern. (94)

There are two problems that might arise in a student's mind in describing Hinduism as a colonial construct utilizing a term that was not used until the late eighteenth century at the earliest. The first is that nothing meaningful can be said about Hindu beliefs before its systematization, and that its beliefs are 'created' as a part of the defining and thus nothing identifiably Hindu can be seen to exist before that time. The second is that Hinduism explored today is completely coherent with that which was described in the colonial project, or that any elements that seek to systematize Hinduism have been rejected as colonial accretions over the years. Neither of these points is correct. In the next part of this chapter, we explore the term Hindu, and more specifically the roots of Hindu beliefs throughout history to the Indus Valley Civilization or the Harappan Civilization. The chapter then returns to an exploration of the term Hinduism, whether it is an accurate term and how elements of modern Hinduism may or may not have been influenced and reified by the inherited traditions of colonialism.

Hindu

Brian Pennington (2005) suggests problems with the claim of Hinduism merely being a colonial construct:

> The claim that Britain invented Hinduism grants altogether too much power to colonialism; it both mystifies and magnifies colonial means of domination and erases Hindu agency and creativity. Second, the assertion that Hinduism is a concept and reality foreign to India prior to the arrival of the British introduces an almost irreparable disruption in Indian traditions that can only alienate contemporary Indians from their own traditions.

> I regard the appropriation of the authority to pronounce some version of a tradition an impostor as an illegitimate intervention of academic historiography into the sphere of religion itself, a sphere over which practitioners alone should have custody. Many hundreds of millions of people today identify themselves as Hindu and resonate with the literary and ritual traditions that they associate with the idea of Hinduism. The claim that Hinduism is merely a modern invention is tantamount to a theological statement about the normative constitution of religious identity, hardly the appropriate or customary turf of the historian. (5)

There is much in Pennington's statement to agree with, but read from a certain point of view it might suggest a positive interplay between the colonizer and the colonized. This is not to suggest there was not an interplay, but the power dynamic at play cannot be ignored, and even if, as he later suggests, some Hindus were complicit in this construction, it does not make the process acceptable. Neither does the fact that there are centuries of history through which Hindu teaching and practice flourished. The need for systematization was a Western imperative, rather than one instigated by Indians themselves. It is possible for both to be true – that the process of systematization was an act imposed by the British, and that centuries of Hindu agency and creativity can find expression within the resultant belief system. It can also be true that this was an act of violence, and that it has been accepted and developed over the past three centuries.

It is patently obvious that Hindu beliefs were evident prior to the eighteenth century, similarly that there were people who were known as Hindus. A student of Sikhism would know that Guru Nanak's reported first words after his river experience are that 'God is neither Hindu nor Muslim', and as such there was the concept of being a 'Hindu' prior to the colonization of India by Great Britain, even though there are some who would suggest that 'the word "Hindu" did not exist in any language till its use by foreigners gave Indians a term for self-definition' (Tharoor, 2021, 4). It could be that Tharoor is recognizing its first use as a geographic designator by the Achaemenid Empire in the sixth century BCE (see below) but the suggestion is as a religious designator, which does not quite tell the whole story.

The history of the term 'Hindu' is linked throughout history as a designation for a people's geographical location. Referring to what today is called the River Indus in Western books, but is also known, and was throughout history as the 'sindhu' meaning 'river', a word used in the *Rig Veda* in approximately 1200 BCE, but whose etymology is unknown (see Witzel, 1999). Although the use of sindhu is evidently much older, as mentioned earlier the Achaemenid Empire certainly used 'hindu' as a geographical designator of people in the sixth century BCE as inscriptions have been found, but its oral use is most probably evident from about 1000 BCE. After the Achaemenid Empire, Audrey Truschke (2023) suggests that '"hindu" was adopted in other languages in Western Asia to describe parts of India geographically' (4). Wendy Doniger (2009) suggests that it was used by 'Herodotus (in the fifth century BCE), the Persians (in the fourth century BCE), and the Arabs (after the eighth century CE)' (30). It is possible that its use within the area it designated was not found, and a word unknown within India. However, an understanding of the geographical significance of its people could be suggested to be found in the *Laws of Manu* where dharma (see Chapter 2) seems to apply in this context:

> That (country) which (lies) between the Himavat and the Vindhya (mountains) to the east of Prayaga and to the west of Vinasana (the place where the river Sarasvati disappears) is called Madhyadesa (the central region). But (the tract) between those two mountains (just mentioned), which (extends) as far as the eastern and the western oceans, the wise call Aryavarta (the country of the Aryans). That land where the black antelope naturally roams, one must know to be fit for the performance of sacrifices; (the tract) different from that (is) the country of the Mlekkhas (barbarians). Let twice-born men seek to dwell in those (above-mentioned countries); but a Sudra, distressed for subsistence, may reside anywhere. Thus has the origin of the sacred law been succinctly described to you and the origin of this universe; learn (now) the duties of the castes (varna). (2:21–25)

Interestingly, the author also identifies 'Mleccha' or 'barbarian' as a designator for those outside of these areas. Just as those outside India are using the language of other in the word 'Hindu', those within India are also developing a terminology of 'them' and 'us'.

The term Hindu continues to be used geographically throughout the following centuries. However, there does begin to be a racial connotation to its use, and possibly a recognition of a difference of belief between Indian beliefs and practices and those from the outside. Indeed, de Bruijn (2012) notes that in poetry around the beginning of the second millennium, it was used to designate those people with a dark skin, in contrast to the Turks, who were of a lighter skin. There were also negative comparisons made with the 'positive' view of Turks.

It could also be argued that around this time, some observers began to draw the differences between Islam and the 'religion' found within India. Al-Biruni begins to draw a comparison between Muslim and Hindu (though the use of the word Hindu may be a later translation, and a more correct translation could be 'the people (al-hind)' Truschke, 2023, 4):

> For the reader must always bear in mind that the Hindus entirely differ from us in every respect, many a subject appearing intricate and obscure which would be perfectly clear if there were more connection between us. The barriers which separate Muslims and Hindus rest on different causes. (al-Biruni, 1910, 17)

That this includes religion is clear a few pages later:

> Secondly, they totally differ from us in religion, as we believe in nothing in which they believe, and vice versa. On the whole, there is very little disputing about theological topics among themselves; at the utmost, they fight with words, but they will never stake their soul or body or their property on religious controversy. On the contrary, all their

fanaticism is directed against those who do not belong to them – against all foreigners. They call them *mleccha*, i.e. impure, and forbid having any connection with them. (19)

This, however, did not become a widespread usage of the word Hindu. It is interesting to note that when Muslims encountered the peoples of India, it is evident that beliefs and practices differed significantly from their own. The geographic usage continued, but it can also be seen that its usage for what is termed 'religion' today may have become more common from those outside India, and also those within. Truschke (2023) notes:

> Between 1400 and 1600 CE, Indian authors invoked 'hindu' in certain contexts to denote a religious community in Sanskrit and vernacular languages. Such usages were few and far between. They did not supplant older senses of 'hindu' for people from a geographical region or, alternatively, a type of king. (8)

It would be easy to argue that the differences between 'Hindus' and Muslims indicate a recognition of two separate religions. It could be that Muslims are identified as a discrete religion, but in defining 'Hindu' it would seem much more likely to be identifying that which is not Muslim, i.e. the religions of the people that are identified as Hindu. However, the identification by 'Hindus' of others as mleccha indicates a shared religious belief between 'Hindus' (see below the discussion about Hinduism). Arguing against those that would suggest that there was no sense of 'Hindu' religious beliefs forming an identity prior to the nineteenth century, David Lorenzen (1999) argues that Sanskrit literature

> establishes a Hindu religious identity through a process of mutual self-definition with a contrasting Muslim Other. In practice, there can be no Hindu identity unless this is defined by contrast against such an Other. Without the Muslim (or some other non-Hindu), Hindus can only be Vaishnavas, Saivas, Smartas or the like. The presence of the Other is a necessary prerequisite for an active recognition of what the different Hindu sects and schools hold in common. (648)

Just as the concept of a geographic area became defined against the 'other' or in encounter with the 'other', so too, it would seem did the sense of religious identity that came to be known as Hindu. This is not to suggest that there was a homogenized belief system, this book will explore different aspects of Hindu belief and practice, it will be very evident that there are vast differences within Hindu communities and traditions. There are essential aspects that enable Hindus to self-identify and find themselves in a religious kinship with others. It is too simplistic to suggest that in Indian history, a Hindu is not a Muslim, but this gave a foil against which to judge. There is evidence within Jain literature of the delineation between Muslim and Hindu rulers; how the difference is drawn is unclear, it could be geographic, but it could also have religious connotations. This duality of geographic and religious difference is shown in the writings of Vidyapati:

> Hindus and Turks live together (hindu turuke milala vasa)
> One's dhamma funny to the other

> One calls the faithful to prayer. The other recites the Vedas
> One butchers animals saying bismillah. The other butchers animals in sacrifices.
> Some are called Ojhas, others Khojas
> Some read astrological signs, others fast in Ramadan.
> Some eat from copper plates, others from pottery.
> Some practice namaz, others do puja. (Truschke, 2023, 9)

The development from geography to religion is highlighted in the Eknath's sixteenth-century poem *Hindu-Turk Samvad* which begins:

> The goal is one; the ways of worship are different,
> Listen to the dialogue between these two!
> The Turk calls the Hindu 'Kafir!'
> The Hindu answers, 'I will be polluted – get away!'
> A quarrel broke out between the two;
> A great controversy began. (Zelliot, 2003, 64)

It would appear that the idea of 'Hindu' belief or practice is older than the British occupation. This does not mean that the belief systems were organized, but that there was an idea of a unifying belief. Truscke (2023) does suggest that in Eknath's poem, Hindu and Brahmin are used synonymously, and as such, the religion spoken of may be more clearly associated with one interpretation and one strata of society. In this way, the wider application of Hindu as a religious term used as broadly as it was a geographic term is not necessarily borne out. This development also runs parallel to the development of the concept of religion identified in the Series Editor's Foreword. To attach a religious system of organization, orthodoxy and orthopraxy would be anachronistic at this time. To recognize that there are identifiable differences by which people self-identified is important in exploring the appropriateness of designating something or someone as Hindu.

In the above-mentioned examples, and further examples up until the eighteenth century, while the term Hindu was used, it was done so irregularly; more so by observers but sometimes by people who would be identified as Hindu. In the late eighteenth century, the term Hindu (or Hindoo) began to be used by the British, both as a geographic and religious term (though at first it was very much a regional identifier). At this point in the history of 'Hindu', it became identified with the use of the systemic term 'Hinduism' to which we now turn.

Hinduism

As highlighted earlier, there is a debate about the use of the term 'Hinduism' in teaching about and describing the religion of Hindus. As can be seen from the title of this book, *Understanding Hinduism*, I will be using the term throughout. This does not mean that it is used uncritically, nor that it is universally accepted. Among Hindus themselves, there are different attitudes towards its use. Consider the following comments from different Hindus:

> Hinduism is a unifying and academic term to describe the major faith rooted in the Indian sub-continent.

> Hinduism implies it is a religion with compact belief system with one book, one prophet and Actually all three are ok but Hinduism is modern and recognized one God. Whereas Hindu Dharma is a confederation of religions practiced in India for millennia with diverse school of thoughts.

> The term 'Hindu' was given to us in recent centuries. Our philosophy of life is based on a set of moral and ethical values collectively known as dharma, and 'sanatana' means eternal. Dharma is the best term and it has always existed therefore it is sanatana. Hindu is what others call us and therefore not preferred.

This same level of diversity is exemplified in writings about Hinduism:

> There are clearly some kinds of practices, texts and beliefs which are central to the concept of being a 'Hindu', and there are others which are on the edges of Hinduism . . . 'Hinduism' is not a category in the classical sense of an essence defined by certain properties, there are nevertheless prototypical forms of Hindu practice and belief. The beliefs and practices of a high-caste devotee of the Hindu god Vishnu, living in Tamilnadu in south India, fall clearly within the category 'Hindu' and are prototypical of that category. The beliefs and practices of a Radhasaomi devotee in the Punjab, who worships a God without attributes, who does not accept the Veda as revelation and even rejects many Hindu teachings, are not prototypically Hindu, yet are still within the sphere, and category, of Hinduism. The south Indian devotee of Vishnu is a more typical member of the category 'Hindu' than the Radhasoami devotee. (Flood, 1996, 7)

In discussing the use and development of the term and categorization of 'Hinduism', the colonial background is evident. However, to suggest that it was purely a British attempt to define the religions of India is to miss the complex interplay of the colonizer and the colonized. Robert Frykenberg (2005) has suggested:

> For purposes of this analysis, therefore, 'modern Hinduism' is seen as that form of corporate and organized and 'syndicated' religion which arose in south India and by which highly placed and influential groups of Brahmans, supported by Brahmanized Non Brahmans, did most of the defining, the manipulating, and the organizing of the essential elements of what gradually became, for practical purposes, a dynamic new religion. Moreover, this process of reification, this defining and organizing of elements which they did, occurred with the collaboration, whether witting or unwitting, with those who governed the land . . . In course of time, these very ingredients of the state rulership, both European and Native, served to bring modern Hinduism into being. (89)

This is not to lay 'blame' but to highlight that while the British established the need to define and structure, it was not only the British that brought Hinduism into existence. It is also possible when studying Hinduism to look at the various forces at play, and that an effort to try and separate modern from premodern aspects is fraught with danger and bias. Without negating the need to explore the various aspects of history which are so significant in Hinduism, it is also important to recognize the Hinduism of today.

Having explored the colonial history of the term Hinduism, it is then possible to look at its use today. As Ludwig Wittgenstein argued: 'One cannot guess how a word functions. One has to look at its use and learn from that' (1968, 109); summarized as the advice: 'don't ask for meaning ask for use', although it is doubtful that Wittgenstein ever used that phrase (Hallett, 1967). The use of Hinduism is now accepted in the lexicon of religion, and its overwhelming use is descriptive rather than pejorative. Is the way that the term is used today enough to overlook its invention? The question of whether there is such a thing as Hinduism seems to have been answered in its development over the past three centuries. Chakravorty (2019) suggests that while at its inception the term held little meaning beyond that which was being suggested by the British; today its meaning is much clearer:

> Similarly, whether Hinduism was 'invented' or not, whether it was a convenient category (or container) created to hold a very diverse population with a great variety of self-identities, it is a social reality now. Hinduism may not have existed in 1800, but it does now, and because of that, it is possible to call oneself Hindu. (81)

It has become a term of self-identification, as well as a helpful shorthand that most people would be able to identify. Wendy Doniger (1991) argues that 'Naming is always a matter of the convenience of the namers, and all categories are constructed' (36).

However, there are many who would suggest that its initial use as an expression of power means that it can never be decoupled from its colonial background. The power of a name is explored by different writers. Salman Rushdie (1991), not writing about Hinduism, suggests:

> To give a thing a name, a label, a handle; to rescue it from anonymity . . . in short to identify it – well, that's a way of bringing the said thing into being. (63)

This does seem to reflect precisely the history and use of the term Hinduism, and the idea expressed by Chakravorty (2019) that in 1800 there was no such thing, but today it is immediately identifiable. In continuing its use, are we guilty of perpetuating a colonial power dynamic, or even accepting as structured or reified something that was never meant to be such? Romila Thapar (2005) describes this process of systematization over the centuries as 'Syndicated Hinduism' and the resultant object to be less diverse and more concrete than its predecessor prior to its naming ever was.

> Today the Hindus of the Parishads and the Sanghs Hinduism, would look upon atheists and animists with suspicion and contempt, for the term Hinduism is being used in a different sense. Hinduism as defined in contemporary parlance is a bringing together of beliefs, rites and practices consciously selected from those of the past, interpreted in a contemporary idiom in the last couple of centuries and the selection conditioned by historical circumstances. This is not to suggest that religions with a linear growth are superior to what may apparently be an ahistorical religion or one with multiple historical roots, but rather to emphasise the difference between the two. (56)

This links with the point made within the Series Editor's Foreword where Prime Minister Modi was seen to be establishing a norm for the celebration of Diwali. In its encounter with the world's religions and the modern world, it could be argued that there is less room for diversity within today's Hinduism. That is not to say there is no diversity, only that boundaries are being set where perhaps there were none before.

The beliefs that are seen to be a part of Hinduism today have a much longer history than the eighteenth century. Just as the term 'Hindu' has its roots hundreds, if not thousands, of years ago, so too do many of the beliefs that might be seen to be within, or the precursor to, modern Hinduism. Axel Michaels (2004) outlines six epochs through which 'Hinduism' developed. These will provide a useful framework within which to identify the different influences and beliefs that can be found within Hinduism today.

First epoch: Pre-Vedic period (up to 1750 BCE)

In this period there is what is known as the Indus Valley or Harappan Civilization. There is evidence that 'Much of what we now call Hinduism may have had roots in cultures that thrived in South Asia long before the creation of textual evidence that we can decipher with any confidence' (Doniger, 2009, 66). The Harappan or Indus Valley Civilization was large, covering a land mass of 750,000 square miles, with up to 40,000 inhabitants. There is evidence of an advanced culture; Kim Knott (2016) suggests that:

> The archaeological evidence suggests that the religion of these cities involved temple rites, fertility rituals, the use of animals, perhaps for sacrifice, and ritual bathing in a large pool constructed of stone. Tiles or seals have been found depicting an early undeciphered script and religious symbols that raise various questions. (5)

Aspects of this civilization and its interpretation have led many to suggest a religion that has imagery and beliefs that point forward to Hinduism as it is known today. For example, there are many female figures that may be evidence of the worship of the Divine feminine, and there are images such as that of a horned deity that may be an early portrayal of Shiva, along with a phallic symbol which may be emblematic of the later linga. Doniger (2009) sounds a note of caution:

There is, in fact, a general resemblance between this image and later Hindu images of Shiva. The Indus people may well have created a symbolism of the divine phallus, or a horned god, or both. But even if this is so, it does not mean that the Indus images are the source of the Hindu images. We must keep this caution in mind now when we consider the images of women in the IVC. (76)

Although there is no direct physical link between the 'religion' of the Harappans and Hinduism, it does appear that for Hindus themselves, there is this link, and it is evidence of a longevity of beliefs and rituals. This is an important step for Hindus in understanding themselves and the civilizations that developed or served as a precursor to Vedic religion or Hinduism today.

This end of this period of Indian history, and the movement into the Second Epoch, has been the subject of much misinformation that still persists in teaching today (see Insight UK, 2021) in the sense that there was an 'Aryan invasion' beginning in 2000 BCE and being responsible for the collapse of the Indus Valley Culture. This idea, which suggested that an advanced 'Aryan' race invaded primitive northern India and established civilization, and supplanted its 'culture', is patently false based on the archaeological evidence of the Indus Valley Culture. Witzel (2005) has suggested that it served the British purposes for a time to support this version of history:

> The theory of an immigration of [Indigenous Aryans] speaking Arya ('Aryan invasion') is simply seen as a means of British policy to justify their own intrusion into India and their subsequent colonial rule: in both cases, a 'white race' was seen as subduing the local darker coloured population. (348)

In reality, it was a migration over a period of years that led to an Aryan presence within India, which led in turn to the development of Sanskrit, which has links to Indo-Aryan and Indo-European languages; there appears to be a common root. There are various arguments made that disprove the replacement of Indus Valley Civilization by Aryans:

> (a) None or hardly any specific settlements of the Aryas can be proved; (b) skeletal remains indicate no phenotypically distinct features of Aryas as opposed to so-called non-Aryas, thus indicating that Arya is not a biological or racial demarcation . . . (c) the language of the Indus Valley seal was already Indo-European; (d) the painted grey ceramic and iron can be proved already in the first epoch. (Michaels, 2004, 33)

This leads Michaels (2004) to suggest 'processes of acculturation' (33). The problem also seems to be accentuated by nineteenth- and twentieth-century views of Aryan as a superior race, suggesting India as inferior. This should not be taught in classrooms, and the advanced nature of the Indus Valley Culture can provide a useful background.

Second epoch: Vedic period (1750–500 BCE)

It is recognized that the Indus Valley Culture ended, and from 1750 BCE there was a development of a new culture that became known as the Vedic period, named for the texts that were developed and written during this time. There is a question about the continuity between the Indus Valley Culture and that found during the Vedic period. Some suggest that there is no continuity (see Michaels, 2004) while Doniger (2009) recognizes discontinuities in systems of administration and building she also recognizes that:

> someone succeeded in preserving on the journey south and east some of the cultural patterns nurtured in the Indus cities, for some of these patterns lived on long after the cities themselves were gone. The Indus civilization may not have simply gone out like the flame of a candle or, at least, not before lighting another candle. (83)

These would include elements of imagery that can trace an element of continuity in belief from a Hindu perspective. It is important to note that the Hindu beliefs expressed today, while believed by Hindus to be contiguous, are not carbon copies of what has been believed throughout history.

The Vedic period is so named because it is believed that the Vedas (see Chapter 5) were composed, passed along and written down during this period. It is possible to note a shifting in the approach to beliefs, in the sense that culture moves from an oral and symbolic tradition to one that began to be written down. Witzel (1999) suggests three different phases:

- Between 1700 and 1500 BCE, the Rig Veda began to be composed.
- Between 1500 and 1350 BCE, other sections and the Yajurveda were composed.
- Between 1350 and 1200 BCE, the later parts including some of the Upanishads were composed.

The dating is noted according to elements of culture that were mentioned, or not. For example, in the first part of the Vedic period, the Rig Veda did not mention things like bricks or cities; contrary to the Indus Valley Culture, there is little evidence of the civilization in which the Vedas were composed.

The deities of the Vedas, such as Indra, Agni, Usha and Surya, are usually associated with the weather. The content of the Vedas will be explored in Chapter 5, but at this point, it is important to note that they established aspects of the cosmology and cosmogony (see Chapter 3) of Hinduism and established some of the ritual practices, focusing on the roles of Brahmins.

In a similar way to the first epoch, this period of time is seen by many Hindus as being contiguous with many beliefs and practices today. It is important to note that this is only one interpretation, and there need to be readings of the Vedas that reimagine or rename some of the deities, beliefs and practices including animal sacrifice that would seem anathema today. Indeed, Doniger (2009) outlines:

> The great gods of later Hinduism, Vishnu and Shiva (in the form of Rudra), make only cameo appearances in the Veda. By contrast, the most important gods of the Veda, such as Agni, Soma, Indra, and Varuna, all closely tied to the Vedic sacrifice, become

far less important in later Hinduism, though they survive as symbolic figures of natural forces: fire, the moon, rain, and the waters, respectively. (129)

It is also possible that the earliest versions of the Ramayana and Mahabharata began to be composed (though elements of both are suggested to be as late as 300 CE).

Third epoch: Ascetic reform period (500–200 BCE)

While Brahminism and elements of Vedic religion continued into the third epoch, there also began to be so-called 'ascetic reform' movements. The two most well-known today surround the lives of Mahavira and Siddhartha Gautama in what came to be known as Jainism and Buddhism, respectively. Both became known as *nastika*, rejecting the authority of the Vedas and the existence of Brahman or its equivalent (see Chapter 2). It was about this time that elements of the Upanishads continued to be developed, and an ascetic tradition similarly developed. In the sense that

> the Upanishads did not replace but merely supplemented the earlier religion . . . so Vedic Hinduism (sacrificial, worldly) continued to exist alongside Vedantic Hinduism (philosophical, renunciant). The tension between householders and renouncers begins here and exerts an enormous influence over the subsequent history of the Hindus . . . Certain words from earlier periods – karma, tapas – took on new meanings at this point, though their original meanings never disappeared, resulting in a layering that served as one of the major sources of multiplicity within Hinduism. (Doniger, 2009, 167–168)

This period also becomes important later as defining Hinduism is easier as it has things that it is not.

Fourth epoch: Classical Hinduism (200 BCE–1100 CE)

Michaels (2004) suggests that at this stage of the development of Hindu ideas 'many elements of the Vedic religion were lost' (38). In this period, there appears to be an approach or development of Hinduism that could be termed a 'restoration' where 'Brahmans, as high priests or advisors, were increasingly summoned to courts that sought to preserve or revive the Vedic religion' (Michaels, 2004, 39). Hiltebeitel (2002) suggests that this time might be known as 'A period of consolidation, sometimes identified as one of "Hindu synthesis," "Brahmanic synthesis," or "orthodox synthesis,"' which 'takes place between the time of the late Vedic Upanisads (c. 500 BCE) and the period of Gupta imperial ascendancy (c. 320–467 CE)' (12). This synthesis was the fusion of Brahmanical ideas and Vedic rites with the developing ideas of bhakti, the writing of the Epics, and to some extent an interaction with Jainism and Buddhism. It is in this stage that 'classical Hinduism' and its many ideas and traditions begin to be developed in forms that would be recognizable today. The various darshanas (see below) are codified, and traditions such as Shaivism and Vaishnavism develop. The Vedas and their deities are drawn upon, as deities are identified with Shiva or Vishnu as the Absolute. The Hinduism of this time develops and consolidates ideas such as smrti and sruti texts (see Chapter 5), varnashramadharma (see Chapter 1), the Four Purusarthas (aims of life): artha, kama, dharma and moksha (see Chapters 1 and 4), and the darshanas (see below).

This is not to suggest that 'Hinduism' emerged fully unified and formed within this period. As is evident throughout this book, 'Hinduism' is a big tent where many different, often opposing views are accepted. There does, however, begin to be an awareness of a way of life that is distinct from others that surround it, and the 'Vedic-Brahminic Hindu religion is now concerned with itself' (Michaels, 2004, 42).

Fifth epoch: Sects of Hinduism (1100–1850)

It is argued that in its encounters with Islam, and the Muslim rulers of India, Hinduism began the process of developing into sects. Not that there was unity beforehand, but that the coalescence around individuals perhaps began during this period. There had been teachers such as Shankara before this point, but in the development of sects there seemed to be an 'implied allegiance to religious, charismatic or poet saints, without an organised following, as for example Tulsidas (about 1532–1623), Dadu (1544–1660), or Caitanya (1486–1533)' (Michaels, 2004, 44). The teachings of people such as Shankara were also highlighted and developed into 'sects' of Hinduism. This is an important development of Hinduism, just as in the use of the word 'Hindu', there was an 'other' against which to define and celebrate Hindu beliefs and history. Indeed, Andrew Nicholson (2014) suggests that solely identifying Hinduism as a colonial construct is 'a slap in the face' for Hindus, and ignores everything that came before, and further that:

> Between the twelfth and sixteenth centuries CE, certain thinkers began to treat as a single whole the diverse philosophical teachings of the Upanisads, epics, Puranas, and the schools known retrospectively as the 'six systems' (*saddarsana*) of mainstream Hindu philosophy. The Indian and European thinkers in the nineteenth century who developed the term 'Hinduism' under the pressure of the new explanatory category of 'world religions' were influenced by these earlier philosophers and doxographers, primarily Vedantins, who had their own reasons for arguing the unity of Indian philosophical traditions. Before the late medieval period, there was little or no systematic attempt by the thinkers we now describe as Hindu to put aside their differences in order to depict themselves as a single unified tradition. After this late medieval period, it became almost universally accepted that there was a fixed group of Indian philosophies in basic agreement with one another and standing together against Buddhism and Jainism. (2–3)

Sixth epoch: Modern Hinduism (from 1850)

This epoch is the development of Hinduism from a colonial perspective, in response to colonialism, and in the system of world religions. In some ways, this could be described as the clash between Hinduism and the West. Within this period, there have been, and continue to be, developments within Hinduism. Separate traditions such as Aryo-Samaj, ISKCON, Swaminarayan Hinduism and others develop, as well as efforts to develop a 'syndicated Hinduism', or approaches to Hinduism that take account of the modern world, its communications and also the recognition of cultural accretions that may need to be jettisoned. This modern 'Hinduism' is ancient, in the sense that it has developed and identified itself in relation to all of the past epochs, as well as the time within which it finds itself today.

The suggestion in outlining the recognition of what is termed Hinduism today throughout history is to recognize that Hinduism is far more than a colonial construct and builds on generations of understandings over thousands of years. It is also important to note that Hinduism did not arrive in the nineteenth century as a carbon copy of what had come before; there had been evolution, reformation, restoration and identification against the other.

Thoughts for the classroom

The use of the terms Hindu and Hinduism is not settled, and maybe the use of the term *sanatana dharma* (eternal dharma) would be more accurate. It has been suggested that the term Hindu dharma may be a useful compromise in recognizing the difficulty of a colonial inheritance, while using a term that was in evidence for centuries before and is recognizable today. When teaching within the classroom, it is important to recognize the contested nature of these terms. In teaching Hinduism as a religion, we are already utilizing a colonial inheritance that utilized a Western Christian lens. A religion that, as suggested, was not identified as a unified religion until the eighteenth or nineteenth century suggests that an act of colonial violence constructed Hinduism in a way that it began to be understood as a reified system. Beginning any study of Hinduism by problematizing it in this way is an important step. It will then allow terminology to be used in a critical way. We are perhaps at a stage where teachers need to use bridging terminology so that students can understand. I recognize this is slightly at odds with the discussion above that we should use the language that Hindus would use themselves, such as mandir instead of temple, dharma instead of duty and so on. One of the wrinkles in this discussion is the cementing of certain terminology within the Hindu community. For example, even though it is the goal of this book to use mandir instead of temple (for example), it will be noted that Hindu authors, Hindus and communities use that term themselves. This is just so with Hindu and Hinduism. It is an important step for teachers to recognize the background to the words Hindu and Hinduism and to use them in a way that recognizes their contemporary nature.

What is also essential when teaching about Hinduism and Hindus is that the diversity is highlighted. While recognizing an increasing syndication of Hinduism, to use Thapar's term, the diversity which was evident at the beginning of its defining should be recognized and a central part of any discussion of Hinduism.

Different traditions within Hinduism

It becomes important for those studying or writing about Hinduism, or even for Hindus themselves, to be precise when speaking of Hinduism. What specific aspect of Hinduism is being referred to? Thapar (2005) suggests that we might focus on groups such as

> Brahmanism, Bhakti, Tantrism, Brahmo-Samaj, Arya-Samaj, Shaiva-Siddhanta, or whatever. These are not comparable to the sects of Christianity or Islam as they do not relate to a single sacred text and its interpretation. Many are rooted in ritual practices and beliefs rather than in texts include and it has been argued that a characteristic difference relates to the orthopraxy of Hinduism rather than to an orthodoxy. (56)

The diversity is not necessarily the result of a linear development; rather, the diversity was already there, but there was an attempt to fit them into the same boxes that are now failing, not that they ever really succeeded.

Indeed, in terms of the census categorizations as well as a person's self-identification, there can be seen in the nineteenth century the development of boundaries of Hinduism. As noted in the Series Editor's Foreword, in the nineteenth century there was the conscious separation of Sikhs from Hinduism by Sikhs themselves, and also an attempt to define Sikhism in contrast to Hinduism (see Holt, 2023a). There are also suggestions of Jainism and Buddhism as nastika forms of Hinduism, but that they developed into such a distinct worldview that they could no longer be found within the bounds of Hinduism or even no longer desired to be within that family of belief systems.

Linked with the development of Hindu ideas explored earlier in this chapter, it is possible to suggest different expressions and traditions within Hinduism. The main delineations between Hindus that we see within the world today focus on Vaishnavism, Shaivism, Shaktism and Smartism. In 2013, Todd Johnson and Brian Grim outlined the numbers of Hindus throughout the world with some degree of diversity recognized, with Vaishnavism having 640,806,845 adherents (67 per cent of all Hindus), Shaivism having 252,200,000 adherents (26.6 per cent of all Hindus) and Shaktism having 30,000,000 (3.2 per cent of Hindus) (400–401). There will be a greater exploration of the different forms of Hinduism in later chapters (especially Chapters 9 and 10), but at this point, it will be useful to explore the basic differences between the movements. These movements are generally seen to have developed over the many centuries of Hindu history. There are newer expressions within each, but they generally find themselves within the larger tradition; one example of such is Swaminarayan Hinduism which arose in the early nineteenth century, which, while somewhat distinct, would find itself in the Vaishnavi tradition.

When exploring Vaishnavism and Shaivism, Heinrich von Stietengron (2005) has noted:

> A number of new religions gained prominence when *bhakti* became popular in the first centuries B.C. as a new emotional approach to salvation. Out of these, often in a process of incorporating related smaller cults into larger units, Vaishnavism and Saivism emerged in the long run as dominant religious forces. Like other bhakti religions they have a monotheistic doctrine in spite of the apparent plurality of existing gods. In each of these religions there is only one highest god, only one ultimate reality. Other gods or godlings belong to lower levels of existence, they often simply represent manifestations of different divine functions of the one deity, and they are dependent on god's will and subject to death and rebirth . . . [T]he Highest God (an all-pervading Visnu, an all-embracing Siva) is far beyond this functional *trimurti*. There are many divine functions with a name given to each, but in theology monotheism remains strictly preserved. Only in Saktism this monotheism is party replaced by a fundamental dualism. (43)

Vaishnavism

The nature and role of Vishnu, either as a manifestation of the Divine or as the Supreme Being, will be explored in Chapter 2. At this point, it is to be noted that those Hindus within Vaishnavism focus their worship and devotion on Vishnu and his various manifestations and teach that Vishnu is Supreme:

> Vaisnavism, like Saivism and Sakta religion, has appropriated for its philosophical basis the Vedanta materials, such as the *Brahmasutras* of Badarayana, and for its devotional basis the *Bhagavadgita*. Vaisnava teachers of all branches have extensively commented on these two most important texts. Together with other Upanisadic materials they provided the understanding of the nature of the ultimate reality which for the Vaisnava teachers is none other than the Visnu-Narayana. Thus the idea of Brahman which appears in the *Brahmasutras* and the Upanisadic texts as an abstract notion is personified in the form of Visnu. The abstract characteristics that are associated with the nature of Brahman, such as brhatva and brahmanatva (greatness), svarupa, nirvisesa, nirguna and saguna natures, are attributed to Visnu as Purusottama (Supreme Person) and the one who is the embodiment of infinite auspicious qualities and free from all imperfections. (Kumar, 2008, 920)

To suggest that it is one tradition would be incorrect; there are aspects of belief that are held in common, but there are many different approaches within Vaishnavism. Flood (1996) suggests that there are five groups or orders that are viewed as most important:

- *Sri Vaishnavas*. In this tradition, Sri refers to Lakshmi, Vishnu's consort. As such, the focus of this form of Vaishnavism is both Vishnu and Lakshmi. Flood (1996) suggests that the founder of Sri Vaishnavism is Nathamuni, a tenth-century acharaya. Based on the Vedas, the most well-known teacher of the tradition is Ramanuja (approximately 1017–1137). The most obvious distinction between Sri Vaishnavas and other Vaishnavas relies upon their interpretation of the Vedas and the Puranic texts. While the Vedas use the examples of deities such as Indra and Bhagra, these are to be interpreted as different names of Vishnu (who is also known as Narayana). Thus, the Vedas become solely focused on Vishnu.

Over time the group split into two, 'called the "northern culture" (*vatakalai*) and the "southern culture" (*tenkalai*). The *vatakalai* emphasised the Sanskrit scriptures and salvation through traditional *bhakti-yoga*, that is devotion to the temple icon, while *tenkalai* emphasized the Tamil scriptures and surrender to the Lord through his grace' (Flood, 1996, 137).

- *Gaudiya Vaishnavas*, also known as Chaitanya Vaishnavism, arose in the Gauda region of Bengal and has its roots in the teachings of Chaitanya Mahaprabhu. Chaitanya Mahaprabhu is believed to be an avatar of Krishna and Radha (Krishna's consort). It is within the Vedanta tradition, and bhakti yoga is a central aspect of its expression. Bhakti devotion to Krishna and Radha through the chanting of 'Hare Krishna' is particularly evident. The International Society for Krishna Consciousness (ISKCON) is possibly the largest expression of Gaudiya Vaishnavism today.
- *The cult of Vithoba*. Traditionally, followers of Vithoba are seen as a Vaishnava tradition because of their focus on Vithoba as a representation of Krishna. In this form he is often a dark young boy. It is a tradition that tends to be non-ritualistic and focuses on bhakti. There is also a group within the cult of Vithoba called the Vakari, who see Vithoba as a combination or unity of Shiva and Vishnu. So, to call all devotees of Vithoba Vaishnava would be erroneous. Further, Sand (1990) outlines that for many, 'Vithoba is neither Visnu nor Siva. Vithoba is Vithoba' (34). Within the Vithoba traditions, caste and gender distinctions are unimportant, and Vithoba is approached by devotees sometimes as male, sometimes as female.
- *The cult of Rama*. As the name suggests, this tradition focuses on the worship of Rama. He is a popularly revered avatar of Vishnu (see Chapter 2), and this group of devotees is often referred to as Ramanandi Sampradaya. Believed to have been founded in the fourteenth century by Ramananda and often refers to Rama as the Absolute.
- *The northern Sant tradition*. Flood (1996) suggests that in Maharashtra and its environs there emerged a number of sants in the fourteenth–sixteenth centuries who taught of a nirguna Lord who is variously known as Ram, Krishna, Hari and other names of Vishnu. Examples include Kabir, who encouraged followers to meditate in order to attain liberation.

To suggest, however, that each of these groups is the sum total of Vaishnava traditions would be erroneous. There are many more groups and traditions that would be described as within Vaishnavism. One such example is Swaminarayan expressions of Hinduism that see Vishnu as the Absolute and the Supreme Lord. Indeed, to strictly delineate the groups is problematic, the lines, if indeed there are lines, are fuzzy and expressions of Vaishnavism cross over and are not clear-cut. Consider the example of Sadh Vaishnavism, which is not found within Flood's five most important groupings, yet is translated as 'True' Vaishnavism and is the basis for many aspects of Vaishnava teachings and beliefs. Sadh Vaishnavism is based on the teachings of a thirteenth-century sant, Madhva, and is seen to be a source for Chaitanya's teachings. As such, Gaudiya Vaishnavism may be an expression of Sadh Vaishnavism. For teachers who are used to viewing religious groups through a Western lens where there are strict delineations, this will be a challenge to not see the groups as competing but interrelated and complimentary with shared traditions. The lines that observers draw may not be obvious or even desirable from within.

Shaivism

Shaivism is seen by some to be the oldest existing form of Hindu religion. Bhatt (2008) argues that:

> In the religious history of India, no religion has had such a long and continuous tradition as Saivism. On the basis of archaeological and literary evidence it is possible to show that the religion of Siva has persisted in India, without a break, since the pre-Vedic times. Few living religions in the world, if any, can boast of such a long and unbroken tradition. (43)

This may be overstating the case slightly, but as has been evidenced by the evidence from the various epochs of Indian history, it could be suggested that the linga of pre-Vedic times and Rudra of Vedic times are the older manifestations of Shiva. Shaivism, in a similar way to the view of Vishnu in Vaishnavism, worships Shiva as Supreme or Absolute (his place as such will be explored in Chapter 2). Looking at the development of what is today called Shaivism, it can be suggested that it is both textual/Vedic and also tantric. Gavin Flood (2003) suggests that:

> While the texts of revelation are important, it is above all the revelation as the living tradition of the guru lineage that animates the tradition and through which the grace of Siva is believed to flow. Here text becomes performance and the texts' teachings embodied in the human guru . . . [T]his structure which places such great emphasis on the teacher–disciple relationship. (203)

While this indicates one element of Shaivism, there are many different expressions of Shaivism that emphasize different aspects and approaches. Alexis Sanderson suggests that there are two umbrella traditions:

> The teaching of Siva (sivasasana) which defines the Saivas is divided between two great branches or 'streams' (strotas). These are termed the Outer Path (Atimarga) and the Path of Mantras {Mantramarga). The first is accessible only to ascetics, while the second is

open both to ascetics and to married home-dwellers (grhastha). There is also a difference of goals. The Atimarga is entered for salvation alone, while the Mantramarga promises both this and, for those that so wish, the attainment of supernatural powers (siddhis) and the experience of supernal pleasures in the worlds of their choice (bhoga). (664)

However, breaking these down, Das (2002) suggests that there are five main traditions:

- *Pashupatis*: It is suggested that Pashupata Shaivism developed in the first two centuries CE and has strands that are focused on bhakti and asceticism. The two main traditions are the somewhat mendicant ascetic Maha Pashupatas and the Lakula Pashupata. Within the Pashupata worldview, the goal of life is union with the Divine, often found through the intellect:

    Union is a conjunction of the soul with God through the intellect, and is of two degrees, that characterised by action, and that characterised by cessation of action. Of these, union characterised by action consists of pious muttering, meditation, and so forth ; union characterised by cessation of action is called consciousness. (Madhava Acharaya, 1882, 107)

    Many of the beliefs of the Pashupatis developed and were inherited by Shaiva Siddhanta.

- *Shaiva Siddhanta* is mainly found in South India and Sri Lanka today. The goal of Shaiva Siddhanta is similar to Pashupata, in that devotees seek union with Shiva; however, some of its traditions are monistic, rejecting the dualism of other traditions. There are seen to be four steps through which union can be found.

    1. *Dasamarga*: 'the slave's way, consists of practices such as cleaning a Siva temple, smearing its floor with cow dung, weaving garlands of different kinds of flowers for the decoration of the image of Siva, uttering the praises of the Lord, lighting the temple lamps, maintaining flower gardens and offering one's services to any devotee of Siva. This is the beginner's form of Siva bhakti.'
    2. *Satputramdarga*: 'the true son's way, prescribes the preparation of the articles necessary for Siva paja and meditation on Siva as of the form of light.'
    3. *Sahamarga*: 'the associate's way, and consists of yoga: withdrawal of the senses from their objects, breath control, suspension of mind activities, recitation of mantras and directing the vital breaths through the six body centres.'
    4. *Sanmarga*: 'the way of truth and reality: bhakti in the form of Siva knowledge has now been fully developed and is identical with liberation and bliss.' (Klostermaier, 2007, 193)

    This tradition is still followed by millions of people today.

- *Kashmiri Shaivism*: is seen to share some similarities with monistic forms of Shaiva Siddhanta in its rejection of dualism. Though it almost died out, it was 'reclaimed' and rejuvenated in the twentieth century by people such as Swami Lakshman Joo and his disciple Acharya Rameshwar Jha. Kashmiri Shaivism is focused on tantra, and while practised today, it had a huge influence on the development of Srikula Shaktism (see below). The yoga practised by Kashmiri Shaivites focuses on becoming one with Shiva.

- *Virashaivism (the Lingyats)*: literally meaning heroic or firm devotees of Shiva, one of the visible aspects of Virashaivism is the wearing of a Shiva-linga (Ishtalinga) around the neck, hence they are being known as Lingyats. Virashaivism has its roots in the twelfth century and the teachings of Basava. They reject any elements of caste and Vedic ritual, while adhering to a strict vegetarianism often associated with Brahmins. Although there have been efforts by some to place them outside of Hinduism, their focus on Shiva and many other beliefs has avoided this for many observers. By wearing the Shiva-linga, they believe that they will be united with Shiva following death.
- *Shaiva Asceticism*: 'Shaiva has long been connected with rigorous asceticism. Well-known are the nake Nagas. Many yogis are Shaivites. Prominent are the Nathapatris, followers of Gorakhnatha, and the Aghori who deliberately contravene moral norms' (Das, 2002, 135).

As with Vaishnavism, there are many more groups and individual devotees within Shaivism, and the list above only begins to scratch the surface of those who worship Shiva.

Shaktism

> The Shakta cult is one of many in which the divine is worshipped in the form of the Divine Mother. (Vanamali, 2008, 13)

In both Vaishnavism and Shaivism, there is a worship of the Goddess or of the Divine Feminine, but she is ancillary to or dependent on Vishnu and Shiva, respectively. In Vaishnavism, she is experienced as Lakshmi, the consort of Vishnu, along with Radha and Sita, who are avatars of Lakshmi alongside Krishna and Rama, who are avatars of Vishnu (see Chapter 2). In Shaivism, Shakti is experienced as Parvati, Durga, Kali and others. Although they may be ancillary within these traditions, 'it is through them that one encounters Shaktism in which the supreme universal entity is the Goddess who rules all. Shiva himself, in this religion, is subservient to Her and Her might.' In exploring her role in Shaktism, Shakti 'has a power unsurpassed in any other theistic cult' (Chitgopekar, 2022, 16). In the *Devi Gita*, she describes herself as the 'supreme Brahman':

> The Goddess spoke:
> May all the gods attend to what I have to say.
> By merely hearing these words of mine, one attains my essential nature.

> I alone existed in the beginning; there was nothing else at all, O Mountain King.
> My true Self is known as pure consciousness, the highest intelligence, the one supreme Brahman.
> It is beyond reason, indescribable, incomparable, incorruptible. (Mackenzie Brown, 2002, 53)

While Flood (1996) suggests that Shaktism is 'less clearly defined than Saivism or Vaisnavism' (175), there are seen to be two main traditions: *Srikula* (family of Tripura Sundari) and the *Kalikula* (family of Kali).

Srikula focuses their devotion towards Shakti as manifest in Lalita-Tripura Sundari. She is seen to be benign and beautiful. Brooks (1992) outlines these aspects of her character:

> Sakti in her supreme aspect (parasakti) manifests as benign (saumya) and beautiful (saundary), rather than as terrifying (ugra) and horrifying (ghora). Thus, Lalita is deliberately contrasted with such figures as Kali and Durga. Lalita Tripurasundari, however, is a totalization of great goddess conceptions. In other words, Lalita is identified with every aspect of the goddess in every possible form and mode of depiction. While primarily depicted as benign, she is also described as terrifying; similarly, she is both auspicious and inauspicious. These oppositions, as Frederique Marglin has pointed out, are not mutually exclusive but encompassing and dynamic. (61)

Within Srikula there are different traditions; some are focused on bhakti of the goddess, while others including Srividya adopt the Tantric Path and utilize tantras (see Chapter 6) which 'include meditation, the repetition of name(s) of the goddess (japa), the spell of mantras and the focus on yantras' (Ferrari, 2008, 737). While often identified with her consort, Shiva, she is often seen to be independent and able to be worshipped as Absolute, by herself. Though, one of the most famous yantras used in tantras is the sriyantra (see Figure 0.1) which is symbolic of both Sundari and Shiva. The yantra has nine interlocking triangles surrounding the bindu (central point), four of which point upwards representing Shiva, and five pointing down representing Shakti.

Kalikula

As the name suggests, devotees within Kalikula are the family of Kalki. June McDaniel (1989) outlines the view of Kalki and all of her forms:

> The devotional strand involves personal love of the goddess, who has created the universe and is infinitely beautiful inwardly, although her outer forms may reflect death and destruction. The devotee wishes to remain the child and worshiper of the goddess forever, at death entering her paradise, which is called Kailasa, or Manidvipa, or Pancakasa. (90)

The deities who are a focus for worship and tantric devotions in the Kalikula traditions include Kali, Chandi, Bheema, Tara and Durga. Worship of Kali is usually in the form of

Figure 0.1 Sriyantra by printcolouring (Creative Commons).

Tantric devotions (see Chapter 6); they come with the recognition of Kali as supreme. Ramakrishna suggests:

> Kali is none other than Brahman. That which is called Brahman is really Kali. She is the Primal Energy. When that Energy remains inactive, I call It Brahman, and when It creates, preserves, or destroys, I call It Shakti or Kali. What you call Brahman I call Kali. Brahman and Kali are not different. They are like fire and its power to burn: if one thinks of fire one must think of its power to burn. If one recognizes Kali one must also recognize Brahman; again, if one recognizes Brahman one must recognize Kali. Brahman and Its Power are identical. It is Brahman whom I address as Shakti or Kali. (Nikhilananda, 2000, 734)

Shaktism is the smaller of the three larger traditions, but as noted earlier, elements of Shaktism are found throughout Hinduism. It is also important to note that 'In the twentieth century, new forms of Saktism emerged, particularly in Diaspora Hinduism, and within new forms of religions' (Ferrari, 2008, 741). While many will worship Shakti alone, devotion to her can be found across traditions.

Smartism

The Smarta tradition is seen to have developed in the first centuries of the Common Era. Indeed, some see Adi Shankara as one of its 'founders' or first proponents or codifiers. It focuses its worship on five deities to try to avoid the sectarianism or rivalry that seemed to have been, and is sometimes today evident, in what is termed Hinduism. Indeed, Bruce Sullivan (1997) describes it as 'non-sectarian' (213). The five deities are:

- Ganesha
- Shakti
- Shiva
- Surya
- Vishnu

Within Smarta, it is interesting to note the choice of the five Ishvara or deities that are worshipped. Although traditionally ascribed to Shankara, it would appear that *pancayatanapuja* (five shrine worship) predated him. In worship, the arrangements of the deities usually has one in the centre surrounded by the other four. This type of approach to the five deities is found in the Puranas. The *Narada Purana* outlines:

> When he worships Visnu in the middle, he shall worship Vinayaka, Ravi(Sun) Siva and Siva outside them. When he worships Sankara in the middle, he shall worship the Sun, Ganesa, Amba and Hari outside them. When he worships Siva in the middle, he shall worship Isa, Vighnesvara, the Sun and Govinda outside. If he worships Gananayaka (Ganesa) in the middle he shall worship Siva, Siva, the Sun and Visnu outside. When the Sun is worshipped in the middle he shall worship Ganesa, Visnu, Amba, and Siva respectively. Thus he shall worship respectfully the five deities every day. (1997, 936)

Sometimes Smarta is particularly associated with Shiva, as Shankara is seen to be one of his avatars. Lola Williamson (2010) suggests, however, that a sixth deity can be added:

> The ninth-century reformer Adi Shankara attempted to bring the different sects of Hinduism together by establishing the Smarta tradition. This tradition, which is followed by the Shankaracharyas and their students today, worships five principle deities: Shiva, Vishnu, Surya, Ganapati, and Devi along with a sixth, an impersonal God existing without form (nirguna). Scriptural authority for the idea of an impersonal God comes from the Upanishads, and authority for worshipping the five deities comes from the Puranas. (89)

This is perhaps a misnomer, in the sense that in reality this nirguna form of God is the reality, and that in his theology Shankara taught the Brahman as impersonal and the ultimate reality. He did, however, recognize that the worship of an Ishvara (sagun or with qualities) is an intermediary step that leads to the worship of the Absolute. In reality, it is Brahman that is worshipped but through an Ishvara, which is an accessible form of the Divine that has attributes; Alf Hiltebeitel (2002) suggests the relationship between this 'sixth' deity and the others:

> Sankara fostered a rapprochement between Advaita and *smarta* orthodoxy, which by his time had . . . developed the practice of *pancayatanapuja* ('five-shrine worship') as a solution to varied and conflicting devotional practices. Thus one could worship any one of five deities (Visnu, Siva, Durga, Surya, Ganesa) as one's istadevata ('deity of choice') . . . As to the god (or gods) of *bhakti*, Sarikara views the deity (*Isvara*) as essentially identical with brahman and real relative to empirical experience. But by being identified 'with qualities' (*saguna*) God can be no more than an approach to the experience of brahman 'without qualities' (*nirguna*). Viewed from the experience of the self as *nirguna brahman*, which 'sublates' all other experiences, the deity is but the highest form of *maya*. (29–30)

As a reflection of elements of Vedanta philosophy (see below), this approach to the nature of the Divine is the one that is perhaps taught most often in schools, without being recognized as a principle of Smarta. Das (2002) has suggested that while 'Many Hindus may not identify as Smartas but, by adhering to Advaita Vedanta as a foundation for non-sectarianism, are indirect followers' (137). The idea of one Supreme Being manifested in different forms is found in all of the forms of Hinduism identified so far, but it is important to recognize that this is one interpretation of the Divine

Darshanas

Another way that Hinduism is sometimes divided is through philosophical schools. Sometimes described as theological schools, neither term fully captures the meaning and scope of the darshanas. Darshana comes from the root 'drs' which means 'to view' or 'to see' and is often described as 'ways of seeing'. Gavin Flood (1996) has suggested that a darshana is 'a system of thought expressed through a tradition of commentaries upon fundamental texts, and *anviksiki*, analysis or investigative science within the field of Vedic knowledge, particularly used with reference to logic (*nyaya*)' (224). There are six astika (accepted/orthodox) schools of darshana based on the logic of the Vedas, and a number of nastika (heterodox) darshanas which include Buddhism and Jainism. The six astika darsanas are:

- *Samkhya*: Traditionally seen to begin with the sage Kapila in the sixth or seventh century BCE, samkhya suggests a dualistic view of reality. In its exploration of the 'cause of the universe', it asserts that the cause is non-sentient. Samkhya philosophy outlines the dual nature of *prakriti* (sometimes translated as matter) and *purusha* (soul). These two are the only two aspects necessary to explain the universe.

    > Prakriti is the primordial 'stuff' of the entire unmanifest and manifest world, whereas purusa is the presupposition of individual consciousness.30 Thus, there is only one prakriti but a plurality of purushas. Also important to note is that purusa is not

> 'self' in the sense of intelligence, ego, or mind. These categories or principles are rather emergents or 'evolutes' of prakriti. Purusa is simply pure consciousness which exists apart from prakriti. (Larson, 1979, 12)

The main idea behind this philosophy is that purusha uses prakriti as a way to attain moksha or liberation. When prakriti and purusha come together, this state is known as *jiva*. The interplay within this context will be explored in terms of the gunas in Chapter 3. In samkhya, knowledge is developed through perception, inference and reliable testimony. While it could be suggested that samkhya is 'no longer a living force in contemporary Indian culture', it has an impact on various Hindu traditions, beliefs and practices (Larson, 1979, 1).

- *Yoga*: is based on the teachings of Patanjali, a mystic who lived somewhere between the fourth and second centuries BCE. Patanjali is believed to have collected together the Yoga Sutras, and much of the philosophy of yoga is based on the dualism of samkhya. Recognizing the duality of purusa and prakriti, and the gunas. The philosophy suggests that there may be an imbalance between the various aspects of a person (see Chapters 3 and 6). The *Katha Upanishad* teaches:

> Only when Manas (mind) with thoughts and the five senses stand still, and when Buddhi (intellect, power to reason) does not waver, that they call the highest path. That is what one calls Yoga, the stillness of the senses, concentration of the mind, It is not thoughtless heedless sluggishness, Yoga is creation and dissolution. (2.6.10–11)

It is only later in the development of yoga that it was seen as a separate tradition from samkhya.

- *Nyaya*: teaches four ways through which knowledge is developed: perception, inference, comparison/analogy and testimony. Knowledge is central in this philosophy; wrong knowledge causes suffering, while right knowledge can lead to moksha. Moksha is attained as part of a five-stage process, through which the previous stage is overcome: '1. Suffering, 2. Birth, 3. motivational acts (or the merit and demerit derived from motivational acts), evil dispositions, and 5. Wrong conceptions. Here we find a causal chain . . . which are accountable for the perpetuation of life' (Matilal, 1997, 353). Nyaya is believed to be based on the teachings of Gautama (not the Buddha), a Hindu sage who lived sometime between the sixth century BCE and the second century CE. Francis Clooney (2001) has suggested further that:

> Nyaya is the traditional school of Hindu logic. In the early centuries BCE the Nyaya logicians undertook the project of describing the world in a coherent rational fashion and without reliance on revelation or a commitment to any particular deity.

Nyaya's primary text, the Nyaya Sutras of Gautama, can be read as a neutral analysis neither favouring nor opposing the idea of God. (18)

Within Nyaya, there are writings that support the existence of a deity, and some that do not, but the universe is composed of five elements: earth, water, air, fire and space (see Chapter 3).

- *Vaisheshika* is closely linked to Nyaya and outlines two reliable ways of attaining knowledge: direct observation and inference. The Vedas are a source of this knowledge within Vaisheshika. One of its most observed teachings is that everything in the universe is made up of, or can be reduced to, paramanu (atoms). The interplay of these paramanu creates reality. Vaisheshika is based on the teachings of Kanada, who lived between the sixth century and second century BCE. Although he did not speak of the Divine, later philosophers such as Udayana suggested that the ordering of the atoms was initially caused by a supreme deity.
- *Mimamsa*, sometimes known as purva (earlier), focuses on the earlier Vedic texts. Unlike the previous darsanas, there are believed to be five sources of knowledge: inference, comparison/analogy, implication, reliable testimony and, for some, negative proof. The main aim of mimamsa is the articulation of dharma based on Vedic texts. Its beginnings are believed to be traced to Jaimini, a Hindu sage who lived between the fourth century and second century BCE. It can be seen as a reaction to Buddhism and Jainism (nastika darsanas) that rejected the authority of the Vedas. It recognizes the eternal and active nature of the self or soul.
- *Vedanta* is also known as Uttara Mimamsa which deals with 'one eternal principle, that of Brahman or the supreme spirit. It is called Vedanta because the word means "end or summary of the Vedas"' (Prinja, 1996, 159). Though based primarily on the Vedas, expressions of Vedanta can be seen to be based on the Prasthanatrayi, meaning the Upanishads, the Brahma Sutras and the Bhagavad Gita. There are different expressions of Vedanta, but it has been suggested that there are common elements across the traditions:

    > The Vedanta schools do, however, hold in common a number of beliefs: the transmigration of the self (samsara) and the desirability of release from the cycle of rebirths; the authority of the Veda on the means of release; that brahman is both the material (upadana) and the instrumental (nimitta) cause of the world; and that the self (atman) is the agent of its own acts (karma) and therefore the recipient of the fruits (phala), or consequences, of action. (Stefon & Doniger, 2015)

    The three main traditions of Vedanta are Advaita Vedanta, Visistadvaita Vedanta and Dvaita Vedanta. Advaita Vedanta is monistic in the sense that Brahman is the ultimate reality and that the atman is a part of Brahman. Everything is part of this oneness. Important thinkers within Advaita are Shankara, Vidyaranya and more recently Vivekananda. The purpose of existence is to destroy maya and ignorance through attaining the knowledge of Brahman which can be developed by *svadhyaya* (a study of the self and the Vedas) which in turn has four stages: *viraga* (renunciation), *sravana* (listening to teachings), *manana* (reflection on the teachings) and *nididhyasana* (meditation on the Upanishads).

Visistadvaita Vedanta is seen to be based on the teachings of Ramanuja. This is seen as a qualified non-dualism, meaning that it recognizes Brahman as the ultimate reality, but it is expressed and manifested in diversity. Bhakti is the sole means to moksha within Visistadvaita.

Within Dvaita Vedanta, there are seen to be three parts to reality: Brahman, chit (souls) and achit (the universe). In turn, Brahman controls, chit enjoys and achit is enjoyed. Dvaita adopts a dualistic approach to reality, and the goal is for the soul to unite with Brahman.

These darshanas have been only briefly touched upon here, and they have been explained separately. As the remainder of the book is explored, it will be evident that different aspects of the darshanas are focused on or developed within different teachings, practices and expressions. These darshanas are not separate from the different traditions outlined above, rather they often find expression within such.

Thoughts for the classroom

The exploration of the diversity of Hinduism, as has already been suggested, lies at the heart of teaching within the classroom. It is impossible to authentically teach Hinduism if we attempt to do so based on a monolithic expression. It may make it easier, but the recognition of different influences and expressions will make it more real and respond to the lived reality and development of Hindu ideas. Hinduism is a way to explore religion in the classroom in a different way that will also have a reciprocal effect as students see the diversity expressed in a religion that did not emerge 'oven-ready' or as neatly meeting the categories traditionally associated with religion. It did, and has, become a way to unify people, such that the initial colonial feel to 'Hinduism' is disappearing:

> Being 'Hindu' became 'a way to be a person, to experience oneself, to live in society'. Hence, people who had earlier identified themselves in other terms – usually by jati, loosely defined by profession, clan, marriage, or local faith practices – were now able to call themselves 'Hindu'. The creation of a new social category – a new religion with a new label – became the fulcrum of history and politics for the entire time that followed. (Chakravorty, 2019, 60)

This approach is not without its challenges. For some students, the utilization of 'some' and 'many' will be enough, and the purpose of this chapter may be to problematize the teaching of Hinduism for teachers. For others, this discussion will provide a useful basis for future learning. It will be in the various teachings and practices that will enable the full .implications of the above to be realized. It is to this task that the book now turns.

Part 1

Key Concepts in Hinduism

Chapter 1

Dharma

Deciding where to start in exploring Hindu beliefs is not an easy task. There are many beliefs and practices that could begin this discussion. In naming Hinduism alternately sanatana dharma or Hindu dharma, there could be seen to be the suggestion that dharma lies at the heart of Hinduism. Indeed, one Hindu has commented:

> Hinduism is about following dharma, i.e. lead your life in the righteous path.

Others support this centrality:

> There are many religions, and we are Hindus who follow the same dharmas as our previous generations. Those who follow those dharmas are Hindus.
>
> Being a Hindu comes down to your values in life. It is all about dharma, and everyone has their own. For me, my dharma is to pray to god, and do our duty, take care of our family, and taking time every day to be with lord, and spend some time with devotion. Also being kind to everyone.

The term dharma is purposefully used, rather than any translation, as none of the utilized terminology such as duty or religion seems to capture its meaning and importance for Hindus. When exploring its etymology, it appears that it comes from the root word 'dhri', can be translated as 'to sustain' or 'that which is integral to something'. Within Hindu cosmology (see Chapter 3), it can be seen that as something fulfils its dharma, it is able to gain positive rebirth and in the case of humans positive karma leading to positive rebirth. As a simple example, looking at the animal world, the dharma or integral nature of a dog may be to be loyal, to be protective. It quite naturally does this and so the atman which may be part of that dog will naturally have a positive rebirth because it has fulfilled the measure of its dharma. This could also be seen in every aspect of the natural world. Humanity is distinct in the natural world because it appears that they alone have the ability to ignore their dharma, and to gain positive and negative karma which will affect future rebirths and the path to moksha. It is this approach to life that enables a view of Hinduism that focuses on orthopraxy rather than orthodoxy. There is not really the concept of 'right' belief as there are so many different expressions of Hinduism (though for further discussion of this, see Chapter 2); however, Hinduism seems to reflect upon and encourage the fulfilment of dharma and the various responsibilities that form a part of that.

The concept of dharma arises out of the Vedas and the Puranic literature, and there are seen to be two sources of phases in their development. Firstly, *dharmasutras* which are 'rules of conduct for various social groups, moral duties, rights, and obligations. These were composed as collections of aphorisms, some so brief that they virtually presuppose commentary, and were written between the seventh and second century B.C.E.' These were linked very closely with the Vedic rituals as they were the final part of the *Kalpa Sutra* which outlined religious practices and sought 'to provide an ordered way of life by delineating each person's rights and duties' (Lochtefeld, 2002, 192). The main dharmasutras and their authors are named as:

- Apastamba (450–350 BCE) which has 1,364 sutras.
- Gautama (600–200 BCE) which has 973 sutras.
- Baudhayana (500–200 BCE) which has 1,236 sutras.
- Vasishtha (300–100 BCE) which has 1,038 sutras.

The range of topics that are covered is vast, and includes aspects such as rituals, ethics, criminal law, civil law and many other topics. In some ways, the construction of the dharmasutras addressed the questions of epistemology outlined in the darshanas centuries before. 'A question that loomed large in the minds of all these authors was an epistemological one: Where can we find these guidelines? What are the sources of dharma?' (Olivelle, 1999, 39). Could their source be solely the Vedas, or could inference and other skills be utilized to define dharma? What became evident in the dharmasutras is that there are different dharmas, meaning in different contexts and for different people, the dharma may be different. This was linked with the concept of varna (see below).

The dharmasutras laid the basis for the dharmashastras, which 'expanded the sutras, put them into verse, and were intended to serve as an actual code of law for the members of the community' (Lochtefeld, 2002, 192). The four main extant dharmashastras are:

- The *Manusmrti* (composed in the second to third centuries) also known as the *Laws of Manu*.
- The *Yajnavalkya Smrti* (composed in the fourth to fifth centuries).
- The *Naradasmrti* (composed in the fifth to sixth centuries) is very much focused on judicial matters.
- The *Vishnuusmrti* (composed in the seventh century) focuses on the bhakti tradition.

Lochtefeld (2002) suggests that

> the Dharma Shastras purported to lay down rules for all members of society. They . . . profess to lay down universal truths. In keeping with this emphasis, the surviving Dharma Shastras are all attributed to mythical sages – Manu, Yajnavalkya, and Narada . . . The Dharma Shastras thus mark the study of dharma (dharmashastra) as a discipline distinct from the earlier Vedic literature, and applied to society as a whole. (191)

It is also of note that the Puranic literature is often focused around dharma; indeed, the *Bhagavad Gita* teaches that a reclamation of dharma is the purpose of Vishnu's avatars:

> Whenever there is a decline in [dharma] and an increase in [adharma], O Arjun, at that time I manifest Myself on earth. To protect the righteous, to annihilate the wicked, and to re-establish the principles of dharma I appear on this earth, age after age. (4:7–8)

Together, there can be seen to be ten different areas which the various sutras and shastras address (Sharma, 2008):

1. Religious rites.
2. Religious duties.
3. Justice.
4. Moral virtues.
5. Varna-specific duties.
6. Ashrama-specific duties.
7. Duties particular to certain groups such as stridharma.
8. Duties particular to a time.
9. Duties with universal application.
10. Those actions that are beneficial for now and in the hereafter.

It would be impossible to explore every aspect of dharma, but as an outworking of the various aspects of dharma explored in the dharmasutras and the dharmashastras, it is possible to suggest two types of dharma (though it is possible to break the concepts down further): that of sadharana (universal) dharma and svadhama (personal) dharma. It is to these two types that we now turn.

Sadharana dharma

Sadharana dharma or universal dharma, sometimes termed universal morality, is the aspect of dharma that applies to all. There can be seen to be two types: *yama* (prohibitions) and *niyama* (recommended practices). The *Vamana Purana* outlines both kinds.

> The sages said: Non-violence, truth, non-stealing, charity, forbearance, self-restraint, tranquillity, non-miserliness, purity and austerity, O great demon, constitute the ten limbed Dharma to be followed by all castes. (14:1–2)

The Vishnu smrti outlines alternative or complementary principles:

> Forbearance, veracity, restraint, purity, liberality, self-control, not to kill (any living being), obedience towards one's Gurus, visiting places of pilgrimage, sympathy (with the afflicted). Straightforwardness, freedom from covetousness, reverence towards gods and Brahmanas, and freedom from anger are duties common (to all castes). (2:16–17)

The ten focused on can also be found in *Vishnu smrti*, they are usually summarized and explained as below.

Yamas

The five yamas are:

- *ahimsa* (non-violence) meaning not causing harm to any living being, and by extension not even having the desire to do so.
- *satya* (truthfulness) meaning to avoid any kind of dishonesty.
- *asteya* (not stealing).
- *brahmacharya* (chastity) meaning that a person restrains themselves in sexual activity, normally meaning celibacy or fidelity.
- *aparigraha* (non-attachment) meaning freedom from materialism.

As universal principles in the expression of morality, these will be explored in much greater detail in Chapter 7. Here, it is important to note, as outlined in the *Vamana Purana*, that these are 'to be followed by all'. While there may be differences of interpretation in certain contexts, they are universal principles of morality that should be followed.

Niyama

The five niyamas are:

- *shauca* (purity) suggesting that a person should be pure physically and spiritually. Cleansing oneself of bad habits, and anything that could be considered adharma.
- *santosha* (contentment) suggesting a contentment with what one has, and the avoidance of wanting more.
- *tupas* (discipline or ascetic practices) often through persistent meditative practices.
- *svadhyaya* (study of oneself) meaning that a person is able to look within and find the truth about themselves.
- *Ishvara-pranidhana* (contemplation of the Divine) and striving to become one with the Divine.

As universal principles in the expression of dharma and spirituality, these will be explored in much greater detail in Chapter 6.

Svadharma

Svadharma, or personal dharma, is that aspect of dharma that is particular to the individual, in contrast to the universal principles of sadharana dharma. In commenting on Bhagavad Gita 2:31 and the identification of Arjuna's svadharma as a warrior, Swami Mukundananda (2014) outlines what svadharma is:

> Swa-dharma is one's duty as an individual, in accordance with the Vedas. There are two kinds of swa-dharmas, or prescribed duties for the individual – para dharma, or spiritual duties, and apara dharma, or material duties. Considering oneself to be the soul, the prescribed duty is to love and serve God with devotion. This is called para dharma. However, since a vast majority of humankind does not possess this spiritual perspective, the Vedas also prescribe duties for those who see themselves as the body. These duties are defined according to one's ashram (station in life), and varna (occupation). They are called apara dharma, or mundane duties. This distinction between spiritual duties and material duties needs to be kept in mind while understanding the Bhagavad Gita and the Vedic philosophy at large.

The aspect of dharma that suggests a loving devotion to the Divine will be explored in Chapter 6. At this stage we will explore what is termed 'apara dharma' or those aspects of dharma relative to the personal physical life, especially those outlined in ashramas (stages of life) and varnashramadharma. It is important to note that these aspects are contextual.

> the pervasive concept of dharma is understood polycentrically across the tradition, not least through the 'open' notion of sanatana dharma, which is invested with specific content when it is applied to different empirical contexts. The vaunted 'subtlety' of dharma in the texts points to a hidden, universal principle of prescriptive and descriptive order that manifests 'to different kaleidoscopic effect in different lives, or at different times in the same life' through such determinate notions as anasarca dharma, stri-dharma, grhastha-dharma, ksatriya-dharma etc. 'Properly, one can only act dharmically in the round, so to speak, allowing each centre of dharma that is circumstantially active in one's life to interact with other such centres'. (Lipner, 2010, 374)

Although the idea of dharma is universal and central, it is also incredibly personal.

Ashramas

One aspect of svadharma is determined through the four *ashramas* (or stages of life). These specific ashramas enable a person to understand and live their personal dharma. It should be noted that in the past these stages were focused on men and that there were three stages in the female *stridharma* (see below). The four ashramas are:

- *Brahmacharya* (student): this stage traditionally begins with the sacred thread ceremony and marks the beginning of study. Yoga, scriptures, arts and sciences would all be studied alongside a simple and celibate life. As a way of living svadharma today, most Hindus in this stage will develop knowledge and learning in whichever situation they find themselves. In the UK, this would be by attending schools and learning at home and in the mandir. The traditional age range for this ashrama is up to about the age of twenty-four, though it should be noted that the duties attached to the ashrama are fluid.

- *Grihastha* (householder). In this stage, a Hindu will be married and assume the responsibilities of a householder. Marriage is a part of Hindu's dharma as a way of sustaining social and religious obligations. The aspects of the householder stage are what would be expected in the running and maintenance of a home based on religious teachings and values. These would include: earning an honest wage; spending money wisely and for the benefit of the household and others; keeping the home clean; observing religious celebrations and so on. This ashrama highlights the integrated nature of Hindu living; there are no 'religious' and 'other' duties; every aspect of the life of a Hindu has dharma as an integral part, rather than additional responsibilities.
- *Vanaprastha* (retirement). When the children of a Hindu are grown and able to take responsibility for their own lives, a Hindu will enter the retirement stage of life. Anciently, this would have meant becoming a 'forest dweller' meaning that worldly concerns are renounced and people are able to devote time to quiet; study sacred texts and meditate. These are generally no longer carried out in the forest but can be adopted in a home. People in the retirement stage are greatly respected.
- *Sannyasin* (renunciation). This stage is often not entered into as it is the complete renunciation of material food and the devotion of the person's entire life to seeking moksha. In this stage, a Hindu might become a wandering holy man, and this can be entered into at any stage of life.

Although seemingly universal in application, there is a suggestion that the ashramas are linked to a person's varnashramadharma (see below) as the *Varama Purana* suggests that 'a brahmana may pass through all four ashramas, a ksatriya the first three, a vaisya the first two and a sudra only one, that of the householder' (Sharma, 2008, 49). The breaking down of these barriers will be discussed below in a discussion of the varnas and caste.

There is also an expectation in the past that these four were not appropriate for women and that there would be three stages of stridharma all in relation to others. Her duties would begin as a daughter and her duties to her father, then as a wife and her responsibility to her husband, and as part of this stage as a mother with responsibilities to her children. The stage of widowhood is the third stage. This approach to stridharma is outlined in the *Laws of Manu*, and it could be suggested that in reality the role of a woman was much more powerful than this suggests. This would certainly be seen to be the case today, and perhaps the four ashramas above may be beginning to have application regardless of gender (see Chapter 7), though manuals on the duties of a wife are still to be found today.

This type of role is celebrated in the person of Sita in the *Ramayana* where 'Sita's decision to follow Rama into the forest, despite his protestations, and her chaste commitment to him during her time in Ravana's court are the proper actions of a devoted and dutiful wife (*dharma-patni*)' (Knott, 2016, 42–43).

Each part of the ashrama is inextricably linked with the life cycle rituals, which will be explored in Chapter 7.

Varnashramadharma

The concept of varnashramadharma is focused on the dharma or responsibilities of those within a particular varna. The varnas are the divisions within society that are often misreported as castes (see below). Varnas were seen to be an organization of society based on its needs, and also the aptitudes of its people. The division of society into four varnas is seen as suggested and justified in the *Rig Veda*:

> When they divided Purusa how many portions did they make?
>
> What do they call his mouth, his arms? What do they call his thighs and feet?
>
> The Brahman was his mouth, of both his arms was the Rajanya made.
>
> His thighs became the Vaisya, from his feet the Sudra was produced. (10.90.11–12)

This passage tells the story of the division of Purusha, at creation. This is one story that is told of creation; Purusha is seen as the universal principle, or cosmic force that was divided into all of the different elements of the universe at creation. The passages that surround those outlined above explain how the moon came from the mind of Purusha, the sun from his eyes. Further, Indra and Agni came from his mouth. It is unlikely to be viewed as literal, but the truths that it teaches in the universal presence of the Divine throughout creation and the universe are still important today (see Chapters 2 and 3).

Prinja (1996) suggests that in the story of Purusha:

> The whole of society is conceived to be one composite entity, with head, hands, stomach and belly, and feet – from the top of the head to the tips of the toes. All these organs make one complete person. According to this concept the teaching, preaching and guiding section of society was called the 'head' – the Brahmin. When there was danger of attack on the Society-Person from outside, the hands defended and protected the person; those who performed this work were called Kshatriya. But the body cannot live only by head and hands. There must be food in the belly in order to sustain life. The third class was enjoined to produce food, which was considered to be the most inestimable wealth of a nation; this class was called 'Vaishya'. Finally, the feet which have to carry the whole burden of this Society-Person were called 'Shudra'. (70)

At its inception each of the varnas was equal and each person was seen to play a valuable role within society. There was no concept of touchability or untouchability within society, and people were free to mix. People were able to fulfil the role in society which best suited their ability. One Hindu today has suggested:

> What you are is defined by what you do. A brahmin who doesn't follow brahminism is not a brahmin. But someone of a different caste who follows brahminism can still be considered a brahmin. Caste is defined by your actions. For example, sage Vishwamitra, was born a Kshatriya, but he became a Brahmin by doing puja and devoting himself to god.

A major figure in Valmiki's 'Balakanda' section of the *Ramayana* (see Goldman & Goldman, 2021), Vishwamitra was a king of the Kshatriya varna, who became a great sage/rishi known for his great austerities, and the author of most of Mandala 3 of the *Rig Veda*. Such an ancient movement between the varnas suggests that the delineations were fluid rather than the fixed boundaries imagined in later years.

In the dharmashatras and the Itihasa, the importance of dharma according to one's varna is highlighted and explained. Indeed, both the *Ramayana* and the *Mahabharata* have dharma as a central topic. For example, Rama put Sita through purity tests because he was conscious of his dharma as a ruler. Similarly, Dhasharatha's acquiescence to the boon that he promised to Kaikeyi is again based on his responsibilities or dharma as a ruler. In the *Mahabharata*, especially in the *Bhagavad Gita*, a dharma based on one's varna is a central theme:

> When a dynasty is destroyed, its [dharma] get vanquished, and the rest of the family becomes involved in [adharma] . . . Through the evil deeds of those who destroy the family [dharmas] and thus give rise to unwanted progeny, a variety of social and family welfare activities are ruined. (Bhagavad Gita 1:40, 43)

In both of these sacred texts, Vishnu has descended to earth to re-establish dharma in the face of adharma. Dharma is necessary for the orderly functioning of society and the regulation of the functions of one's varna.

Over time, a person's varna came to be determined by their birth rather than their abilities. Within each varna, there came to be *jatis* or *upjatis* which were subdivisions based on various professions within each varna. At different points, the concept and practice of untouchability were found in Indian society. There were roles outside of the varnas that were seen to be ritually impure; as such, those in the varnas were made unclean by contact with the untouchables, and the untouchables made others unclean through contact. Many Hindus today would say that the system became less than it originally was:

> The caste system nowadays is biased, and is based on what you are doing. If a soldier is doing his job, then he is within a certain caste. The caste system is based on your dharma and what you do. In ancient times, it was based off of profession, but then it became by birth. People follow it blindly, but don't know the meaning. It should be

based upon deeds, not birth. I think this is more due to the way old towns and villages were set up and both to make things more efficient and for the high-ego people to exert control, this system was set up. I do not believe it is what is a 'Hindu' way of life/philosophy.

This aspect of the nature of humanity is controversial throughout the Hindu world, particularly in modernity, and its manifestation as the concept of caste. It is an area that is often taught in the classroom (see Insight UK, 2021). Insight UK suggests that issues of caste and untouchability are taught as part of Hinduism, but it is suggested that it 'is a social issue, not a religious one and is not limited to any one community' (27). Insight UK and others suggest that the teaching of caste should be removed from the study of Hinduism. Wendy Doniger (2009) reflects this view and places the reification of caste firmly as a result of colonial ignorance or misinformation:

> The false Orientalist assumptions that India was timeless and that the classical texts of the Brahmins described an existing society led to the equally false assumption that the village and caste organization of colonial or even contemporary India was a guide to their historical past. (83)

In this way, it could be suggested that an over-reliance on texts, in this case the *Laws of Manu*, influenced the way the British viewed both Indian history and contemporary Hindu society. This is seemingly supported by some of those involved in the governance of India. Governor-General Lord Canning in 1857 suggested that caste made it easier to govern:

> As we must rule 150 millions of people by a handful (more or less small) of Englishmen, let us do it in the manner best calculated to leave them divided . . . and to inspire them with the greatest possible awe of our power and with the least possible suspicion of our motives. (in Sharma, 2019, 32)

One of the census administrators in the early twentieth century suggested:

> We pigeon holed everyone by caste and if we could not find a true caste for them, labelled them with the name of hereditary occupation. We deplore the caste system and its effect on social and economic problems, but we are largely responsible for the system we deplore. (in Sharma, 2019, 21)

To suggest, however, that caste was a colonial creation is not accurate. It was harnessed and used for their benefit, and perhaps its perpetuation and rigidity into the twentieth century can be laid at the feet of the British, but there are elements that suggest both a historical and contemporary identification with Hinduism, and wider Indian society. Despite recognizing its modern roots in Orientalism, Doniger (2009) suggests its continuing relevance: 'Caste, the most important of the allegiances by which the people whom we call Hindus do identify themselves most often, is closely regulated by religion' (26). Indeed, in the course of research for this book, many Hindus recognized the place of caste in the past, and to some extent today:

> The caste system caused a lot of discrimination. In a way, if we never had a caste system that would have been good, however, since it's there people now justify it.
>
> Caste system in my opinion is formed based on various professions people do. They are these people where they inherit specific skills from previous generations. We are all the same and in my opinion, human community as a whole would great if we stick to our professions.

However, many others reflected a nuanced view of caste, which suggests it has little or no relevance today:

> The caste system was originally thought about as being part of profession. Over time, it turned more into a birth based system, which is now used as a weapon to discriminate. Ideally, discrimination based on caste should be abolished, and the purpose of caste itself needs to be questioned. All human beings are created equal so why should there be a caste system?
>
> The caste system is unnecessary, everyone is human and equal, everyone is made equal. Everyone has the right to pray to god.

This diversity of views is perhaps to be expected in a religion that is defined by its differences. There are many who would baulk at the inclusion of the concept of caste within a book that purports to strive to be an accurate representation of Hinduism. To ignore it, however, would be to leave teachers ill-equipped to address the perpetuated understanding of it as a part of Hindu identity.

The term caste, however, is certainly problematic and indicative of the colonial inheritance it evidences. The word 'caste' is of European origin. It reflected a society that was divided into rigid classes and divisions, that, it could be argued, were more reminiscent of British society than the way that Indian society had been organized.

Adi Shankara

At different points in history, there have been teachings and movements that have argued against the system that had become somewhat ingrained within society. One example in the eighth century is that of Shankara reflected in the writing of the *Manisha Panchakam*. In this story, the sage, Shankara, is returning to a temple after bathing in the Ganges. On the road, he is approached by a chandala (or untouchable). At which point, his Brahmin companions ask Shankara to tell him to move. The chandala replies with two questions about what it is that Shankara wishes him to move:

> To move this body from that body, or to separate this consciousness from that consciousness? O sage, which do you want me to move away when you say, 'Go! Go'?

> If the sun is reflected in the waters of the Ganga, or in a stream flowing through a slum, is there any difference? Or for space in a golden vessel and space in a clay pot? With regard to atma, the tranquil, natural ocean of limitless consciousness, How can one say 'He is a brahman, he is an outcaste'? Such distinctions are erroneous.

This causes Shankara to reflect and recognize the truth of reality. The following verses all recognize the truth that the chandala has taught Shankara, including:

> I am indeed brahman. This entire world is a projection of pure consciousness. Because of ignorance, all this has been projected by me. One whose mind is firmly established in this blissful, eternal, absolute, pure truth, he is my guru, be he an outcaste or a brahman. Thus is my conviction. (Adi Shankara, 2010)

The exchange ends when Shankara helps the chandala to his feet and bows before him, reflecting the recognition of the fluidity of varna and the incorrectness of untouchability. To suggest that Shankara's views opposed the delineation of varnas would be to go too far, but his teaching of the unity of the Advaita philosophy suggests that he might accept the basis of varna as being beyond hereditariness. There are examples, however, where Shankara seems to affirm the restrictions that caste presented. In his *Brahma Sutra*, he says: 'This is another reason why the Sudra has no right: By the Smrti he is debarred from hearing, studying, and acquiring the meaning of the Vedas' (Gambhirananda, 2009, 234).

Other reformers throughout history and in the contemporary world have included Siddhartha Gautama (the Buddha) and Guru Nanak (the first guru in human form of Sikhism). Both of these figures arose from the background of what would today be called Hinduism, and aspects of their teaching focused on the equality of all (see Holt, 2023a, 2023b). Although they are generally seen as separate from Hinduism, both the Buddha and Guru Nanak's rejection of caste reflects the society of the time that seemed to function on the basis of these rigid structures, and the ideas of untouchability (particularly in the various experiences of Guru Nanak).

Caste and colonialization

As outlined earlier, the rigidity and centrality of what is today termed the caste system were established by the British as they sought to colonize and govern India. One of the elements of colonialism and Orientalism explored in the Series Foreword suggests that at this time, and in the world religions paradigm, the British sought to understand the 'other' through their own cultural lens. As Christians who placed great emphasis on a book, the Bible, they expected to find such an approach in the colonized people and communities. Sanoy Chakravorty (2019) suggests that 'The inventions were done by first elevating selected and convenient Brahmanvadi Sanskrit texts like the *Manusmrti* to canonical status, and later through the census and its categories. Both were acts of convenience and simplification' (21). Chakravorty continues:

It had no relationship with ground reality. In fact, it is doubtful that caste had much significance or virulence in society before the British made it India's defining feature. In the last quarter of the nineteenth century, the newly established census and its categories and counts firmly established these made-up social categories – both of religion and caste – and set India on a path to an ever-expanding politics of identity. (21–22)

It is here that the complex relationship between the colonizer and the colonized is drawn into sharp focus. Many of those Indians who were in the administrative positions were from Brahmin families, and as such were beneficiaries of the solidification of such a system within society as indicated in the Introduction to this book. Robert Frykenberg (2005) highlighted this:

> Brahmans have always controlled information. That was their boast. I It was they who had provided information on indigenous institutions. It was they who had provided this on a scale so unprecedented that, at least at the level of All-India consciousness, a new religion emerged the likes of which India had perhaps never known before. (89)

It served the needs of the high-caste Brahmins to portray a Hinduism that benefited them, and for the British to reinforce this hierarchy that served their purposes. This is not to suggest that the Brahmins were to blame; rather, that caught in an oppressive system, they were 'forced' to make the best of it for themselves.

The discussion about varna and caste is an important aspect of learning about Hinduism. For many, the various samskaras (see Chapter 7), ashramas and wider aspects of personal dharma have some relation to varna and the story of Purusha. To eliminate the concept of varna from Hinduism would be to strip various aspects of what has laid the basis for various practices throughout history. It is possible to recognize the interplay between religion and culture, but over the many centuries, they have become fused. Varnashramadharma does still seem to have an important part to play in a discussion of a person's personal dharma. This is not to suggest, however, that the concept of caste does, and there may be a need to explore earlier understandings of dharma and varna when exploring Hinduism.

Thoughts for the classroom

The question could be asked as to whether the caste system should be taught in the classroom. At various times, it has been described as an 'atrocity' that deserves to be condemned in the 'harshest [of] terms' (Lakhani, 2007). It is suggested that it has no relation to Hinduism but is a societal expression that became falsely enmeshed or identified with a Hindu way of life. Jay Lakhani (2007) continues that:

> Just as crusades or inquisitions committed in the name of Christianity should not be equated to Christianity the hereditary hierarchical caste cannot and should not

be equated to Hinduism. The caste system is a socio-economic feature; it does not originate from religion.

Therein lies the difference; the so-called caste system, as reflected and viewed through a hierarchical lens, is different from the varnas that were, and are, seen to be egalitarian in nature. The continuation of the teaching of 'caste' as Hindu could be seen as an act of colonial violence against the community. By accepting its existence as rooted within Hinduism, and as supporting Indian society in its hierarchical form, it can be seen to reinforce or 'add to the sense of inferiority that many Indians feel about their own culture' (Tully, 1992, 7); conversely, this is the result of the colonial approach to India in the nineteenth and twentieth centuries that European, and Christian, culture was far superior. It would appear that if something is repeated often enough, those involved begin to accept it as truth.

The recognition that difference is not something to be denigrated is important. There have been movements throughout history that have tried to recapture what would be seen today as the essence of the varnas. This continues today in areas of Hindu and Indian society, with untouchability now illegal, and laws to try to address the historical discrimination against the scheduled castes.

While the above suggests that acceptance of how varna is viewed today, it would be wrong to accept a wholesale revisionist view of caste throughout history and modern times. It was reinforced by colonialism and perhaps given a greater focus, but throughout history, there has been evidence of the caste system being imbued with validity by religious beliefs and practices. It is at this point that a worldview approach to the teaching of Hinduism can be helpful. To simply say that any vestiges of caste are the result of societal and cultural influences, rather than religion, is to ignore the complex relationship that these forces have had throughout history and in contemporary society. As noted earlier, some of those Indians in positions of power within the colonial system reinforced the system adopted by the British as it reinforced their place within the structures. Throughout history, the nature of untouchability as ritually unclean was highlighted by the inability of untouchables to enter into temples. A person's dharma became associated with their varna by birth, rather than their varna by aptitude. Rules, both religious and social, became associated with the various jatis and varnas. The caste system was not created by colonialism, rather it was given concrete status, as it enabled an adoption of the view that European society and culture was superior, and also enabled an 'easier' ruling of the peoples. The censuses that did so much to reinforce and reify ideas of religion fulfilled much the same task with regard to caste. It is important to note the way that religious beliefs and practices are mediated through culture and society.

One area where it might be interesting and valid to teach about the development of what is termed 'the caste system' is through a sociological lens. Within a Marxist approach to society, the system of the varnas can be seen, when they are 'corrupted' to be evidence of the superstructure of society. Its identification with Hinduism may well have helped people to come to a sense of meaning about their position in life, but it did so in a way that benefited the ruling classes. Consequently, Marx argued that the primary function of religion, and in this case the varnas, is to reproduce, maintain and make legitimate class inequality. According to Marx, religion serves as a means of controlling the working population by promoting the idea that the existing hierarchy is natural, God-given and therefore unchangeable – in other words, the rich are rich and powerful while the poor are poor and powerless because this is God's will. It is this that leads Marx to make his oft-quoted maxim that religion is 'the opium of the people'. He continues to suggest that:

> The abolition of religion as the illusory happiness of the people is the demand for their real happiness. To call on them to give up their illusions about their condition is to call on them to give up a condition that requires illusions. The criticism of religion is, therefore, in embryo, the criticism of that vale of tears of which religion is the halo. (Marx & Engels, 1975, 175–176)

For Hindus, the abolition of a Hindu way of life would be anathema; however, the illusory accretions that were added to the concept of varna would be given up. Many Hindus now see the concept of 'caste' to be a corruption that, throughout history and especially in the context of colonialism, was developed in a way to subjugate the masses and keep people happy with their lot in life.

Conversely, or perhaps attendant to this view, the teacher could explore the purpose of society and its organization through the writings of Durkheim. He describes elements of religion as totemic, meaning shared symbols that unify and give meaning to a community. The varnas can be seen as a way that society has unified itself around 'external and tangible form'; it becomes 'the sign by which each clan distinguishes itself from others, the visible mark of its personality, a mark that embodies everything that belongs to the clan in any way, men, animals and things' (2001, 154). Society becomes intertwined with the religious aspects of life, and the varna society can be seen as a positive influence of regulation and identity.

Returning to the wider principle of dharma, as it is central to Hindu identity, so too should it be central to the teaching of Hinduism within the class. As two Hindus have noted:

> Being a Hindu is a way of life, and is mostly made of dedication and discipline.
>
> It is a philosophy of life, which is based on concepts communicated through stories (Upanishads) like Ramayana and Mahabharata. Some of the core concepts are – doing your dharma (your role, responsibility, your work), being a good human (various morals depicted through stories), and not worrying too much about the results (as your destiny is already determined from previous deeds/karma, perhaps in previous lives).

In exploring the concept of dharma, this chapter has pointed forward to expressions of belief in devotion (Chapter 6) and the ethical dimension expressed in morality (Chapter 7).

The concept of dharma also draws on sacred texts (see Chapter 5) and also reflects on ideas of the Divine (see Chapter 2). In some ways, it is the unifying feature of all of the different strands of the Hindu way of life. Recognizing this in the classroom enables the teacher and the student to draw things together. As different concepts and practices are taught, the relation to dharma would be advantageous. To take just one example from the classroom, where the Ramayana may be taught as the victory of good over evil, this may be true on one level; the recognition of the exemplification of dharma, and the need for adharma to be overcome, changes ever so slightly the focus of the teaching. Similarly, when teaching about yoga or bhakti, the links with the niyamas would provide important context. It will be interesting for the reader as they read the rest of this book to keep dharma in mind and begin to make those links for themselves.

Chapter 2

The Nature of the Divine

> Then Vidagdha, the son of Sakala, asked him. 'How many gods are there, Yajnavalkya?' Yajnavalkya decided it through this (group of Mantras known as) Nivid (saying), 'As many as are indicated in the Nivid of the Visvadevas – three hundred and three, and three thousand and three.' 'Very well,' said Sakalya, 'how many gods are there, Yajnavalkya?' 'Thirty-three.' 'Very well,' said the other, 'how many gods are there, Yajnavalkya?' 'Six.' 'Very well' said Sakalya, 'how many gods are there, Yajnavalkya?' 'Three.' 'Very well,' said the other, 'how many gods are there, Yajnavalkya?' 'Two.' 'Very well,' said Sakalya, 'how many gods are there, Yajnavalkya?' 'One and a half.' 'Very well,' said the other, 'how many gods are there, Yajnavalkya?' 'One.' 'Very well,' said Sakalya, 'which are those three hundred and three and three thousand and three?'. (*Brihadaranyaka Upanishad* 3.9.2)

In reciting this conversation between Vidaghda and Visvadevas, the complexity of Hindu belief in the Divine is expressed. There is a multiplicity in unity, and perhaps this would account for the diverse range of responses that Hindus would give when asked about the nature of the Divine.

The concept of 'God' and the nature of the Divine encapsulates the undesirability, as well as the almost impossibility of placing Hindu beliefs into the neat little boxes designed for religions in the world religions paradigms spoken about in the Series and Volume Introductions above. It is very difficult to avoid the words 'God' or 'gods' in a discussion of the divine within Hinduism, but it is important to note that as a word 'God' conjures up different images and meanings. As with each individual religion, and the interpretations thereof, the inexact and competing definitions of specific words can lead to different interpretations. When speaking of Hindu beliefs about the Divine, it is possible to observe writers who use 'God' with a capital 'G' for the one God, and 'gods' or 'goddesses' with a lower case 'g' for the different manifestations of the one God. The understanding of the 'one' and the 'many' will form the main bulk of this chapter, and although it would be tempting to adopt this approach in a way to differentiate between the understandings of the Divine, this book will strive to use specific terminology for the 'one' that does not adopt the use of the term 'God' (though it will be used on occasion), and will tend to use deities in relation to various manifestations. For some, this may appear to be an unnecessary distraction; even though Hinduism with its colonial connotations is used, the reasons for its use having already been explored, there are other colonial hangovers that will not be perpetuated. Indeed, some of the terminology that I will avoid using has been used by Hindus themselves, but I think they have been used to help non-Hindus (especially those with a Christian background) understand Hinduism in a way that is intelligible for them. Thus, a Brahmin becomes a priest, or Brahman becomes God. Each of these terms is 'Christian' or 'Western' and as such come loaded with certain connotations and understandings. Rather than making Hinduism intelligible on Christian terms, an approach that continues the legacy of colonialism, I think it is important for non-Hindus to understand Hinduism on Hindu terms. I will strive as much as possible to avoid non-Hindu terminology. Where original writers or translators have used such terms, I will keep the original language, but it will be in the context of this caveat.

In the Introduction to this book, we explored aspects of the historical development of Hindu beliefs. It is not the purpose of this chapter to cover the same ground. Rather, this chapter will seek to explore the various approaches to the Divine that are found within Hinduism today.

It is usual in the classroom to begin an exploration of the nature of the Divine within Hinduism with a discussion of Brahman. Although the term Brahman is often used as a shorthand to describe the universal force or power that is within and beyond everything, Brahman might actually be more correctly described as one of three features of the Divine. Together, the three features are:

- Brahman (everywhere)
- Antayarami (within)
- Bhagavan (outside/beyond)

Rasamandala Das (2002) suggests that while these three features might lie at the heart of all schools of Hinduism, they are given different emphasis and understood in different ways. He suggests a difference between advaita and dvaita schools (see Introduction). On the one hand, advaita traditions adopt a monistic approach and 'consider the soul one with God in all respects. The numerous deities are considered more or less imaginary, representing aspects of the formless, all-pervading world soul (*Brahman*).' Whereas, dvaita traditions would be considered dualistic and 'consider the soul and God to be eternally distinct even though both are *Brahman* (spirit). God is *saguna*, possessing spiritual attributes such as form, personhood, and activity' (22). The other deities are manifestations of the Divine personhood observing a pantheon that might be termed 'inclusive monotheism' or 'henotheism' (Das, 2002, 22). Both terms suggest the idea of a supreme deity, with subordinate deities which can reflect some of the attributes of the supreme.

This is a nuance or description that may not ordinarily find discussion in the classroom. It is easier and more common to explain that there is one Supreme deity (Brahman) who is understood and personified in many different ways. It is possible to suggest that the other deities are created or imagined to better understand qualities of the Divine. In this way, Brahman is likened to the light entering into a prism, and the resultant colours that emanate are just aspects that help humans understand that which is outside of understanding.

Sometimes as teachers it is possible to prioritize a knowledge of what Hindus believe and therefore miss the lived reality of the experience of Hindus. Consider the Year eight Hindu child who tells their teacher that they believe in many deities. The teacher, who is a Hindu herself, suggests to them that they have misunderstood the teaching and that there is only one 'God'. The teacher, though well-intentioned, is prioritizing their own interpretation of Hindu beliefs over what may be perceived as more 'folk' teaching. It is important that when belief in the Divine is being taught, that while there is a more accepted interpretation, there are many different ways to understand what the Divine is and how it can be worshipped.

It is against this background that this chapter will discuss the Divine and the associated deities. Both approaches should be recognized, and when speaking of certain expressions or manifestations of the Divine, their 'reality' can be interpreted in different ways. One note of caution should be surrounding the term 'reality' in relation to the various deities. For worshippers, the deities are 'real' in the sense that they either exist or are manifestations of aspects of the Divine to enable Brahman to be understood. At no point does the question of their existence reduce their importance in the worship of, and devotion to, the various deities. All of the actions towards them are seen to be efficacious.

In exploring the three aspects of the Divine suggested above, with Brahman being everywhere, Antaryami referring to being within the individual and Bhagavan as being outside of the universe and transcendent, it is important to note that this is only one interpretation, and that often the shorthand of Brahman is used to cover all of the different aspects.

Brahman

As indicated earlier, as an aspect of the Divine, Brahman is to be found within all living beings and throughout the universe. The *Mundaka Upanishad* outlines:

> That Brahman is in front and in back, in the north, south, east, and west, and also overhead and below. In other words, that supreme Brahman effulgence spreads throughout both the material and spiritual skies. (2.1.1)

When speaking of the Divine, it is usually Brahman that Hindus refer to, and that the manifestations of the Divine are different aspects to help understand that which is ineffable. In many traditions of Hinduism, Brahman is nirguna, meaning that without form and without characteristics, Brahman just is. The *Chandogya Upanishad* outlines this belief:

All this is Brahman. (1.1.1)

It then goes further in making Om/Aum synonymous with Brahman:

> The full account, however, of Om is this: – The essence of all beings is the earth, the essence of the earth is water, the essence of water, the plants, the essence of plants man, the essence of man speech, the essence of speech the Rig-veda, the essence of the Rig-veda the Sama-veda, the essence of the Sama-veda the udgitha (which is Om). (1.1.1–2)

Aum is the sacred syllable, the symbol of Brahman, the source of all existence. In this form, it has become the recognizable symbol of Hinduism. For some Hindus, it is the sacred syllable/sound, the sound that something makes when it is making no noise, whether it is a person, an animal, a tree and so on. As such, it is an apt symbol of Brahman, as the Absolute that is within everything, and gives life to the universe.

Kim Knott (2016) outlines this view of Brahman:

> This [Brahman] originally referred to creative power or truth. . . . By the time of the early Upanishads, it had come to refer to the impersonal cosmic principle or absolute reality. (16)

Within dualistic and monistic approaches within Hinduism, the relationship between Brahman and the atman (soul) is most different. In monistic views, everything is Brahman, and the atman is naturally included in this. The *Chandogya Upanishad* outlines this:

> All this is Brahman. Let a man meditate on that (visible world) as beginning, ending, and breathing in it (the Brahman). Now man is a creature of will. According to what his will is in this world, so will he be when he has departed this life. Let him therefore have this will and belief . . . He is my self within the heart, smaller than a corn of rice, smaller than a corn of barley, smaller than a mustard seed, smaller than a canary seed or the kernel of a canary seed. He also is my self within the heart, greater than the earth, greater than the sky, greater than heaven, greater than all these worlds. (13.14.1,3)

Figure 2.1 AUM the unicode consortium, Public domain.

In some ways this is pre-empting the discussion of antaryami below, but the monism is the idea that Brahman is everything and everything is Brahman. Whereas within a dualistic approach, while linked, and there is a desire to be united with Brahman, Brahman and the atman are distinct (this will be explored further in Chapter 4).

As will be explored later in this chapter, the idea that Brahman has many manifestations enables the Divine to be both nirguna (without qualities) and sagun (with qualities). In some ways, this can be similarly delineated as Absolute and personal understandings of Brahman; in reality, however, it is the Absolute that is supreme; Sarvepalli Radhakrishnan (1968) adopting a qualified dualism suggests that:

> Both the Absolute and the Personal God are real, only the former is the logical prius of the latter. The soul when it rises to full attention knows itself to be related to the single universal consciousness, but when it turns outward it sees the objective universe as a manifestation of this single consciousness. (79)

Antayarami

Antayarami is the concept within Hinduism that the Divine is within the heart, explained in the *Bhagavad Gita*:

> The Supreme Lord dwells in the hearts of all living beings, O Arjun. According to their karmas, He directs the wanderings of the souls, who are seated on a machine made of material energy. (18:61)

Das (2002) explains this from an ISKCON perspective; the Divine is:

> 'the controller within' and refers to God residing within the hearts of all beings. He is sometimes called the Supersoul, Paramatman. The Katha Upanishad likens the soul and the Supersoul to two birds sitting within the same tree (i.e. the heart). The Supersoul is initially perceived in various ways, through memory, instinct, intelligence, inspiration, and exceptional ability. He is the object of meditation for many mystic yogis. This feature of God represents his cit (knowledge) aspect. (20)

The idea of Brahman or the Divine within the heart means that a person is guided by the heart, in Das' discussion by 'the controller within', or maybe the body is a vehicle which is driven by the atman, signified by the heart. This understanding of the Divine is very close to the idea of Brahman within every living thing, but at the same time highlights the interconnectivity between Brahman and the atman, usually from a monistic perspective, though it could reflect a dualistic approach. The heart is seen to be the 'housing' for the soul in the *Katha Upanishad*:

> The Purusha of the size of a thumb, the internal atman, is always seated in the heart of all living creatures; one should draw him out from one's own body boldly, as stalk from

grass; one should know him as pure and immortal; one should know him as pure and immortal. (2.3.17)

The symbolism of the heart and of antaryami is not explored in detail within Hindu writings; Jayaram (n.d.) suggests that the presence of the Divine in the heart has five meanings that can be summarized as:

1. The heart houses the soul.
2. It is the place that the atman goes to at the time of death.
3. It is the source of all thoughts and emotions.
4. It is intelligence, enabling a person to see through maya.
5. It enables a person to connect with Brahman.

Each of these aspects of the heart is the role of Brahman, and antaryami serves to remind the Hindu that they are intimately connected with the Divine. While Brahman may be Absolute, Brahman is also personal. This finds expression in the teachings of Ramanuja who built on the monism of Shankara, developed a qualified dualism that recognized monism but also taught that people are different from one another, and different from Brahman as this is the experience of our own senses and feelings. He taught 'that ultimate reality is internally qualified (vishishita). What is more, ultimate reality is not impersonal and without qualities' but is 'the Lord, the one who is desired by all those who seek to escape suffering' (Knott, 2016, 29), and is the supreme person (*purusha*).

Bhagavan

Bhagavan is often translated as 'Lord' or 'The Adorable One' and is often used interchangeably with 'God'. It is not unusual to hear Hindus speak of Bhagavan as a shorthand for the Divine, or indeed for a title, for example Bhagavan Krishna or Bhagavan Swaminaraya. When hearing or seeing the title used, it is important to note the context and the object of its use. It is also used to define or identify the being that is Absolute, or Supreme, that which is transcendent and outside of time and the universe.

In the *Vishnu Purana* VI.5, Bhagavan is defined thus:

That essence of the supreme is defined by the term Bhagavat: the word Bhagavat is the denomination of that primeval and eternal god: and he who fully understands the meaning of that expression, is possessed of holy wisdom, the sum and substance of the three Vedas. The word Bhagavat is a convenient form to be used in the adoration of that supreme being, to whom no term is applicable; and therefore Bhagavat expresses that supreme spirit, which is individual, almighty, and the cause of causes of all things. The letter Bh implies the cherisher and supporter of the universe. By ga is understood the leader, impeller, or creator. The dissyllable Bhaga indicates the six properties, dominion, might, glory, splendour, wisdom, and dispassion. The purport of the letter va is that elemental spirit in which all beings exist, and which exists in all beings. And thus this great word Bhagavan is the name of Vasudeva, who is one with the supreme Brahma, and of no one else. This word therefore, which is the general denomination of an adorable object, is not used in reference to the supreme in a general, but a special signification. When applied to any other (thing or person) it is used in its customary or general import. In the latter case it may purport one who knows the origin and end and revolutions of beings, and what is wisdom, what ignorance. In the former it denotes wisdom, energy, power, dominion, might, glory, without end, and without defect.

It can be seen that Bhagavan is used by Vaishnavites to refer to Vishnu as Lord, whereas Ishvara is used in relation to Shiva by Shaivites. The division of use is not as simple as this, and Bhagavan is used by many different Hindus as a word synonymous with 'Lord' or the Supreme Being and can be found to be used by Shaivites, or to refer to Adi Shakti in Shaktism. Bhagavan can also be used in reference to manifestations of Vishnu such as Krishna, who is seen as the Supreme Being. Ramanuja is one of the thinkers who identifies Vishnu with Brahman and Purusha, and he does this by using aspects of the *Vishnu Purana*:

> The question in essence is 'What is Brahman?' The answer making a decisive declaration of the nature of Brahman follows. 'The universe originates from Vishnu and exists in him. He is its maintainer and controller. He is the world. He is greater than the greatest. He is supreme. He is the Paramatman. He dwells in the selves. He is beyond all characterizations in terms of form, colour, etc. He is beyond decay and cessation, beyond modification, increase and characterizations in terms of forms, colour, etc. He is beyond birth. He can be described only as the 'Ever-existent'. He dwells in all and all things dwell in him. Therefore the wise name him 'Vasudeva'. He is the supreme Brahman, eternal, unborn, imperishable and undecaying. He is always of the self-same form, free from evil, and thus pure. He is all this and has both this manifested and unmanifested as his form. And also he exists as the individual spirit and time. (1978, 48)

Supreme Being is different from the presentation of Shiva, Vishnu or Shakti as a manifestation of Brahman; whichever deity is seen to be Bhagavan or sometimes as Purusha, they are the Absolute, or the supreme manifestation of the power of Brahman within the universe. There are many interpretations that may be adopted.

It is therefore evident that teaching the nature of the Divine is complex and multi-faceted. As indicated earlier, the approach adopted within Hinduism, and within the classroom, will focus on Brahman as the Supreme Being and that other deities are only manifestations of various qualities. If Shakti is used as an example of how the difference between a manifestation and the Absolute can find expression within Hinduism.

Shakti, as the Divine feminine, is seen by some Hindus to be supreme. Vanamali (2008) describes her thus:

> Shakti, the mother power or divine energy, has many forms and symbols. All beauty and all ugliness flow from her. She is Lakshmi, the auspicious, bestower of boons and beauty. She is Saraswati, the giver of all wisdom and art. She is Tripurasundari, the most beauteous in the three worlds. But she is also Kali, the destroyer, whose wrath ignites the storm, the thunder, and the lightning. She is Mahishasuramardini, killer of the demon Mahisha. She is Chandika, the terrible, who lets loose the typhoon, the flood, and the tidal wave. (12–13)

As the Supreme Being, she is seen to contain the three cosmic principles of *prakriti*, *shakti* and *maya*.

> In terms of power the Divine Mother has a dual aspect: one as avidya, or cosmic delusion, and one as vidya, or cosmic deliverance. She binds us with her bewildering maya (cosmic illusion) in this world-play of birth, death, and enjoyment. On the other hand, it is she who releases us from this wheel of existence. Artists have depicted her as holding a noose in one hand, with which she binds us, and a sword in the other, with which she cuts the knot. (Vanamali, 2008, 14)

Further defining these three qualities or principles associated with Shakti:

> Adi Shakti or Parashakti is believed to be the divine energy of creation. She is known as 'Prakriti' meaning she who gives rise to all life forms. She is called 'Mahamaya' or one who creates the illusion of this world. Her name is Mahavidya meaning the greatest knowledge that frees one from the illusion of this world.
>
> In ancient times Adi Shakti was revered and worshipped above all the gods. She was the Mother Goddess who commanded the love of her children and showered them with blessings. Shakti represents consciousness and intellect. She is compassionate, merciful and nurturing as well as furious, vengeful and violent. (Puri, 2018, 4)

She has all of the qualities and aspects of the Divine, and is worshipped by many as such. In the *Devi Bhagavata Purana* 1:8, her supremacy is outlined, even above those traditionally described as the trimurti:

> Thus the omnipresent Sakti, the wise call by the name of Brahma. Those who are verily intelligent should always worship Her in various ways and determine thoroughly the reality of Her by every means. In Visnu there is the Sattviki Sakti; then He can preserve; otherwise He is quite useless; so in Brahma there is Rajasi Sakti and He creates; otherwise He is quite useless; in Siva, there is Tamasi Sakti and He destroys; else He is quite useless.

In many traditional depictions of Hinduism, the feminine is dependent on the masculine. Thus, Parvati and Sati are the consorts of Shiva, whereas in those aspects of Hinduism that see Shakti as supreme, it is the masculine that is dependent on the feminine. This is outlined by Chitgopekar (2022):

> One of the most important works in Shaktism, besides the Devi Mahatmya, is the Sanskrit text, the Devi Bhagavata Purana. It celebrates the divine feminine as the primary divinity, the origin of all existence, the preserver and the destroyer of everything, and the one who empowers spiritual liberation. (156)

Although Shakti is never addressed as Bhagvana, it is evident that her supremacy is an important aspect of Hinduism for many. This is illustrated in *The Adoration of the Divine Mother* from *Savitri* by Sri Aurobindo (2000):

> For one was there supreme behind the God.
> A Mother Might brooded upon the world;
> A Consciousness revealed its marvellous front
> Transcending all that is, denying none:
> Imperishable above our fallen heads
> He felt a rapturous and unstumbling Force.
> The undying Truth appeared, the enduring Power
> Of all that here is made and then destroyed,
> The Mother of all godheads and all strengths
> Who, mediatrix, binds earth to the Supreme. (3:2)

Conversely, there is dispute about the interconnection between the various manifestations of the Divine Feminine and Shakti. On the one hand, Puri (2018) suggests that 'All other goddesses in the pantheon are manifestations of her various strengths and attributes' (4). Whereas Kingsley (1986) suggests otherwise:

> I have tried to resist the theological assumption found in much scholarship on Hindu goddesses that all female deities in the Hindu tradition are different manifestations of an underlying feminine principle or an overarching great goddess. There are, indeed, certain Hindu texts, myths, and traditions that assert this position unambiguously. But to assume that every Hindu goddess in every situation is a manifestation of one great goddess prevents us from viewing such goddesses as Laksmi, Parvati, and Radha as deities containing individually coherent mythologies, theologies, and meanings of their own. (14)

This diversity of understanding is similar to that found throughout Hinduism more widely. It is possible that both are found within the various traditions of Shaktism. Shakti alone is supreme, but she can be understood in that one supreme sense in the various ways that she is pictured and worshipped within Hinduism more widely, and Shakti more narrowly. Within Shaktism, there are various forms that are recognized and worshipped by different traditions. These include, but are not limited to, Ambika, Durga, Kali, Sita, Parvati, Tripurasundari, Mahatmaya, Tara, Tulsi and Ganga. Whichever interpretation is accepted, the Divine feminine becomes important in Hindu belief and practice. The story of Sati will be narrated below in relation to Shiva Yogiraj, but as she died and the 108 separate pieces of her body fell to the earth, each place became a pitha (seat) where the force of Shakti is particularly strong (though the numbers differ according to authority):

> While noting that she is omnipresent and thus accessible to devotees everywhere, the Goddess provides a lengthy list of over seventy sites that are especially sacred to her. These sacred sites are referred to as sthanas, 'abodes' or 'dwelling places.' These places manifest a different ambience from the sacred sites known as tirthas ('fords' or 'crossings') associated especially with Shiva. Tirthas, often situated at river crossings, furnish access to a realm beyond this world, allowing the pilgrim as it were to cross from this human realm to the divine. Sthanas are not crossings but seats (pithas) of the Goddess, her habitations in this world, located under trees, beside a pond, in caves, or at the entrance to a village. The pilgrim seeks the Goddess at such places not with the otherworldly concerns of final liberation, but with the pressing issues of this world. (Mackenzie Brown, 2002, 25)

Examples of these Shakti pithas are:

- Tarapith (seat of Tara) which is the site of Sati's cornea.
- Vajreshvari Devi which is the place where Sati's breast fell.
- Kalimath and Kamakhya both claim to be the site where Sati's vulva fell to the earth.
- Hinglaj is the site of the crown of Sati's head.
- Jwalamukhi is the place where Sati's tongue fell.

As noted, the number and sites of pitha differ, but it should also be emphasized that

> the sites are spread throughout the subcontinent, from Baluchistan in modern Pakistan, to Assam in the far east, to deep in southern India . . . From this perspective, the entire subcontinent is seen as a single cohesive unit, with the network of sites connected to one another as are the parts of the body. (Lochtefeld, 2002, 252)

In this short discussion of understanding Bhagavan as Lord, it is important to note that many Hindus may approach Vishnu, Shiva, or Shakti as the Supreme (see below), and that other deities are linked to him or her. As we move onto a discussion of the various manifestations of the Divine, it is important to keep this diversity of understanding in mind.

Manifestations of the Divine

Throughout this chapter, it has been reiterated that an understanding of the Divine varies according to the different traditions within Hinduism, or even between families and individuals. The first part of the chapter suggested that there are many deities – both devas and devis. The various interpretations suggest that these deities are 'creations' that enable Hindus to personify or picture different qualities of Brahman. Whereas an inclusive monotheism, or henotheism, suggests that there is a Supreme Lord, and that there are many deities that help understand Brahman, but exist in relation to that Supreme Being.

One of the first things that is often taught within the classroom about Brahman is that while there are many ways by which 'they' can be known, it is through three main expressions; namely the Trimurti or Trideva: Brahma the Creator, Vishnu the Preserver and Shiva the Destroyer. This is a shorthand that is often used, but may not be entirely accurate in the impression that it gives. Vasuda Narayanan (2015) argues that while the idea of the Trimurti 'brings together the three great functions of a supreme god and distributes them among three distinct deities' it 'is misleading in two ways':

> First, it suggests that Hindus give equal importance to all three gods, when in practice most focus their devotions on a single supreme deity (whether Shiva, Vishnu, the Goddess, or a local deity who may be unknown in other parts of India) and consider the other deities secondary. Furthermore, Brahma is not worshipped as a supreme deity. Though portrayed in mythology as the creator god, he is only the agent of the supreme deity who created him; that deity, at whose pleasure Brahma creates the universe, may be Vishnu, Shiva, or the Goddess, depending on the worshipper's sect.
>
> Second, the 'polytheistic' interpretation of *trimurti* suggests that creation, preservation, and destruction are functions that can be performed separately. But in fact these functions are three parts of an integrated process for which one particular supreme god is responsible. In this context, destruction is not unplanned, nor is it final: it is simply one phase in the ongoing evolution and devolution of the universe. The cycle of creation will continue as long as there are souls caught up in the wheel of life and death. It is in this sense that devotees of Shiva, Vishnu, or the Goddess see their chosen deity as the creator, maintainer, and destroyer of the universe. (299)

This is often not recognized. The approach often undertaken does not contain this nuance; consider this extract from a textbook in describing the nature of the Divine:

> There is one universal spirit called Brahman which pervades the whole universe and is symbolised in the syllable OM. There are three main aspects to Brahman, called the Hindu triad of Brahma the creator, Vishnu the preserve and Shiva the destroyer . . . The Hindu triad of gods Brahma, Vishnu and Shiva are the three aspects of the life force of Brahman: creating, preserving and destroying and re-creating the universe. (Voiels, 1998, 22 and 25)

There is a simplicity in teaching Hindu beliefs about the Divine in this way. It is somewhat easily understood, and the various aspects of the Supreme Being are given expression. Other examples of teaching Hindu beliefs prioritize one view over another. In the textbook *Hinduism for Schools*, Seeta Lakhani (2005) rejects the idea of henotheism or inclusive monotheism suggested by Das (2002), but recognizes a religious pluralism (not plurality of gods):

> Religious pluralism is a uniquely Hindu idea. It suggests that every one relates to God in a different way. As we are all different, individually or as groups, the way we relate to God has to be necessarily different. . . . The concept and approach to God that we adopt has to reflect our inclinations including out social and historical backgrounds, it cannot be otherwise. (Lakhani, 2005, 11)

Lakhani is very much influenced by Vivekananda and Ramakrishna, and as such, the approach of the textbook reflects their teachings about the Divine, often termed neo-Vedanta. It has been suggested that this approach to Hinduism has been influential in the West and that it has also been 'Western-influenced' (King, 1999, 69). Care should be taken by the teacher in considering expressions of 'orthodox' Hinduism, as the recognition of diversity is at the heart of what is to be taught. Of interest is that within this textbook the representation of the Brahman and the trimurti is similar to above:

> The same God fulfilling three different roles is called *Trimurti*, 'three in one'. One God is depicted as three in the forms of *Brahma*, *Vishnu* and *Shiva*. (Lakhani, 2005, 13)

However, Vivekananda would reject their independent existence from Brahman, or as he uses the term 'God'; Lakhani (2005) further explains:

> The third approach to God in Hinduism is to think of Cod as formless, *nirakara*, as well as without attribute, *nirguna* . . . This approach takes pluralism to the other extreme. It moves dramatically away from the idea of God as a personality, to the idea of God as a principle. The idea that God has a particular form or that he has superhuman attributes like omniscience or omnipotence is seen as human limitations imposed on the concept of God. As we are human, the only way we can relate to God is in human terms, and thus we give him various human forms and superhuman attributes like being 'all compassionate', Some people recognise the limitations of such monotheistic approaches and thus prefer to adopt this third approach. The word 'God' is now replaced with the term 'Ultimate' or 'Cosmic Reality' – *Brahman*.

> Vivekananda has emphasised the importance of moving away from the idea of God as a personality to the idea of God as the principle that underpins everything. Modern thinking man will find is easier to relate to spirituality if this third approach is promoted. (20)

A similar textbook that explains the nature of the Divine from the perspective of ISKCON (International Society for Krishna Consciousness) highlights the slight nuance of approach depending on the source:

> In the material world there are three principal deities called the trimurti (literally 'three deities'). They correspond to God's function of creation, sustenance ad destruction. God also exists beyond this world, as an impersonal force and/or as the Supreme Person. Most commonly that transcendent Supreme is identified with Vishnu, or one of his forms (i.e. Krishna, Rama or Narayana). (Das, 2002, 48)

Here, Vishnu is seen to be identified with Brahman or the Supreme Being. This belief of Vaishnavism is also found in the *Bhagavad Gita* when speaking of Krishna:

> Arjun said: O Shree Krishna, I behold within Your body all the gods and hosts of different beings. I see Brahma seated on the lotus flower; I see Shiv, all the sages, and the celestial serpents. I see Your infinite form in every direction, with countless arms, stomachs, faces, and eyes. O Lord of the universe, whose form is the universe itself, I do not see in You any beginning, middle, or end. (11:15–16)

A similar view of Shiva is articulated in the *Brahmanda Purana*:

> We [Vishnu and Brahma] made obeisance, with palms joined in reverence, to the trident-bearing Siva (Sarva), the lord of extremely terrific voice, of terrible features and curved fangs, to that great unmanifest lord. 'Obeisance to you, O lord of worlds and Devas. Salutations unto you, O lord of Bhutas, O highly noble soul. Obeisance to you, O lord who have achieved permanent Yogic powers. Hail to you, O Lord established over the universe. You are Paramesthin (the highest deity), the supreme Brahman, the imperishable great region; you are the eldest one. You are Vamadeva, Rudra, Skanda and Lord Siva. (Tagare, 1958, 262–263)

In this example, Shiva is Supreme, while Brahma and Vishnu (and others) are expressions of him, and dependent upon him. This leads Andrew Nicholson to highlight this approach:

> Worshippers in an extremely pluralistic theological environment to coexist and acknowledge one another's gods, though typically not as equals. For the Vaisnava, all the benefits bestowed on the worshipper of Siva come ultimately come from Visnu. And for the Saiva, the fruits of devotion to Visnu have their ultimate origin in Siva. (2014, 186)

Indeed, in the *Ishvara Gita*, essentially a retelling of the Bhagavad Gita from a Shaiva point of view, reiterates the words of Krishna, but they come from Shiva (Nicholson, 2014, 234):

> As everything is submerged in me and as I am the *Atman* of all, I assume the bodies of all the gods and become the enjoyer (recipient) of all *Havis* (sacrificial offerings) and the dispenser of the fruits thereof. (*Kurma Purana* 2.4.8; Tagare, 1981, 351)

An approach to teaching that does not recognize diversity in understanding the Divine would be flawed, accepted as it is by some Hindus. Teachers need to be aware of the need to recognize the incomplete presentation of Hindu teachings when focusing on one approach. As has been suggested in the Series Editor's Foreword, the use of 'man', 'most' or 'some' would be a starting point with children of any age to articulate that what is being taught is not all there is in the realm of Hindu teaching.

All of this discussion serves as a background to the discussion of the various manifestations of the Divine. How these manifestations are understood is within the context of how Hindus see the Supreme, or the reality of the manifestations. In the exploration of some of the manifestations, their characteristics, acts and their devotees will be explained, but how their 'existence' is to be understood will be according to the worldview of the individual Hindu.

As indicated at the beginning of this chapter, there are millions of manifestations of the Divine; in this chapter, we will necessarily focus on only a small number. In so doing, their 'reality' will not be commented upon as we have recognized the variety of approaches to this question. The way that their symbols, stories and roles are understood is consistent whether they are considered to have independent or dependent existence.

Brahma

Within Hindu belief, Brahma is described as the Creator. In short, it is believed that he created the world and everything that is on it. He creates every new world that is made. Although this would be accepted by many, if not most, Hindus, Brahma is the creator in relation to the Supreme Being who is the ultimate creator. The story of creation in the Brahmanda Purana is narrated by Shalini Srinivasan (1971):

Figure 2.2 Brahma (Courtesy of Tim Evanson from Cleveland Heights, Ohio, USA, CC BY-SA 2.0 via Wikimedia Commons).

> In the very beginning, there was water everywhere and nothing else. From this water emerged a golden egg. The egg split and out of it came Brahma, who had created himself within the egg. He is called 'Swaymabhu', meaning self-born. From the first half of the egg, Brahma created the earth . . . and from the second, heaven. Brahma placed the earth in the water and started to create time, the eight directions and language. He made the sky, the clouds, thunder and lightning . . . After fourteen pralayas, Brahma goes to sleep, and everything he has made dissolves. All creation is returned to the eternal ocean from which Brahma created it. And with this, night falls for Brahma. He sleeps alone in the dark, dreaming of the next day when he will awake and create a new world. (2–4, 31)

In some stories following the creation of the universe, Brahma created Saraswati, his consort. And from their marriage, they gave birth to Manu, the first human. Brahma endowed him with the gifts of the five senses, movement, the power of procreation and the gift of thought.

In many of the murtis depicting Brahma, similar imagery and symbols are utilized. He appears seated on a lotus and is shown with four heads facing the four directions, symbolizing that he created the entire universe and, in many traditions, the four Vedas. He holds the Vedas in his hands, which help him create the universe. The water pot (*kamandalu*) is used in prayer to show that people can direct their thoughts to more spiritual matters. The *mala* (beads) he holds help people to meditate. His vehicle is a swan (hans), which is known for its judgement between good and bad and is said to be able to separate water and milk. Sometimes Brahma is shown riding a chariot drawn by seven swans.

Although at different points in history Brahma has been the focus of worship, he has few worshippers today. Swami Achuthananda (2018) outlines how he is viewed and worshipped today:

> Brahma is invoked in Hindu rituals and resides in almost every temple of Shiva or Vishnu, usually in the northern wall. However, despite being an important member of the Trimurti, only a few temples have Brahma as the chief deity. The famous ones include the Brahma temple at Pushkar, Rajasthan; the Erawan Shrine of Bangkok (Thailand); and the Brahma temple at Tirunavaya, Kerala. Temples dedicated to Brahma can also be found in the temple compound of Prambanan, located in Java, Indonesia, and within the complexes of Angkor Wat, Cambodia. (7–8)

There are different reasons suggested as to why Brahma is less focused upon than in the later centuries BCE. These range from the development of Vaishnavism and Shaivism that made Brahma dependent as creator on the figures of Vishnu and Shiva respectively. A different creation story highlights Brahma's dependence on Vishnu:

> Vishnu, as soul of the entire cosmos, produces countless universes from his breathing and the pores of his skin. He enters each universe, as the universal soul. From his

navel springs a lotus flower, upon which is born Brahma. Brahma performs austerity and creates the world from sound, beginning with the Gayatri-mantra.

Before he commenced creation, Brahma wanted to perform yajna (sacrifice) since the universe is created and maintained only through sacrifice. As yet, he had no ingredients. Therefore, the Supreme Lord agreed to become the necessary ingredients. Through that yajna, all species were created, as well as human society, with its places of residence, its languages, and so on. Brahma also created the various occupations and the corresponding system of four varnas. Thus the brahmanas represent the head of the Supreme Lord; the kshatriyas are his arms, the vaishyas his thighs and the shudras his legs. (Das, 2002, 35)

Different versions of this story include Shakti waking Vishnu, suggesting that it is time for creation. Although principally about Vishnu, this story highlights the contingent nature of Brahma in Hindu cosmology today. As an aside, this is not dissimilar to the view of Brahma within aspects of Buddhism, where Brahma may actually see himself as 'necessary' in the sense of Supreme and uncreated, but that even he is subject to the maya of existence (see Holt, 2023b).

There is also the suggestion that as the creator, his work is complete for this time, and there may be little benefit in worshipping him; he is seen to be acting 'primarily in an advisory capacity' (Bailey, 2008, 112). Less recognized reasons for his lack of worship focus on his originally having five heads. Becoming obsessed with one of his daughters, he made her the subject of unwanted attention and Vishnu chopped off one of his heads in punishment though in some retellings the object of his affection is Parvati, the consort of Shiva who is the one to administer the punishment. Another story from the *Shiva Purana* suggests that Brahma is punished with a lack of devotees and mandirs for deceiving others into thinking he is Supreme.

Vishnu

Vishnu, as the sustainer or preserver, is the usual way of describing his place in the trimurti of Hindu deities. Throughout the texts, Vishnu has many names, and from a Vaishnava perspective, many of the names used to describe the Supreme Being refer to Vishnu. In the *Vishnu Purana*, we read:

I bow unto Him that is holy and eternal – the supreme Soul who is every uniform, – even Vishnu, the Lord of all . . . even him who bringeth about creation, maintenance and destruction to everything. I bow unto him that is uniform yet hath a multiplicity of forms; who is both subtle and gross; – who is manifested and unmanifested; unto Vishnu, the cause of salvation. I bow unto Vishnu, the supreme Soul, who pervadeth the universe and who is the fundamental cause of his creation. (Dutt, 1896, 5)

Alongside other interpretations of Brahman and the Supreme Being, Vishnu is seen as both nirguna and saguna. Vishnu has many names; in the *Mahabharata* he is identified as such by the name Narayana:

I am Narayana, the Source of all things, the Eternal, the Unchangeable. I am the Creator of all things, and the Destroyer also of all. I am Vishnu, I am Brahma and I am Sakra, the chief of the gods. I am king Vaisravana, and I am Yama, the lord of the deceased spirits. I am Siva, I am Soma, and I am Kasyapa the lord of the created things. And, O best of regenerate ones, I am he called Dhatri, and he also that is called Vidhatri, and I am Sacrifice embodied. Fire is my mouth, the earth my feet, and the Sun and the Moon are my eyes; the Heaven is the crown of my head, the firmament and the cardinal points are my ears; the waters are born of my sweat. Space with the cardinal points are my body, and the Air is my mind . . . In consequence of my energy from my mouth, my arms, my thighs, and my feet gradually sprang Brahmanas and Kshatriyas and Vaisyas and Sudras . . . Moved by my own maya, I create gods and men, and Gandharvas and Rakshasas, and all immobile things and then destroy them all myself (when the time cometh). For the preservation of rectitude and morality I assume a human form, and when the season for action cometh, I again assume forms that are inconceivable. (CLXXXVIII)

The supremacy of Vishnu does not negate the possibility that other deities exist. The story is told in the *Bhagavata Purana* of Bhigru the sage being tasked to find out which of the deities was the greatest. After initially trying to recuse himself from the task because he was the son of Brahma, Bhigru was convinced otherwise and set about his task. He first visited Mount Meru and the court of Brahma. Upon arriving at Mount Meru, he did not treat his father with the respect that would have been expected and required. Brahma became angry at the slights that Bhigru had been guilty of, and it was only over the course of time that Brahma was able to calm himself; Bhigru apologized and left his father. He next went to Shiva in his court at Kailash. Shiva greeted him as a brother, yet Bhigru did not reciprocate. Shiva became angry and reached for his trident. Only with the intervention of Parvati was Shiva able to calm down. Bhigru next went to Vaikuntha and the court of Vishnu. Here he found Vishnu asleep whereupon he jumped on Vishnu's chest (despite Lakshmi's protestations). Vishnu awoke and jumped up, apologizing profusely to Bhigru for not greeting him appropriately, and expressed concern for Bhigru's feet and whether they had been hurt by connecting with his chest. Vishnu began to massage Bhigru's feet. The sage had found his answer. Vishnu was the greatest of the deities. The story is obviously told from a Vaishnava perspective and is focused on a particular set of qualities that might be best suited to Vishnu:

Diplomacy and equanimity are requirements for Vishnu's role as preserver of the universe, just as impulsiveness serves Shiva well in his role as the destroyer. So, strictly speaking, Bhrigu was testing a quality that was a prerequisite for the preserver role. (Achuthananda, 2018, 40)

When looking at the murtis of Vishnu, they generally have common characteristics such as his skin being blue to indicate he is as endless as the sky. His vehicle is the swift-flying bird Garuda. Vishnu is usually shown sitting on a large snake with many heads. The snake is called Ananta, which means 'endless' or 'eternal'. This shows that, even when the world is destroyed, Vishnu will be waiting to create it again. In some interpretations, when Ananta is coiled, creation ceases to exist. The *Bhagavata Purana* identifies Ananta as an avatar of Vishnu (1.18:19).

Vishnu generally holds a conch shell (*sankha*) indicating the spread of the divine sound *Om/AUM*. He also holds a discus (chakra), a reminder of the wheel of time, and to lead a good life; there is also a lotus (Padma), which is an example of glorious existence, and the fourth hand holds a mace (gada), indicating the power and the punishing capacity of Vishnu if discipline in life is ignored. He also carries the sword of wisdom, and sometimes he has a bow, which represents the cosmic senses (Bailey, 2008).

It is evident from the passage above from the *Mahabharata* about Narayana and others that in the person of Vishnu, 'For the preservation of rectitude and morality I assume a human form' meaning that, as viewed within Hindu teaching, he takes upon himself mortal form to preserve or sustain the world:

> Although I am unborn, the Lord of all living entities, and have an imperishable nature, yet I appear in this world by virtue of Yogmaya, My divine power. Whenever there is a decline in righteousness and an increase in unrighteousness, O Arjun, at that time I manifest Myself on earth. To protect the righteous, to annihilate the wicked, and to re-establish the principles of dharma I appear on this earth, age after age. (Bhagavad Gita 4:6–8)

Swami Achuthananda (2019) explains what this means:

> Avatar means descent and generally refers to the incarnation of a god into an earthly form, such as an animal or a human. It is a hallmark of the Hindu god Vishnu. Hindus believe Vishnu has descended to Earth on many occasions. However, ten such descents are considered more significant than the rest and are collectively known as Dashavataras, or ten descents. (1)

The identification of the Dashavataras as the main or significant avatars of Vishnu is shown in Figure 2.3, but this does not preclude other examples of avatars or manifestations of the Divine on the earth. Indeed, Ramakrishna accepted Jesus as a manifestation or avatar of the Divine (Bassuk, 1987), though this is contested and not without its controversy. More accepted within Hinduism is the place of Swaminarayan (see below). The focus here will be on the Dashavataras as these are accepted by the majority of Hindus. The ten avatars are:

- Matsya the fish saved creatures of the world from being drowned in a great flood.
- Kurma the tortoise helped the gods live forever.
- Varaha the boar rescued the earth when it fell from its place.

Figure 2.3 Vishnu and his avatars (Courtesy of Raja Ravi Varma, Public domain, via Wikimedia Commons).

- Narasimha, half man and half lion, killed a demon who attacked Vishnu's worshippers.
- Vamana, the beautiful dwarf, defeated the demon king Bali.
- Parasurama the warrior not only destroyed fighters but also put an end to war itself.
- Rama the king showed how to rule justly and live simply.
- Krishna the cowherd is loved by humans for his beauty, love and sense of fun.
- Buddha, the teacher, is revered by Hindus as well as Buddhists because he taught non-violence.
- He is to come to earth once more as: Kalki, the slayer, who will come to bring this age to an end and destroy all that is evil.

There are many accounts of the lives and actions of the various avatars. One mention in modern literature is found in Chapter 9 of *The Rise of Nine* by Pittacus Lore, where all of the Dashavataras are described, and it would be interesting for students to reflect on whether they are an accurate reflection of Hindu belief.

Possibly the two most focused upon avatars of Vishnu, and indeed two that are viewed as manifestations of the Divine in themselves and objects of worship, are Rama and Krishna. Their lives are explored in the *Ramayana* and *Bhagavad Gita* respectively, and it is perhaps the popularity of these that inspire people in devotion to each. Both are objects of worship in their own right, and the worship of Krishna as Supreme, rather than just an avatar of Vishnu, is a principle of ISKCON (see Chapter 8):

> Krishna is known as purnavatara, or the complete descent of the entire divinity into the form of humanity. The Bhagavad Purana declares, 'Krishnastu bhagavan swayam.' Krishna is the Supreme Lord in his completeness . . . Thus, Lord Krishna is not only the sat-chit-ananda, the existence knowledge-bliss of the absolute, without any diminution or contamination of his perfection, he is also the Uttama Purusha, the perfect person, amid all imperfect situations. (Vanamali, 2012, 23–24)

For Rama, he is an ideal:

> In Rama, God took on a human form with all its frailties in order to show us how our aspirations for a dharmic life can be fulfilled. In him we see how we can surmount our frailties and become divine, if we are prepared to completely subjugate the ego, live only for the good of the world, and act in consonance with the duties and obligations of our particular positions in society. Valmiki's Rama is the portrait of a man who shakes off the limitations of mortality and becomes divine by strict adherence to truth and honour . . . [T]he life of Rama shows that when a human being tries to uphold dharma at all costs, he must be prepared to sacrifice all other loves. (Vanamali, 2014, 3, 8)

Shiva

As indicated earlier, Shiva is seen both as the third aspect or destroyer of the trimurti, as well as the Supreme Lord within Shaivism. Only speaking of Shiva as the destroyer is to miss his complexity and depth. It would only focus on his seeming destructive and almost capricious nature, rather than recognizing him as one of the most easily petitioned. It is said that 'When a devotee gives all her heart to him, the Lord in turn becomes equally impatient to give his love to her' (Vanamali, 2013, 38). The separation of the trimurti into creator, sustainer and destroyer seems to miss the importance of Shiva. He is venerated and worshipped for many more reasons than his role as destroyer. Indeed, in Shaivism, he is worshipped as creator, preserver, and destroyer. He is 'best understood in three perfections: *Paramesvara* (Primal Soul), *Parasakti* (Pure Consciousness) and *Parasiva* (Absolute Reality)' (Sharma, 2000, 65). His supremacy is discussed above in a discussion of manifestations of the Divine, and the search by Brahma for his beginning and end. All references to the Supreme in the Puranas and the Vedas are references to Shiva within Shaivism. In this sense, he has come to be identified with Rudra and sometimes Indra from pre-Vedic times. Indeed, references in the Vedas to the 'three eyed one', while being initially identified as Ruda mantra, is known as the Tryambaka mantra, referring to the Shiva as three-eyed:

> We worship Tryambaka, whose fame is fragrant, the augmenter of increase; may I be liberated from death, and, like the urvaruka from its stalk, but not to immortality; let

us worship Trayambaka, whose fame is fragrant, the augmenter of increase; may I be liberated from death like the urvaruka from its stalk, but not unto immortality (Rig Veda VII.59.12).

There are many versions of the creation of the universe that involve Shiva. In the discussion of the creation of Lakshmi below, we see one role of Shiva in creation. One description of Shiva as the source of creation comes from the *Shiva Purana*:

> At the time of Great Dissolution when all the mobile and immobile objects of the world are dissolved everything gets enveloped in darkness, without the sun, planets and stars. There is no moon. The day and the night are not demarcated. There is no fire, no wind, no earth and no water. There is no unmanifest primordial being. The whole firmament is one complete void, devoid of all Tejas elements. There is no Dharma or Adharma, no sound, no touch. Smell and colour are not manifest. There is no taste. The face of the quarters is not demarcated. Thus when there is pitch darkness that cannot be pierced with a needle and what is mentioned in the Vedas as 'The Existent and the Brahman' is alone present. When the present visible world is not in existence, the Sat Brahman alone is present which Yogins observe perpetually in the inner Soul, the inner Firmament. It is incomprehensible to the mind. It cannot at all be expressed by words. It has neither name nor colour. It is neither thick nor thin. . . . The Being, having no form of its own, wished to create, in the course of its own sport, an auspicious form of its own endowed with all power, qualities and knowledge.

> A form that goes everywhere, that has all forms, that sees all, that is the cause of all, that should be respected by all, that is at the beginning of all, that bestows everything, and that sanctifies everything should be created (So it wished) and hence created that form of Ishvara of pure nature. The original Being without a second, with neither beginning nor end, that illuminates everything, that is in the form of Cit (pure knowledge) , that which is termed Supreme Brahman, the all-pervasive and undecaying, vanished. The manifest form of the formless Being is SadaSiva. Scholars of the ancient and succeeding ages have sung of it as Isvara. Isvara though alone, then created the physical form Sakti from his body. This Sakti did not affect his body in any way. (7. 4–9, 15–19 195–196).

The Purana continues with Vishnu arising from the side of Shiva, but being born out of his navel. Brahma also arose out of the lotus in the navel of Shiva. Brahma is said to have awoken in confusion not knowing where he was, but viewed himself as the original being and the creator. This confusion, and the humility of Shiva, can go some way to explain the various stories of creation that reference Brahma or Vishnu. Worship of either of these, or any manifestation of the Supreme, is only worship of Shiva.

> But, O beloved, remember that I myself am the Supreme Brahman, as is Vishnu. Devotion to him or to me is the easiest method of attaining salvation (Vanamali, 2013, 41).

Care should be taken by the teacher to recognize the multi-faceted nature of Shiva. Vanamali (2013) describes the contradiction or complementarity of Shiva:

> He is the Great Lord, Maheswara, and the Great God, Mahadeva. He is one of the Immortals, Unborn and Deathless. The Shiva Purana equates him with the Supreme Brahman of the Vedas. He is also the endearing personal god, Shambunatha, and the innocent Bhola with a naive nature. On the other hand he is Dakshinamurthy, the supreme teacher who gave the teachings of the Vedas, the Shastras, and the Tantras to the rishis. He is also master of every art, the supreme dancer, Nataraja, the supreme musician, composer of the Sama Veda. Though normally pictured in his fierce aspect, he can also take the form of Sundaramurti, the handsome one, and entrance anyone. To the wicked he is Bhairava, or Rudra of fierce aspect. Depending on the needs of the devotees he is capable of taking on many forms. His forms, attributes, decorations, weapons, attendants, and activities are given in great detail so that he becomes a living reality. As Rudra he is full of wrath and destruction, but as Shiva he is filled with all auspiciousness. He has two natures – one wild and fierce, the other calm and peaceful (30–31).

In murtis and pictures, Shiva is often represented in three different forms.

- Shiva Nataraj
- Shiva Yogiraj
- Shiva Lingum

These represent different aspects of Shiva, and each of these forms give some insight to his importance, his attributes and why he is worshipped.

Shiva Nataraj

In this form, Shiva is often known as the Lord of the Dance. As the Lord of the Dance, there are often two poses in which he is shown that show the two opposing forms or forces of Shiva - creator and destroyer. The first is *lasya*, which is often described as a gentle dance and is sometimes more associated with the dance of Parvati. It is said to be the dance of creation. The *tandava* dance is more frenetic and is the form most associated with Shiva, and it is this form that the murtis are traditionally performing. There is a deep symbolism to the dance.

> The dance, in fact, represents His five activities (Paiicakritya), viz: Srishti (overlooking, creation, evolution), *Sthiti* (preservation, support), *Samhara* (destruction, evolution), *Tirohhava* (veiling, embodiment, illusion, and also, giving rest), *Anugraha* (release, salvation, grace). These, separately considered, are the activities of the deities Brahma, Vishnu, Rudra, Mahesvara and Sadasiva. This cosmic activity is the central motif of the dance (Coomaraswamy, 1957, 59).

It is evident from this description, that as Lord of the Dance, Shiva is supreme. He is the creator, preserver and destroyer through his dance, through his power. The ninth tantra of Tirimular's (n.d.) *Tirumantiram* focuses especially on Shiva and his dance. It speaks of the dance of creation, the dance of the Vedas and many other aspects that dance symbolizes. It highlights the various features that would be seen in a Shiva Nataraj murti:

> The hand that holds the drum, (Si)
> The hand that sways, (Va)
> The hand that offers Refuge, (Ya)
> The hand that holds the blazing Fire, (Na)
> The lotus-foot, firm, on Anava Mala planted, (Ma)
> – Thus of the Divine Dance Form. (9278)

Each of these is then interpreted:

> Hara's drum is creation;
> Hara's hand gesturing protection is preservation;
> Hara's fire is dissolution;
> Hara's foot planted down is Obfuscation (Tirodayi)
> Hara's foot, raised in dance, is Grace (Redemption) abiding.
> The flaming fire is He;
> The sparkling light within is He. (2799–2800)

Exploring the various symbols of the murti as outlined above, it is possible to see the reasons for devotion to Shiva as Nataraj, as reflected in *Unmai Vilakkam*:

> Creation starts from the Drum. Protection proceeds from the Hand of Hope. The fire produces destruction. From the Foot holding down proceeds Droupavam; the Foot held aloft gives mukti. By these means, Our Father scatters the darkness of maya, burns the strong karma, stamps down mala (Anava) and showers grace, and lovingly plunges the soul in the Ocean of Bliss. This is the nature of His Dance. (36–37)

This suggests that:

- Shiva holds a drum to represent the pulse of time and the bang that began the universe.
- There are flames symbolizing destruction of ignorance and maya.
- He has one hand raised in blessing of protection to his devotees.
- He has one hand pointing towards his foot symbolizing rising above the demon dwarf, Apasarmara Purasha, who represents ignorance.

Other symbols within the murti include:

- The equanimity and calmness of Shiva are shown in his expression.

- The frenetic nature of the dance is represented by his hair spreading out behind him. One of these strands can be seen to be the deity and river, Ganges.
- Shiva's headwear often has a crescent moon, associated with Chandra, the deity of the moon.
- The fire can also symbolize creation and destruction.
- One hand has the abhaya mudra suggesting fearlessness of evil.

This dance unites Shiva with his devotees, and releases those who worship him from maya. As he is within everything, as a worshipper seeks union with the Divine, they realize that this ongoing dance takes place within the heart. Shiva, as a benevolent deity, as already outlined, seeks to bless those who seek his blessings.

Shiva Yogiraj

Figure 2.4 Illustrates the image associated with Shiva Yogiraj. In this form, he is 'the great ascetic god, the Great Yogi, Lord of Yogis, teacher of yoga' (Kramrisch, 1981, xv). Many of

Figure 2.4 Shiva Yogiraj (nlmAdestiny from Bangalore, India, CC BY 2.0 via Wikimedia Commons).

the stories in the Puranas surround Shiva as Yogiraj. The story of Sati, how she performed *tapayasa* (a form of penance and austerity) so that Shiva as Yogiraj would accept her as his wife. When her father, Daksha, offered sacrifice without Shiva, she gave up her body because her father had offended her Lord. Her body was destroyed and split into 108 separate pieces which fell to the earth, each place is known as a *Shakti pitha* (see above). She sought rebirth and was reborn as Parvati, who similarly performed penance and devotion so that Shiva as Yogiraj would accept her as his bride. Parvati's mother was opposed to the marriage, and in a practical joke, he appeared to Mena in one of his forms as Yogiraj:

> He had five faces and three eyes. His hair was matted and had the crescent moon on it. His body was smeared with ashes. He had ten hands with a skull on one, the trident and sword and many other gory weapons in the others. His upper cloth was a tiger's hide, and the lower one, an elephant's. He was utterly dishevelled. (Vanamali, 2013, 65)

After being convinced to allow the marriage, Shiva appeared to Mena in the form of Sundaramurti, 'the personification of masculine beauty' (Vanamali, 2013, 66).

The symbols most often associated with Shiva Yogiraj are:

- *The moon*: there are different elements of symbolism associated with the moon on Shiva's head. As indicated above, it has links with Chandra, the deity of the moon. The story outlines that Daksha cursed Chandra, but Shiva healed him. Upon Daksha cursing Chandra again, Shiva asked him to take refuge in his hair, where he would be able to constantly rejuvenate, thus Daksha causes the moon to wane, while Shiva causes him to wax; this has led to Shiva sometimes being known as Somnath. This also highlights a link to the drink, *soma*, and being the source of moksha:

    > Those who are inclined to the fruitive activity described in the Vedas worship Me through ritualistic sacrifices. Being purified from sin by drinking the Soma juice, which is the remnant of the yajnas, they seek to go to heaven. By virtue of their pious deeds, they go to the abode of Indra, the king of heaven, and enjoy the pleasures of the celestial gods. (Bhagavad Gita 9:26)

    Soma can also provide an 'intoxication', meaning the state of bliss that yogis can reach through yoga and meditation. In addition to this symbolism, the moon can also be seen as a crown on Shiva's head.
- *The third eye*: Shiva is often referred to as Triambaka because he has a third eye. Through the two eyes, a person is able to experience the physical world, but through the opening of the third eye through the practice of yoga, a person is able to open up another form of perception. This perception enables a person to see beyond *maya* (see Chapter 3) or illusion and see the true nature of existence and reality. It is not that existence is illusory, but the way that people experience is.

- *The trishul* (trident): with its three points, there are many things that the trishul is believed to symbolize. In one interpretation, the points represent the three aspects of Shiva as the Supreme Being, that of creation, sustaining and destruction. A further interpretation might also be body, mind and atman; or possibly will (*icchya*), action (*kriya*) and knowledge (*jnana*). Possibly, most importantly, for the representation of Shiva Yogiraj, are the three most important *nadis*: ida, sushuma and pingala. These are the channels through which energy is believed to travel through the body. Yoga is believed to purify these channels and enhance physical and spiritual health:

  > More specifically, pranayama is said to bring about nadisuddhi ('purification of the channels'). This is first stated in the Nisvasatattvasamhita Nayasutra (4.9) and is taught in several subsequent tantric works. In hathayoga texts purification of the channels is the primary aim of the simple method of pranayama (in contrast with the more siddhi- and liberation-oriented kumbhakas or 'breath-retentions'). (Mallinson & Singleton, 2017, 109–110)

  This purification leads to the rising of *kundalini* (the divine feminine energy) and enable moksha (see Chapter 3).

- *A snake*: Again there are many aspects to the symbolism of the snake that is often wrapped around Shiva's neck. It is symbolic of time and its passing, as it is often coiled, in a similar way to time being cyclical. The snake is often identified as the deity of Vasuki, who was used in the churning of the ocean at creation. In a Yogic sense, the snake is often believed to be symbolic of a filter, to stop poisons entering the body, whether those poisons are wrong ideas, emotions, energies or ideas. This is also seen to be identified as the *vishuddhi* which is centred in the throat:

  > The word vishuddhi literally means 'filter.' If your vishuddhi becomes powerful, you have the ability to filter everything that enters you. Shiva's centre is supposed to be vishuddhi, and he is also known as Vishakantha or Neelakantha because he filters all the poison. (Sadhguru, 2014, 41)

- *Ganga*: The goddess Ganga is often seen coming out of the top of Shiva's hair, representing Shiva as the source of the Ganges. For this reason, he is often known as *Gangadhara* (Bearer of the river Ganga). One narrative suggests that when Mother Ganges fell from the heavens through his hair, Shiva absorbed her power, or in some interpretations, she was imbued with Shiva's power.

- The kamandalu (water pot): this is usually seen to contain amrit and the need to transcend the physical world, and rid oneself of ego; the ultimate purpose of a yogi.

- Nandi the bull: is traditionally Shiva's vehicle and is a symbol of patience, as he sits and waits for Shiva. Patience is one of the ultimate principles of meditation, and Nandi is a reminder of this. In another interpretation, Nandi is a symbol of righteousness and as such Shiva is associated with such.

There are many other symbols of Shiva in the murtis that are created to represent him. It is evident from the small number outlined above how his place as Yogiraj is seen as an inspiration to his devotees. As the 'King of the yogis', he sets an example, but is also a source of inspiration and blessings for those who seek him through meditation and yoga.

Shiva Lingum

The Shiva lingum has been described as the 'most prevalent emblem of Siva, found in virtually all Siva temples. A rounded, elliptical, aniconic image, usually set on a circular base, or pitha, the Siva linga is the simplest and most ancient symbol of Siva' (Subramuniyaswami, 2001, 829). Although the form of Shiva lingum is often expressed as a symbol of fertility, as it is in the shape of a phallus, this is perhaps to view it through a Western lens. It has a much deeper representation with reference to Shiva as the Supreme Being. It is said that he 'can be worshipped through his formless aspect of the *linga*, as well as his aspect with form' (Vanamali, 2013, 25). Thus, in offering devotion to Shiva lingum, a devotee is worshipping the formless Shiva, Ishvara, or Brahman. Vanamali (2013) described the linga as meaning 'a sign' and as such:

> Brahman, the cosmic spirit, has no linga, but since the mind needs something concrete to hold on to, Shiva is depicted in the form of the *linga*. Shiva's *linga* is the divine phallus, the source of the seed of the cosmos, containing within it the entire universe of living and non-living beings. All life is created from it and returns to it. The *yoni*, or sign of the female, forms the base of the linga and together they represent the union of man and woman, Shiva and Shakti, the cosmic spirit combined with the cosmic Prakriti, or nature, through which the whole of creation comes into being. (25)

It is suggested that the lingum represents the three perfections of Shiva: *Parasiva* (Primal Soul), *Parasakti* (Pure Consciousness) and *Paramesvara* (Absolute Reality). It combines the feminine and the masculine, and as such can be seen to be the perfect representation of the Divine. Sometimes, it may be tempting in the classroom to focus purely on its phallic nature, if at all. The reference to the Supreme Being and the seeds of the cosmos is an important distinction to make and will help students understand the depth of its symbolism. Indeed, Swami Sivananda (1945) rejects its symbolism as a sexual organ:

> The popular belief is that the Siva Lingam represents the phallus or the virile organ, the emblem of the generative power or principle in nature. This is not only a serious mistake but a grave blunder. In the post-Vedic period, the Linga has become symbolic of the generative power of Lord Siva. Linga is the differentiating mark. It is certainly not the sex mark. (220)

The lingum enables the worshipper to focus on the formless one, and therefore Shiva. It might also be tempting for the teacher to ignore this aspect of Shiva as it is likely to cause comment or dismissiveness. As the form of the formless one, this is perhaps the most important representation of Shiva that can form an interesting aspect of discussion, but one that should be discussed in a way that is age appropriate.

Avatars

Although less spoken about than the avatars of Vishnu, there are seen to be many avatars of Shiva, though Shaivites may reject such and suggest that there are none, for example in the *Ishvara Gita* (the Shaivite version of the Bhagavad Gita) 'there is not avatar', rather the supposed avatars are but visible manifestations of the deity, suggesting that they might be illusory (Parrinder, 1982, 88). It has been observed in the *Linga Purana* that there have been twenty-eight manifestations or forms of Shiva (Winternitz, 1927, 569), whereas *Shiva Purana* suggests nineteen:

- Piplaad
- Nandi
- Veerbhadra
- Sharabha
- Ashwatthama
- Bhairava
- Durvasa
- Grihapati
- Hanuman
- Vrishabha
- Yatinath
- Krishna Darshan
- Bhikshuvarya
- Sureshwar
- Kirateshwar
- Suntantarka
- Brahmachari
- Yaksheshwar
- Avadhut

Some avatars such as Hanuman are suggested in Vaishnava literature (Lutgendorf, 2007); while other forms, or manifestations, are identified with the founders of certain Saivite traditions. Indeed, Shankara is seen by some as a manifestation of Shiva, though 'his doctrine is far removed from Saivism' (Mayeda, 1979, 4). Though maybe appealing to explore, the focus of Shiva worship is mainly on the three forms highlighted above and as the Supreme Being.

Lakshmi

> Salutations, O Daughter of the Ocean of Milk.
> Salutations, O Support of the Three Worlds.
> Salutations to you of the propitious glance.
> Protect me, for I come seeking refuge. (Song for Lakshmi, attributed to Agastya
> (Rhodes, 2010, 127))

Most discussions of Lakshmi usually begin with a description of her as 'the consort of Vishnu'. Although this is true, it reflects a view of Hinduism that prioritizes its masculinity. Lakshmi is much more than her relationship to her husband. As a devi, she can either be seen as a manifestation of Brahman or of Shakti. In this sense, and in forms of Shaktism, Vishnu is the consort of Lakshmi. The recognition of this type of language and positionality is important in the teacher's description of Hinduism.

Lakshmi is the goddess of wealth and fortune, and as such, is the focus of widespread devotion. Throughout Hindu homes and workplaces, there will often be small images of Lakshmi. These are accompanied by the lighting of an oil lamp or incense sticks and a short prayer. Lakshmi 'requires just this brief obeisance, for she does not insist on onerous fasts, nor does she have wrath that needs appeasing' (Chitgopekar, 2022, 169). Rather, she is popular and loved because she is the source of wealth and good fortune. The *Vishnu Purana* highlights:

> Thus, Brahman, have I narrated to thee, in answer to thy question, how Laksmi, formerly the daughter of Bhrigu, sprang from the sea of milk; and misfortune shall never visit those amongst mankind who daily recite the praises of Laksmi uttered by Indra, which are the origin and cause of all prosperity. (1.12)

She is worshipped as an aspect of Shakti, and is also beloved of Vaishnavites.

Having spoken of her independence, Lakshmi is also tied to Vishnu in the minds and worship of Hindus. The *Vishnu Purana* records:

> For in like manner as the lord of the world, the god of gods, Janarddana, descends amongst mankind (in various shapes), so does his coadjutrix Sri. Thus when Hari was born as a dwarf, the son of Aditi, Laksmi appeared from a lotus (as Padma, or Kamala); when he was born as Rama, of the race of Bhrigu (or Parasurama), she was Dharani; when he was Raghava (Ramacandra), she was Sita; and when he was Krishna, she became Rukmini. In the other descents of Visnu, she is his associate. If he takes a celestial form, she appears as divine; if a mortal, she becomes a mortal too, transforming her own person agreeably to whatever character it pleases Visnu to put on. (1.12)

Thus, she is worshipped in the forms of her avatars (see below the discussion of Sita) and also as Lakshmi herself. Her relationship with Vishnu is not subservient, however. They are seen to be evidence of the accessibility of the Divine as both masculine and feminine. They work in perfect harmony, whether as Lakshmi and Vishnu, Krishna and Radha or Rama and Sita. She is seen as benevolent as the goddess of wealth and auspiciousness, as such she can be seen as an intermediary between devotees and Vishnu. Their symbiotic or complementary nature can be seen in the Bradford Lakshmi Narayan Mandir where they are both the main deities.

In her murtis (see Figure 2.5) there is symbolism that reminds devotees of various aspects of Hindu belief, as well as her role and importance.

Figure 2.5 Lakshmi by Raja Ravi Varma, Public domain, via Wikimedia Commons.

These include:

- Her four arms are symbolic of the four goals of life: dharma, artha, kama and moksha (see Chapter 4).
- Sometimes she is depicted 'carrying rosary, axe, mace, arrow, thunderbolt, lotus, pitcher, rod, Sakti, Sword, Shield, Conch, bell, wine-cup, trident, noose and the discus' (Rajeswari, 1989, 19).
- Sometimes she is seated on a lotus flower, or is holding two of them. Lotus flowers are often a symbol of being able to overcome bad circumstances while maintaining purity and attaining success.
- There are often gold coins falling from one her hands. This is a symbol that she is able to reward her devotees with prosperity.
- Two elephants are often near her and are symbolic of her appearance as Gajalakshmi. Elephants are 'symbols of wealth, strength, and boldness' (Kozlowski & Jackson, 2013, 88).
- In one hand she often holds a water pot (kumbh), which is a symbol of fertility and prosperity.

There are many stories associated with Lakshmi. One of the stories of Lakshmi is often associated with the celebration of Diwali (see Chapter 6). In the story of King Hima, he had a son who it was foretold would die from a snakebite on the fourth day of his marriage. Knowing this, his wife made sure he stayed awake. To do this, she placed piles of silver and gold at her husband's bedroom door, and lights were lit throughout the palace. She kept him awake by telling stories and singing songs. Disguised as a serpent, Yama, the god of death, arrived but was blinded by the dazzling light of the silver and gold that was illuminated by the lights. Instead of entering the bedroom, Yama fell asleep on the coins, soothed by the stories and the songs. He left quietly in the morning. This day is celebrated as 'Yamadipdan' – the offering of lamps to Yama. Lamps are burnt all night. Lakshmi thus has importance in relation to Vishnu and also as the Supreme Goddess, who lies behind everything.

Sita

Auspicious Sita, come thou near: we venerate and worship thee

That thou mayst bless and prosper us and bring us fruits abundantly. (*Rig Veda* 4.57.6)

As an avatar of Lakshmi, Sita is often seen as being defined by her relationship with Rama, whereas there are elements of her story and character that go beyond the dutiful wife. She is seen by many as an ideal, someone who is respectful to her husband, and who fulfils her role as a wife and mother. She is loyal to Rama as she accompanies him into banishment in the forest. Her capture by Ravana is due to the competing demands of dharma; to follow the instructions of Lakshmana, or to fulfil her duty to respond to the petition of an elderly holy man. Throughout the story, she remains pure, and is willing and able to demonstrate her purity through a trial of fire so that she can return to Ayodhya at Rama's side as his queen.

It is at this point that most of the retellings of the Ramayana in the classroom end. There is much more to her story, and her centrality to the events of the Ramayana has led some to reframe it as the *Sitayana* (Srinivasa Iyengar, 1987; Majmudar, 2019). Greater exploration of feminist readings of the story of Sita and Rama can be found below in this chapter and in Chapter 7. At this stage, it is important to note, however, the various elements of the story that happen after Rama and Sita's return to Ayodhya.

The first surrounds the announcement of her pregnancy; Rama's response is similar to that when he defeated Ravana: 'It's not me! It's others who will doubt the faithfulness of Sita.' Instead of speaking to her about this, he orders Lakshmana to abandon Sita in the forest. It is here that she enters the ashram of the sage, Valmiki. She gives birth to her sons, Lava and Kusha, and then raises them. They are trained in martial arts, and some traditions hold that they defeated their father's army before being revealed as his sons. Asking Sita once again to prove her virtue, so that she can return to Ayodhya with him as his queen, she demurs and instead is swallowed up into the earth by Bhumi (goddess of the earth).

Although these events are found in Valmiki's Ramayana, they are rarely told in schools, where the triumphal return suggests a 'happily ever after'. Interestingly, there are other stories of Sita that reflect her link with Shakti as the supreme deity. The *Adbhuta Ramayana* (sometimes called the *Sitayana*) is a Shakta text that is presented as an appendix to the original Ramayana. The story tells that on defeating the ten-headed Ravana, that there is a thousand-headed Ravana from Pushkar, who is the brother of the original Ravana. In battling the thousand-headed Ravana, Rama is about to be defeated; at this point, 'Sita assumes the frightening form of Mahakali, carrying all the marks of Shiva – the third eye, the crescent moon, and the trident. She kills the brutal Rakshasa along with his sons and army' (Chitgopekar, 2022, 27). After her victory, Brahma is reported to have said to Rama:

> She embodies in her divine self the virtues of 'Nirguna' as well as 'Sagun' (i.e., she has a subtle, invisible form having no attributes but incorporating the stupendous powers or Shakti of Nature which controls the working of the entire cosmos, as well as a gross, visible form having attributes as is evident in a colossus and fearful form as Mahakali, the great black Goddess of death, respectively). (Chhawchharia, 2009, 355–356)

The final two Cantos of the Adbhuta Ramayana are Rama lauding Sita with many descriptions of the Divine, and her taking upon herself the mortal form of Sita to return to Ayodhya.

Although Sita is mainly worshipped as part of a couple, with Rama, there are some who worship her independently. There are mandirs dedicated to Sita on her own. These include:

- Janaki Mandir, Janakpur, Nepal, where it is believed Sita lived for a time.
- Sita Mai Mandir, Sitamai, Karnal, India, where the earth opened and Bhima received Sita.
- Sita Kund, Punaura Dham, Bihar, India, where Sita is believed to have been born (found in the earth).
- Seetha Devi Mandir, Pulpally, Wayanad, Kerala, India is also linked to Lava and Kusha who are believed to have played with her.
- Seetha Amman Mandir, Nahe Nuwara Eliya, Sri Lanka, is believed to be where Ravana kept Sita prisoner.

She is prayed to for her loyalty and as a fertility deity. As a representation of Shakti, she 'is an integral part of the Indian woman's psyche. At every stage of an Indian woman's life, her name is invoked' (Bhargava, 2000).

Hanuman

Hanuman is often focused upon in the classroom because of his role in the story of the Ramayana. His role in finding Sita by leaping across the sea, and setting fire to the city in Lanka, as well as the healing of Lakshmana by bringing the Medicine Mountain from the Himalayas to the battlefield, each indicate his role as a support to an avatar of Vishnu, making him worthy of worship. Indeed, in many mandirs, a murti of Hanuman will be found next to Rama, suggesting this close connection. He is worshipped in relation to Rama and to other forms of Vishnu. This closeness is highlighted in the popular image where Hanuman is exposing his heart, and written upon it is the name of Rama (see Figure 2.6).

Vanamali suggests that he is a manifestation of his father Vayu, the deity of wind, one of 'three incarnations to help Lord Vishnu. As Hanuman he helped Rama, as Bhima, he assisted Krishna, and as Madhvacharya (1218–1317), he founded the Vaishnava sect known as Dvaita' (2010, 5). He is also worshipped independently, as well as an avatar of Shiva. Lutgendorf (2007) highlights various stories surrounding Hanuman's birth, one such focuses on the devotion of his mother:

> Intent on obtaining an exemplary son, Anjana performs austerity atop a hill for seven thousand years. Via a celestial voice, Shiva indicates his satisfaction with her and tells her that he will be born to her as the eleventh Rudra. (130)

As such, Hanuman, as a deity, while significant for his role in various stories, is also worshipped today. John Brockington (2008) suggests that his current popularity is based on 'his role as an easily propitiated intermediary, his ability to "get things done", and his providing access to the more remote Rama, which accounts for the common remark that there are more shrines nowadays to Hanuman than to Rama'. (284–285)

Figure 2.6 Rama and Sita in Hanuman's heart.

As indicated earlier, Hanuman is often utilized in the classroom presentation of Hinduism as a character within the *Ramayana*. It is notable that this only begins an exploration of his nature, role and importance. In having 'legs in both camps – Shiva and Vishnu. His father is Shiva and he is the greatest devotee of Vishnu in his avatara as Rama' (Vanamali, 2010, 17) Hanuman has become one of the most worshipped deities within Hinduism. As Vanamali (2010) further notes:

> Hanuman is a specialist to whom people turn for the specific services in which he excels. He is capable of warding off all evil portents and planetary disturbances, so he is slowly creeping into prominence. In fact, in Maharashtra, which is predominantly a state devoted to Ganesha worship, we find that Ganesha's shrines are outnumbered

almost four-to-one by those to Maruti, as Hanuman is sometimes known, since he is the son of the wind god, and the name Maruti is a form of the Sanskrit word for wind. (17)

There are many reasons behind why a Hindu might approach Hanuman in worship. These include:

- His example of the perfect mind and the ability to control it
- His physical strength
- His mastery over many celestial bodies (exemplified by his ability to eat the sun) and cosmic powers or influences
- His connection with healing, as evidenced by his finding of the herb for Lakshmana, as well as a later event where he heals the twin sons of Rama and Sita
- His example of a warrior
- His example of a diplomat
- His example of a perfect student and devotee
- He was a perfect yogi both in terms of laya yoga and karma yoga where he had 'perfect mastery over his senses, achieved through a disciplined lifestyle and as discussed, by a strict adherence to celibacy and selfless devotion. He controlled his mind through absolute faith in the divine' (Vanamali, 2010, 8).
- He is selfless, wise and possessed of a great intellect.

The Hanuman Chalisa is a hymn of praise and supplication directed to Hanuman. These verses highlight the multi-faceted role that Hanuman has and the various reasons people will offer devotion to him:

Every arduous task in this world
becomes easy by your grace . . .

Taking refuge in you one finds all delight,
those you protect know no fear . . .

All disease and pain are eradicated,
brave Hanuman, by constant
repetition of your name.

Hanuman releases from affliction
those who remember him in thought, word, and deed . . .

Give no thought to any other deity-
worshipping Hanuman, one gains all delight.

> All affliction ceases, all pain is removed,
> by remembering the mighty
> hero, Hanuman . . .
>
> Says Tulsidas, Hari's constant servant,
> 'Lord, make your encampment
> in my heart.' (2020, 11–12)

The hymn suggests that Hanuman possesses the eight siddhis or perfections that are similarly exemplified in stories of his life:

- Anima: reducing the body even to the size of an atom
- Mahima: expanding the body to an infinitely large size
- Garima: becoming infinitely heavy
- Laghima: becoming almost weightless
- Prapti: having unrestricted access to all places
- Prakamya: realizing whatever one desires
- Istva: possessing absolute lordship
- Vastva: the power to subjugate all.

Many of the qualities that make him a focus for devotion are reflected in the symbols associated with murtis of Hanuman:

- A giant mace (gada) as a symbol of his strength and bravery.
- The medicine hill that he carried or medicinal herbs.
- An image of Rama and Sita.
- Sometimes he is depicted with five faces suggesting the five directions (including upwards) and that he is able to protect devotees.

As well as being a focus for devotion in personal lives and a central character in many modern stories and films, there are many mandirs around the world that have Hanuman as their titular deity. In the UK, these include mandirs in Leicester, London, Port Talbot and Brentford. In recent years, in India Hanuman has become a focus not just of worship but, in some quarters, a symbol of Hindu nationalism (see Chapter 9) as what has become known as 'Angry Hanuman'.

Thoughts for the Classroom

This chapter has explored only a small number of deities, and there is scope for a much greater focus on manifestations of the Divine within the classroom. With this as a background, it is possible to suggest some ways they can be explored.

Use of murtis

One of the most engaging aspects when teaching Hinduism is its imagery, colour and vibrancy. There are many pictures and images of deities that can be used in the classroom to bring aspects of Hindu belief and devotion to life for the students. This should not, however, be done thoughtlessly. I have suggested elsewhere (Holt, 2022) that the:

> Teacher needs to be very careful how they present such beliefs and practices. One such example is in the use of objects that are held to be sacred or important within religions. . . . They should not be used uncritically. In having children handle them and ask questions of them, or even using them to provide decoration, is it possible that the teacher is making the sacred mundane? (192)

There are many benefits to the use of objects and images in teaching about Hindu deities. Jackson et al. (2010) suggest that their use can 'encourage empathy with the people for whom these artefacts hold religious significance, and . . . generate responses of awe and wonder' (205). The teacher needs to be careful about the blurring of the lines between '"hands-on" learning [and] respect for other people's sacred objects and religious devotion' (p. 205). As such, the teacher needs to be clear about why they are using them, and the safeguards that they are putting in place for their proper use. As Homan (2000) suggests 'Teachers will need not only to sort out the appropriate uses for different objects of religious devotion but also to clarify the extent to which they are prepared to use these objects as a vehicle for experience' (28–29).

The first area of discussion is the terminology that we use in describing objects that we may choose to use. Homan (2000) argues that 'The use of the term "artefacts" frequently conveys a sense of a distant and even dead culture whose human participants are to be understood from the analysis of physical traces' (28). There is a lot to be said for Homan's argument; even if we do not agree there is enough to stop and give us pause in using language that has become uncritically accepted. The term 'artefact' relates to Indiana Jones and as Homan terms it a 'dead culture' rather than the lived reality of religion and belief that these objects come from or are reflective of. If the term 'artefact' is to be avoided, what terminology is appropriate? There are a number of terms that can be used linked with the types of objects used, and the purpose to which they are put:

- Objects of devotion/ devotional objects
- Objects used in devotion/worship
- The name of the object itself
- Objects that are used to illustrate but which may not be religious/sacred in and of themselves, and can therefore be variously described as paintings, pictures, sculptures, etc.

The use of such objects is very important; they provide a window to the spiritual lives of Hindus. That imagery highlights the importance and evocativeness of such objects, but it also highlights a concern with using the first three types of objects that are highlighted above. Homan (2000) argues that in using them the teacher must 'honour the spiritual significance of devotional apparatuses and not merely to regard their ritual functions' (29). With regard to terminology with regard to images of Hindu deities, the word that should be used is 'murti'; there is no equivocation in this. This is the word that is used by Hindus themselves, and as such should be adopted within the classroom. Stephen Jacobs (2008) outlines the importance of murtis:

> The image of the deity in the temple is known as murti or arcavatara. Both of these terms suggest that the infinite, which transcends all form, takes on a defined and limited shape for the sake of the devotee. The image therefore is not simply a representation or a symbol, but is considered to be the deity. In Vaisnavism the murti is considered to be one of the five forms of the deity. (366)

To use such images thoughtlessly, even if they are not installed, would be disrespectful. As such, so would the use of terms such as idols and icons. Such terms have 'negative undertones propelled by the cultural imperialism of monotheism: the idol is seen as that of a "false" god' (Handa, 2008, 359). Further exploration of the nature of murtis will be found in Chapter 6, but recognizing their significance and use in the context of the nature of the Divine is an important consideration for the teacher.

In using the objects as 'artefacts' or even as an educational resource, they are being taken out of their context, and it is important to note that the teacher is having pupils ascribe meaning to them in the role of an outside observer. Joyce Miller (2003) has observed, in relation to art but the same could be said of religious images, that:

> The interpretation of the arts is a complex phenomenon in which it is important to recognise that works of art are not reflections of received truths or facts. They are interpretations and one part of a dialectic between art, the artist and the viewer. Thus, in the classroom, the pupil is the viewer while in the faith community the believer is the viewer. Their understandings may be very different and this raises the question of validity, for there are no clear criteria for judging such matters. (205)

Unless the pupil is a believer themselves, there is no way that they can understand the sacredness that is imbued within the images or objects themselves. There are questions that teachers need to ask themselves when using murtis:

- Why are we using it?
- Do the pupils understand how it is viewed and used within Hinduism?
- How would a Hindu feel about the way that we are using it?

Richard Yeoman's argument about what art can bring to the classroom is equally true of religious objects:

> [Objects] can make a contribution on several levels, and as a teaching tool provides a vivid and effective visual backing to religious education, giving concrete form to religious dogma, expression and attitudes, as well as revealing the social, political and historical dimensions of a religion. [Some objects] while providing some insight into religion, is also something to be enjoyed for its own sake and perhaps its greatest value is its capacity to capture the imagination of the pupil or student. I would suggest that [objects] could provide a more direct and immediate stimulus for the study of religion.
> (Yeomans, 1978, 51)

This raises the question as to how they can be used to explore religion and religious experience and still maintain their integrity as sacred objects. It is impossible for a murti to have the same meaning outside of its context or when used by someone for whom it does not hold significance.

This links with the experiential pedagogy of RE. David Hay (2000) argues that 'For committed believers the experiential dimension is by far the most significant aspect of their religion' (72). Religious experience can be seen as the beginning and sustaining influence of a person's religious life. This experiential aspect of religion does not stand in distinction to the other dimensions of religion and, indeed, is grounded in them, but it does provide the most important aspect of religious practice. Perhaps in reaction to the phenomenological approach, where the observable aspects of religion were being studied, Hay and others felt 'that the experiential dimension of religion was being ignored by RE teachers, or at least treated with kid gloves' (2000, 73). The argument could be advanced: 'How can pupils understand religion if they cannot empathetically experience religion?' On one hand, the experiential approach asks children to spend time looking inward to themselves to experience similar questions and the seeking for answers that are at the heart of religion. As such, stilling or guided activities that encourage pupils to reflect on their own identity and the shaping of their own beliefs can be valuable.

One activity that might be used as an approach to learning using a murti is based on the enquiry approach. In this example, a murti of Ganesh is used and the enquiry question is: 'How is the importance of Ganesh shown through his murti?' or 'Why would some Hindus pray to Ganesh?' The stages of learning would be:

- Pupils investigate the murti (similar to Figure 2.7) and explore the various symbols that they find.

Usually this would be done by having children spend a few minutes with the murti and raise questions such as:

- Why does he have an elephant head?
- Why does he have an axe?
- What is in his other upper hand?
- What is the symbol on his forehead?

Figure 2.7 Ganesh murti (Photo taken by James Holt).

- Why does he wear a crown?
- Why is he sat on a rat?
- Why does he only have one tusk?
- Pupils investigate their questions using appropriate sources. They then begin to suggest answers to the questions they suggested in response to the murti. They may begin to draw tentative conclusions based on their investigation.
- Pupils discuss these conclusions with one another to evaluate their tentative positions.
- Pupils produce work that answers the original question: 'How is the importance of Ganesh shown through his murti?' or 'Why would some Hindus pray to Ganesh?' Answers that might suggest his importance include:

- He is the son of Shiva, as such, the blessings of Lord Shiva can be found. This is indicated by the mark on his forehead (tilak) to symbolize his position as a follower of Shiva.
- He can destroy ignorance, as indicated by his vehicle being a mouse or rat that he is able to overcome. Similarly, there is an axe, which can be used to destroy ignorance.
- Ganesh is a guide for his devotees as shown by the goad, which elephant drivers use to guide the elephant.
- A snake tied around his waist to show his conquering of desires.
- A single tusk to show his single-mindedness.
- Ganesh can remove obstacles which can be removed with his trunk.

- Pupils raise any questions that come out of the investigation.

In this activity, students are able to recognize that the murti is much more than an image, and that the images, in addition to the presence of the Divine, can help focus a Hindu's devotion and worship (for more on worship and devotional activities, see Chapter 6).

Cultural appropriation

It is possible to suggest that there is no concept of blasphemy within Hinduism. Deities are benevolent and angry, they have emotions and have been 'physically' involved in various elements of human history. Images of their exploits are found on the walls of mandirs, and comic books are written about them. There are traditional retellings of tales such as the Ramayana (Pai, 2009) as well as more science fiction or alternative retellings such as Deepak Shekhar Kapur's (2014) *Ramayan 3392AD*. This also extends to film retellings of the stories of deities whether they be live action or cartoon. This means that within the classroom there are a range of activities such as storyboards that can be utilized within the teaching of Hinduism. One activity that is often found in our classroom are Hindu Deities Top Trumps. These are usually created by the individual teacher and are fairly subjective. Table 2.1 shows an example of a Top Trump Card based around Brahma:

It is not to suggest that this is necessarily an appropriate task. There are positives to the type of activity, in that it highlights the diversity of manifestations of the Divine. Conversely, does it minimize or trivialize the role and importance of individual deities? This is especially true in the utilization of scores to prioritize certain aspects of a deity. This raises the question of appropriateness and of cultural appropriation. To some extent, this raises similar issues with regard to the use of murtis within the classroom.

Ganesh is one of the most well-known deities within and outside of Hinduism. The knowledge of him outside of Hinduism was possibly enhanced by his place on the Kwik-e-mart of *The Simpsons*. The character Apu has a shrine to Ganesh in his shop. This highlights one of the dangers of cultural appropriation with regard to Hinduism.

Table 2.1 Sample Top Trumps Card

Brahma

Deity of: Creator (4)

Vehicle: Swan (3)

Devotees: Not many because his work has been done (1)

Defeating of evil: No major stories of overcoming evil (0)

Symbols: He holds Vedas in his hands, which helps him create the universe. The water pot (kamandalu) is used in prayer to show that people can direct their thoughts to more spiritual matters. The mala he holds helps people to meditate (3)

At what point does representation become disrespect? Indeed, the musician Rihanna was criticized for posing without a top on, with a necklace of Ganesh (Addo, 2021), and the K-Pop band Blackpink used his image in a music video (May & Lee, 2020). Further examples in the fashion world include the use of an image of Ganesh on a swimsuit (Cassidy, 2022), and the advertising of trainers by Cardi B posing in the form of Durga

(Dharni, 2020). In the case of Cardi B, it was intended to be a homage to Durga, but this was rejected by many Hindus, resulting in a series of apology videos from the rapper:

> When I did the shoot the creatives told me I was going to represent a Goddess, that she represents strength, femininity and liberation, and that's something that I love and I'm all about, and thought it was dope . . . But if people think I'm offending their culture or their religion I want to say that was not my intent. I do not like offending anyone's religion; I wouldn't like it if someone did it to my religion. When people dress as Virgin Mary and Jesus, as long as they do it in a beautiful, graceful way . . . But I wasn't trying to be disrespectful; maybe I should have done my research. I'm sorry, I can't change the past but I will do more research for the future. (Rani, 2020)

This raises the issue of the intention and thoughtlessness behind such actions with regard to deities. This is not just restricted to non-Hindu representations of Hindu deities, but similar sensibilities surround Hindu content makers. The 2023 film *Adipurush* has been condemned in certain sections of the Hindu community because of its depictions of the figures in the Ramayana in a 'violent' and inappropriate way. The High Court in India has suggested:

> Does anyone imagine the religious characters to be in existence in the way they are shown in the movie? The attire worn by the characters in the movie, do we imagine our Gods to be like this? Ramcharitmanas is a sacred text, people recite it before leaving their homes and you depict it in such a pathetic way? (Satija, 2023)

Further exploration of the muscularity of certain figures, including Hanuman, will be developed in Chapter 9. At this point, it is important to discuss the sensitivity towards the depiction and use of deities and figures in Hindu literature. Without the concept of blasphemy, the teacher needs to be aware that this does not give them carte blanche to use these figures in any way. Every use, description and task associated with them needs to be carefully considered in a way that does not trivialize.

Storytelling

Within an exploration of the sources for the narratives surrounding the events of deities within Hinduism, there is a range of possibilities that arise for their use in the classroom. The stories of the deities are normally narrated in the classroom with little discussion, but in a similar way to the Christian Gospels, the narrations of the lives of the gurus, along with texts from many religions, there are opportunities for critical reading of such. At no point does this mean that the teacher or pupils seek to criticize the role of the Divine.

It is possible in analysing the writing of the text to explore the texts in terms of understanding both the Divine and the communities which produced these texts. One such modern example is the life of Swaminarayan, a nineteenth-century figure who is regarded as Divine by his followers. Manual Parekh suggests that in narrating his life, 'it is very difficult to decide what is strictly historical and what is superimposed by the faith of his followers' (Parekh, 1943, xi). Raymond Williams (2019) illustrates this with reference to his childhood:

> His childhood name was Ghanshyam, which was also one of the childhood names of Krishna. This is thought to be especially appropriate because the legendary stories of the childhood of Ghanshyam resemble the stories in the puranas about the childhood of Krishna. Indeed, some of the stories of Krishna may have been transformed to apply to Ghanshyam. Devotees do not accept this judgment. They maintain that these stories are attributed to Suvasini Devi, Rampratap's wife, who came to Gujarat with the family twenty-eight years after Ghanshyam left home. Therefore, the stories are accepted as accurate accounts of his childhood. (14)

This same approach is reflected in the multiplicity of interpretations of the stories of deities found in sacred texts and oral narrations. There are many stories of creation; differing stories for how Ganesh got his elephant head; and different interpretations as to the historicity of certain figures. For example, was Rama always perceived as an avatar of Vishnu, or is *The Ramayana* a narrative of a man who is seen to have godlike qualities, and as such is regarded as a manifestation of the Divine latterly, rather than being understood as such at the time? A modern corollary to that is the installation of a murti of Sachin Tendulkar in Bihar (see Mishra, 2013). The idea is not that Tendulkar is divine, rather that he possesses qualities that are worthy of focus and emulation.

Within the classroom, there has been a development in the use of hermeneutics in terms of reading sacred texts. As texts that are used within the Hindu community, it is possible to see that the stories can be used in the same way. As we understand a hermeneutic approach to be about 'the art or science of interpretation, concerned with meaning and significance' (Bowie et al., 2020, 3), it is possible to move beyond sacred text to read the stories of deities to see how the narratives are imbued with meaning and significance.

This type of approach should include the reading of the text (most likely in English) to explore the things we learn about the deity from the narrative; what we learn about the community that produced it; what links there are to wider Hinduism; the possible historicity claims that can be made; and how the text links with, and is used, by Hindus today. Pupils in schools are used to having narratives curated or mediated for them, and engagement with the source material helps pupils engage with the narrative in a much more effective and authentic way.

There are many stories told of the deities. There have been volumes filled with stories and there is only the opportunity to draw on brief examples. It should also be noted that throughout this book there have been, and will be, examples from the deities that are used to underpin or illustrate teachings as given expression in Hinduism.

For each of the deities, there are a multitude of stories that could form the basis of an exploration of Hindu beliefs and values in the classroom at all stages of education.

Storytelling lies at the heart of understanding Hinduism. It has to be utilized correctly and enthusiastically by the teacher.

To an extent, stories lie at the heart of religion, and especially of Hinduism. The stories of the deities can be used to frame morality, teachings and also the boundaries of Hinduism. Trevor Cooling suggests that stories are 'big ideas sometimes referred to as a metanarrative, which express our whole understanding of the whole world and help people make sense of their lives' (2002, 45). This is just so with Hinduism. As we reflect on some of the stories, whether it is the Ramayana, the Bhagavad Gita or the story of how Ganesh got his elephant's head, they can help us understand the important aspects of Hinduism. We can understand the nature of existence, the Divine, samsara, through a utilization of stories of the classroom.

As just one example, the story of *The Ramayana* can be explored through many hermeneutical lenses. In its historical lens, it can be viewed from the perspective of different religions in India. Robert and Sally Goldman (2021) highlight that its

> popularity and influence . . . has extended to virtually all the religious cultures of Asia . . . So, in the many Jain versions of the tale, Rama is regarded as a virtuous Jain layman; for the Buddhists of South and South-East Asia, he is a *bodhisattva*, a future Buddha; and for the peoples of the Malay-Indonesian world, he is portrayed as an ideal Islamic prince. (5)

There are opportunities also to engage in different readings within the Hindu tradition. A feminist reading of the Ramayana might focus on the role and place of Sita and what can be learnt about the role of women in history, religion and in the modern world. Examples of such retellings that might assist the teacher include *Sita's Ramayana* written by Samhita Arni (2011). Arni suggests that such a retelling helps place women at the centre of the narrative:

> For once, you get to see the tale of India's most respected prince from a very feminine side. Instances of war and violence, which find so much prominence in other retellings, are relegated to the backbench in my tale. My story looks at Ramayana for its pathos and its impact on the survivors of the Great War – the widows, the orphans, the departed, so on and so forth. It's the human cost that I'm concerned with . . . But if you are a woman - you must live through defeat . . . you become the mother of dead sons, or an orphan, or worse, a prisoner. (Pallapothu, 2018)

Another example is *The Liberation of Sita*, written by Volga (2016); this retelling 'celebrates womanhood and the power to make a choice. Sita achieves inner peace and liberation through questioning the very notions of truth and fidelity' (Pallapothu, 2018). Some of these readings may be challenging to traditional Hindu norms. One example that has challenged Hindus is the fictional retelling Kaikeyi by Vaishnavi Patel (2022), which explores the events of the *Ramayana* from the perspective of the 'evil step-mother'. This retelling humanizes Kaikeyi and portrays her as a multi-faceted character rather than a caricature. In some ways, *Kaikeyi* does for the figure of Kaikeyi what *Wicked* does for the Wicked Witch of the West (Maguire, 1995). Indeed, in the introduction to her novel, Patel (2022) outlines that a family dispute about Kaikeyi's role led to her writing:

> One particular summer, [my grandmother] told us the story of how the noble prince Rama was exiled by his jealous stepmother Kaikeyi, who was convinced to banish him by her wicked servant Manthara. At this, my mother stepped in to add that Kaikeyi had actually helped Rama. Without Kaikeyi, my mother pointed out, Rama would have never achieved his destiny by slaying the demon king Ravana, his main adversary in the Ramayana. My grandmother disagreed, arguing that it was cruel to exile your child, no matter the circumstance. And then we moved on. But their minor dispute stuck with me for years, and I would periodically search for stories told from or studying Kaikeyi's perspective to make sense of the contradiction. I never found them. Eventually, I decided to write my own. I wanted to give Kaikeyi a chance to explain her actions and explore what might have caused a celebrated warrior and beloved queen to tear her family apart. I hope that *Kaikeyi* gives voice not just to its titular character but to the many women who populate the world of *The Ramayana* and have rich and worthy lives of their own. (vii–viii)

In addition to these readings through various hermeneutic lenses, there are opportunities to explore beliefs and practices of Hindus through storytelling. In *Hanuman's Adventures in the Netherworld*, Mahadevan (2005) narrates Hanuman asking questions about his own nature, the purpose of life, the nature of existence and the Divine:

> 'Who am I?' Hanuman asked. 'When I see my own face reflected in the still waters of a pond, I see just another monkey. The same bright beady eyes, the same hairy body, the same long tail as anyone else . . . So who am I? How am I different?'
>
> The wise Jambavan fells Hanuman that he is the son of the great Vayu, Lord of the Winds. Hanuman asks: 'If I am really his son, why does he stay away from me?'
>
> Jambavan replies: But he is always will you . . . he's the life breath of this earth, the prana. He is the sweet-scented zephyr that stirs the leaves of the trees in the forest, the cool gust that songs the first smell of rain. He is the dust dew that dances in the desert the raging cyclone that sinks entire fleets out at sea. Vayu is everywhere. He is the breath in your lungs. That is your father, Hanuman. From him you have the power to leap over oceans. To fly. Who can stop you from going where you please? (10)

Storytelling really does lie at the heart of teaching about and understanding Hinduism. Whether it is the articulation of dharma in Epics such as the *Bhagavad Gita* or the realization of the truth of existence illustrated in the story of Hanuman above.

Learning can be deepened with the use of story. Stories also have many levels of understanding that need to be analysed and studied for academic understanding. The stories that are told help us understand what is important for Hindus then, and today.

Miller Mair suggests that this is so: 'All our stories are expressions of ourselves even when they purport to be accounts of aspects of the world. We are deeply implicated in the very grounds of our story telling' (1989, 257). Hinduism can thus be experienced through its stories. Whatever age of student we are working with, using the stories of the deities can help them understand more deeply, not just the events of the stories, but also the teachings of Hinduism and their importance to Hindus today.

Chapter 3

Hindu Cosmology

Hindu cosmology, properly speaking, consists of two aspects: firstly, *jagadutpatti*, or cosmogony, which explores discussions surrounding the origin of the world. Secondly, *bhuvana-jnana*, or cosmology, which explores the metaphysical nature of the world. As has been explored in Chapter 2, it is evident that in exploring cosmogony there are many different stories, but all link with the expression of the Supreme Being at the heart of the cosmos, as the cause of the universe. How this has been explored and explained differs across different traditions of Hinduism, and at different stages in the expression of those beliefs. Gerald Larson (2011) suggests that:

> God (Ishvara) or the Absolute (Brahman) – or, if one prefers, any of the proper conventional names such as Brahma, Vishnu, Shiva, Krishna, and so forth – plays a crucial role in what might be called 'enabling' the world to unfold and take shape. This is the case in terms of the various conceptualizations of space, time, and deity in Hindu thought. The term 'various,' however, is important here . . . [T]here is no single cosmogony or cosmology accepted by all developing Hindu traditions. There is, rather, a rich pluralism of tales, myths, legends, and speculations, most of which involve God (Ishvara) or the gods in one form or another, but none of which is normative for Hindu religious traditions as a whole. (113)

The important aspect that appears to be common across Hindu traditions is that there is no beginning to time. The universe is in a constant cycle of creation, destruction and recreation. Indeed, across the cosmos, there are many universes, perhaps best described as Hindus recognizing a multiverse. It is subject to the concept of *rta*, which is often seen to represent cosmic order. It is seen to have three aspects:

> In this tradition the cosmic order is called rta which has three features: gati (continuous movement or change), samghatna (a system based on interdependence of parts) and niyati (inherent order of interdependence and movement). (Sharma, 1990, 16)

Rta, as the regulating force of the universe, is the basis for all action, and therefore virtue and dharma. It is sometimes translated as 'law' or 'commandment', suggesting the importance of order and dharma.

The ideas of the structure of the universe also differ widely within Hinduism. In one understanding, based on the *Vishnu Purana*, there is seen to be different aspects or layers represented by the cosmic egg or *brahmanda* (sometimes *Hiranyagarbha*). In some narrations, the cosmic egg is the source from which all existence and life arose. With the earth at its centre, there are different continents that extend horizontally and vertically across different continents, with millions of yojanas (measure of distance) in length and breadth. Looking horizontally, the universe has the earth, and often Mount Meru at its centre. The universe is enclosed in the cosmic egg, and then a description of it working out from the centre is:

- Mount Meru is at its centre.
- Surrounding Mount Meru is the earth, or island of the rose apple tree (Jambu-dvipa). This is split into many regions.
- Then there is a salt ocean.
- Then there are seven further lands of sugar cane juice, wine, ghee, buttermilk, milk and sweet water.
- Realm of darkness and the outer shell of the cosmic egg.

It has been suggested that 'a vertical section' of the cosmic or world egg produces the following layers:

Satyaloka (the true world)
Tapoloka
Janaloka
Maharloka
Svarloka (Planets) is one of the regions of the consequences of work.
Bhuvarloka (Sky) is one of the regions of the consequences of work.
Bhurloka (Earth) is one of the regions of the consequences of work.

Atala (White)
Vitala (Black)
Nitala (Purple)
Gabhastimat (Yellow)
Mahatala (Sandy) Nether worlds
Sutala (stony)
Patala (Golden)
Sesa (the World-snake)
Rauvara etc. (28 narakas or hells)

The cosmos, whose centre is the earth, extends upwards and downwards in many
    lokas ('worlds') (Klostermaier, 2008, 153).

Beings are reborn into these different worlds, and none is permanent.

Each of these understandings of the cosmos and the universe teaches important truths for Hindus. For many, these truths are reflective of a worldview that teaches of reincarnation (see Chapter 4). The interplay between these narratives and science would be seen to be compatible for most Hindus. Although the Big Bang and evolution are not explicitly part of these stories, Hindus would have no problem accepting them as explanations for the creation of the universe and of the created world. Although to the modern mind these stories seem 'fantastic' for the vast majority of Hindus, they are stories that help people understand the nature of the Divine and the universe, rather than scientific truths that need proving. Indeed, when reading the Creation hymn (*Nasadiya Sukta*) in the Rig Veda (10.129), many Hindus would see the compatibility of such:

> Then was not non-existent nor existent: there was no realm of air, no sky beyond it. What covered in, and where? and what gave shelter? Was water there, unfathomed depth of water? Death was not then, nor was there aught immortal: no sign was there, the day's and night's divider. That One Thing, breathless, breathed by its own nature: apart from it was nothing whatsoever. Darkness there was: at first concealed in darkness this All was indiscriminated chaos. All that existed then was void and form less: by the great power of Warmth was born that Unit. Thereafter rose Desire in the beginning, Desire, the primal seed and germ of Spirit. Sages who searched with their heart's thought discovered the existent's kinship in the non-existent. Transversely was their severing line extended: what was above it then, and what below it? There were begetters, there were mighty forces, free action here and energy up yonder Who verily knows and who can here declare it, whence it was born and whence comes this creation? The Gods are later than this world's production. Who knows then whence it first came into being? He, the first origin of this creation, whether he formed it all or did not form it, Whose eye controls this world in highest heaven, he verily knows it, or perhaps he knows not.

The primal seed, or in previous terminology, the cosmic egg, began creation, which expands the universe until it is time for destruction and recreation. The universe contains five primordial elements which coalesce in creation, and then are destroyed within the end of the universe (see below in this chapter *Gunas and* panchamahabhutas).

The attempts made to highlight the compatibility of Hinduism and science are shown in one explanation of the avatars of Vishnu (see Chapter 2). One such example is given by Venkatrangan Gokul (2018). In his reading of the Vedas, Darwin and the avatars of Vishnu, he shows an evolution parallel in their figures (see Table 3.1).

Although some links can be seen, in parts, there is a forcing of the issue; in light of the compatibility of science and Hinduism, however, it is the attempt that is important. Although Gokul (2018) and others (Labh, 2022) have attempted this harmonization by reading it back into the narratives, the recognition that evolution is an explanation for the mechanism of creation is important for Hinduism, and also the teacher in the classroom.

Table 3.1 Avatars of Vishnu and Their Relation to Evolution

Avatar of Vishnu	Stage of Evolution
Matsya	An organism (fish) that originates in the seas.
Kurma	A turtle, or an organism that can live on land or sea.
Varaha	A boar, indicative of the next stage of evolution with land animals.
Narasimha	Half man, half lion, suggesting beings that were 'crude, uncivilized and rough but with humane values' (Gokul, 2018).
Vamana	A dwarf, representing the earliest humans (this is perhaps where elements of the explanations and links become a little forced).
Parasurama	A human who had developed the use of sophisticated instruments such as weapons.
Rama	'Humans became less violent, more matured, calm, and respectful. Humans began having rituals and traditions. The human also started having relationships with other humans' (Gokul, 2018).
Krishna	Representing humans who are more materialistic but also spiritual.
Buddha	Thinking about the nature of existence and the purpose of life.
Kalki	Humans learn to destroy creation.

Gunas and panchamahabhutas

Gunas (qualities) is a word within Hinduism that has two quite interrelated meanings. On the one hand, gunas in the Samkhya traditions of Hinduism refers to three qualities or forces of behaviour and of the nature of things. They are forces found within *prakriti* (matter):

- *Sattva* (goodness): 'is always positive and carries associations with goodness, truth, wholesomeness, health, cognitive thought, and deep-rooted religious life' (Lochtefeld, 2002, 265).

- *Rajas* (passion) 'can be either positive or negative, depending on the context. It is negative when one becomes a slave to one's passions, blinding one to careful and conscious thought. However, one's passions can also help to engender activity and industriousness' (Lochtefeld, 2002, 265).

- *Tamas* (decay): 'is always negative and is associated with darkness, ignorance, sloth, spoilage, and death' (Lochtefeld, 2002, 265).

Everything has these three forces that work together in different ways as part of the nature of a living thing. They will be explored in greater depth in Chapter 4 in relation to the nature of humanity.

The second understanding of gunas refers to qualities of the five primordial elements, though they are less often spoken of as gunas, rather as *panchamahabhutas*; these elements are:

- Space/Ether (akasha)
- Air (vayu)
- Fire (tejas)
- Water (apa)
- Earth (prithvi)

These five physical elements combine in almost infinite ways to form every element and being of existence. It is important, therefore, to keep these five elements in balance along with the three gunas mentioned above (this will be discussed in greater detail in Chapter 4). The importance of these bhutas in worship is shown through the five Shiva lingum mandirs that are dedicated to each bhuta individually. Linking back to the Shiva lingum (see Chapter 2) and its representation of the universe and the cosmic spirit. These mandirs are:

- Ekambareswarar Mandir representing earth, and containing the prithvi/bhumi lingum.
- Jambukeshwarar Mandir representing water, and containing the varuna lingum and an underground stream.
- Arunachaleswara Mandir representing fire, and containing the agni lingum. At the festival of Karthika Deepam, a large beacon is lit symbolizing the Shiva lingum of fire.
- SriKalahasti Mandir representing air, and containing the vayu lingum.
- Thillai Natarajar Mandir representing ether/space, and containing the Indra lingum.

Each form part of the Shaiva pilgrimage elemental tradition.

In some ways, the idea of the panchamahabhutas is analogous to the nature of colours in art, that a person can begin with the three primary colours (and black and white) and an infinite range of colours can be created. With the five bhutas, everything can be created, and just as the universe is created when all of these five elements are brought together, so too is everything within the universe. This has important implications for a Hindu environmentalism, when balance is needed, and the opportunity for the five elements to develop and combine effectively is seen. Outside of the infusion of the natural world with the Divine, it is also possible to see the interrelatedness of all things, and therefore the responsibility that humanity has to the universe (see Chapter 7).

Yugas

As has been indicated, the universe is cyclical in Hindu belief. A kalpa is a measurement of time equivalent to 4.2 billion years, or one day in the life of Brahma (there is a larger measurement known as a mahakalpa, or lifetime of a hundred years for Brahma or over 311 trillion years, or the time of one breath of Vishnu). The calculation of a day of Brahma is based on passages from various texts, including the *Bhagavad Gita*:

> One day of Brahma (kalp) lasts a thousand cycles of the four ages (maha yug) and his night also extends for the same span of time. The wise who know this understand the reality about day and night. (8:17)

Within a kalpa is one thousand 'cycles of the four ages' with each cycle also known as a Yuga Cycle lasting for a total of 4,320,000 years and having four different ages/yugas. These are known as the Satya/Krita Yuga, Treta Yuga, Dvapara Yuga and Kali Yuga. In commenting on the above passage from the Bhagavad Gita, A.C. Bhaktivedanta Swami Prabhupada (1972) notes:

> These four yugas, rotating a thousand times, comprise one day of Brahma, the creator god, and the same number comprise one night. Brahma lives one hundred of such 'years' and then dies. These 'hundred years' by earth calculations total to 311 trillion and 40 million earth years. By these calculations the life of Brahma seems fantastic and interminable, but from the viewpoint of eternity it is as brief ·as a lightning flash. In the causal ocean there are innumerable Brahmas rising and disappearing like bubbles in the Atlantic. Brahma and his creation are all part of the material universe, and therefore they are in constant flux. (428)

There are specific time frames for each, with earth years as well as divine years, based on passages from the Vedas and also the *Mahabharata*:

> A year (of men) is equal to a day and night of the gods . . . I shall, in their order, tell you the number of years that are for different purposes calculated differently, in the Krita, the Treta, the Dwapara, and the Kali yugas. Four thousand celestial years is the duration of the first or Krita age. The morning of that cycle consists of four hundred years and its evening is of four hundred years. Regarding the other cycles, the duration of each gradually decreases by a quarter in respect of both the principal period with the minor portion and the conjoining portion itself. The learned say that these twelve thousand celestial years form what is called a cycle. (12.231. 17, 19–21, 29)

Each age is then split into three with the phases being known as *sandhya* (dawn), main/proper and *sandhyamsa* (dusk). The dawn and dusk are each 10 per cent of the main part of the yuga, leading to the following breakdown:

- Satya/Krita Yuga: 1,728,000 (4,800 divine) years
  - Krita-yuga-sandhya (dawn): 144,000 (400 divine)
  - Krita-yuga (proper): 1,440,000 (4,000 divine)
  - Krita-yuga-sandhyamsa (dusk): 144,000 (400 divine)
- Treta Yuga: 1,296,000 (3,600 divine) years
  - Treta-yuga-sandhya (dawn): 108,000 (300 divine)
  - Treta-yuga (proper): 1,080,000 (3,000 divine)
  - Treta-yuga-sandhyamsa (dusk): 108,000 (300 divine)
- Dvapara Yuga: 864,000 (2,400 divine) years
  - Dvapara-yuga-sandhya (dawn): 72,000 (200 divine)
  - Dvapara-yuga (proper): 720,000 (2,000 divine)
  - Dvapara-yuga-sandhyamsa (dusk): 72,000 (200 divine)
- Kali Yuga: 432,000 (1,200 divine) years
  - Kali-yuga-sandhya (dawn): 36,000 (100 divine)
  - Kali-yuga (proper): 360,000 (1,000 divine)
  - Kali-yuga-sandhyamsa (dusk): 36,000 (100 divine)

It is believed that currently the universe is in the 51st year of Brahma's existence, meaning that it is halfway through the mahakalpa. In terms of the Yuga Cycle, it is agreed that it is currently the Kali Yuga:

> The Kali Yuga began at midnight between February 17 and 18, 3102 BCE. Consequently it is due to end about 427,000 CE, whereupon a new Golden Age will dawn. (Godwin, 2011, 301)

Utilizing 3102 BCE as a yardstick, it is possible to posit the following years for the four yugas:

Table 3.2 The Approximate Dates of the Current Yuga Cycle

Yuga	Beginning	End	Duration (Years)
Satya/Krita	3,891,102 BCE	2,163,102 BCE	1,728,000
Treta	2,163,102 BCE	867,102 BCE	1,296,000
Dvapara	867,102 BCE	3102 BCE	864,000
Kali	3102 BCE	428,899 CE	432,000

The four ages decline in morality as time goes on, and as a result of this, the Kali Yuga is seen to be the worst. Perhaps this is an indication of the decay and deterioration of living things that are subject to time. One indicator of this is the standing nature of the deity Dharma, who is pictured as a bull; in the Satya Yuga, Dharma stands on four legs, in the Treta Yuga it is three, followed by two in the Dvapara Yuga, and in this Kali Yuga it is one. Each of the four ages will be briefly outlined below.

Satya/Krita Yuga

The yuga of truth is the best of all of the yugas. The *Vana Parva* of the *Mahabharata* outlines the circumstances of the Satya Yuga:

> O child, that yuga is called Krita when the one eternal religion was extant. And in that best of yugas, everyone had religious perfection, and, therefore, there was no need of religious acts. And then virtue knew no deterioration; nor did people decrease. It is for this that this age is called Krita (perfect) . . . And, O child, in the Krita age, there were neither gods, nor demons, nor Gandharvas, nor Yakshas, nor Rakshasas, nor Nagas. And there was no buying and selling. And the Sama, the Rich, and the Yajus did not exist. And there was no manual labour. And then the necessaries of life were obtained only by being thought of. And the only merit was in renouncing the world. And during that yuga, there was neither disease, nor decay of the senses. And there was neither malice, nor pride, nor hypocrisy, nor discord, nor ill-will, nor cunning, nor fear, nor misery, nor envy, nor covetousness. And for this, that prime refuge of Yogis, even the Supreme Brahma, was attainable to all. And Narayana wearing a white hue was the soul of all creatures. (CXLVIII)

Treta Yuga

Treta, meaning three things, may have reference to three avatars of Vishnu being present in this age: Vamana, Parashurama and Rama; conversely it could refer to the length of the Treta Yuga being 3,000 divine years. This age of the universe is characterized by wisdom. It is in this stage of the history of the universe that things begin to decline and the power of humanity begins to diminish. For example, instead of the necessities being met through thought, it is necessary to have means to gain these necessities. Similarly, people begin to be less 'religious' or inclined towards the Divine, rather beginning to focus on the material aspects of life, though religious rites begin to become necessary. The Mahabharata outlines this yuga thus:

> In this age, sacrifices are introduced, and virtue decreaseth by a quarter. And Narayana (who is the Soul of all creatures) assumeth a red colour. And men practise truth, and devote themselves to religion and religious rites. And thence sacrifices and various religious observances come into existence. And in the Treta Yuga people begin to devise

means for the attainment of an object; and they attain it through acts and gifts. And they never deviate from virtue. And they are devoted to asceticism and to the bestowal of gifts. (*Vana Parva* CXLVIII)

Dvapara Yuga

Dvapara has reference to two, perhaps because it is twice as long as the Kali Yuga, or perhaps because the bull Dharma stands on two legs. This age is characterized by the performance of yajnas or rituals. Again, the Mahabharata describes the Dvapara Yuga:

> In the Dwapara Yuga, religion decreaseth by one half. And Narayana weareth a yellow hue. And the Veda becometh divided into four parts. And then some men retain (the knowledge of) the four Vedas, and some of three Vedas, and some of one Veda, while others do not know even the Richs. And on the Shastras becoming thus divided, acts become multiplied. And largely influenced by passion, people engage in asceticism and gifts. And from their incapacity to study the entire Veda, it becomes divided into several parts. And in consequence of intellect having decreased, few are established in truth. And when people fall off from truth, they become subject to various diseases; and then lust, and natural calamities ensue. And afflicted with these, people betake themselves to penances. And some celebrate sacrifices, desiring to enjoy the good things of life, or attain heaven. On the coming of the Dwapara Yuga, men become degenerate, in consequence of impiety. (*Vana Parva* CXLVIII)

It is perhaps in the Dvapara Yuga that there is a noticeable drop-off in virtue and morality. People become self-interested and less connected to the Divine, 'few are established in truth' and sacrifices are performed not just for the deity but also for the benefit of the self.

The Dvapara Yuga is seen to end, and the Kali Yuga is ushered in by the battle between the Pandavas and the Kauravas described in the *Mahabharata*. At the end of this age, Krishna returned to Vaikuntha, his divine abode.

Kali Yuga

The Kali Yuga is the yuga in which Kalki (an incarnation of Vishnu) will come at the end to destroy and end the world; this is seen to be the most depraved of the yugas, with Kali meaning 'contention'. This is the age in which humans currently live. *The Vishnu Purana* outlines:

> Wealth [morals] and piety will decrease day by day, until the world will be wholly depraved. Then property alone will confer rank; wealth will be the only source of devotion; passion will be the sole bond of union between the sexes; falsehood will be the only means of success in litigation; and women will be objects merely of sensual gratification. Earth will be venerated but for its mineral treasures . . . dishonesty will be the universal means of subsistence; weakness will be the cause of dependence; menace and presumption will

be substituted for learning; liberality will be devotion; simple ablution will be purification; mutual assent will be marriage; fine clothes will be dignity; and water afar off will be esteemed a holy spring . . . The people, unable to bear the heavy burdens imposed upon them by their avaricious sovereigns, will take refuge amongst the valleys of the mountains, and will be glad to feed upon wild honey, herbs, roots, fruits, flowers, and leaves: their only covering will be the bark of trees, and they will be exposed to the cold, and wind, and sun, and rain. No man's life will exceed three and twenty years. Thus in the Kali age shall decay constantly proceed, until the human race approaches its annihilation. (4.24)

The Kali Yuga is perhaps of most interest in the classroom, and also for the living of Hindu dharma, in the sense that it is the current age. It also provides an idea of how the universe will end. Doniger (1999) outlines its ending:

At the end of the present Kali age, when virtue and religion have disappeared into chaos and the world is ruled by unjust men, Kalki will appear to destroy the wicked and usher in a new age. Often he is pictured as being seated on a white horse, with a naked sword in his hand, blazing like a comet. According to some myths, Kalki's horse will stamp the earth with its right foot, causing the tortoise that supports the world to drop into the deep. Then Kalki will restore the earth to its initial purity. (629)

Thoughts for the classroom

This has been the case throughout all of the discussion of deities, dharma and any Hindu beliefs thus far in this book, and will continue to be so. The messiness or diversity of Hinduism has as much reference to origins and explanations for the universe as it does with anything else. The above system of yugas could be seen as somewhat focused on the avatars of Vishnu, which are one interpretation of time. There are other, less well-known, interpretations, such as the manvantaras:

A day in the life of Brahma is divided into 14 periods called manvantaras ('Manu intervals'), each of which lasts for 306,720,000 years. In every second cycle [(new kalpa after pralaya)] the world is recreated, and a new Manu appears to become the father of the next human race. The present age is considered to be the seventh Manu cycle. (Doniger & Hawley, 1999, 691)

While not incompatible with the yugas, the emphasis in this is slightly different.

The use of the cosmology and cosmogony of Hinduism in the classroom provides a different view of time and of the nature of creation than may be found in classrooms where Abrahamic faiths are the main focus of teaching. In that interpretation, time is somewhat linear, whereas seeing existence and the universe as cyclical is perhaps more reflective of modern science, which suggests an expanding and collapsing universe. It

Table 3.3 Evidence of the Kali Yuga Today

Description of the Kali Yuga	Evidence
Then property alone will confer rank.	
Wealth will be the only source of devotion.	
Passion will be the sole bond of union between the sexes.	
Falsehood will be the only means of success in litigation	
Women will be objects merely of sensual gratification.	
Earth will be venerated but for its mineral treasures.	
Dishonesty will be the universal means of subsistence.	
Menace and presumption will be substituted for learning.	
Mutual assent will be marriage.	
Fine clothes will be dignity.	
People [will be] unable to bear the heavy burdens imposed upon them by their avaricious sovereign.	

also lays the basis for a discussion of the cycle of samsara (see Chapter 4) where the existence and journey of the atman is similarly cyclical.

When looking at creation myths in the classroom, there is often a focus of 'getting to the truth'. Hindu narratives about creation provide elements that may highlight a Hindu worldview, but none are necessarily seen to take priority or seem more true. It is the creation of the universe that enables Hindus to recognize the importance of the universe. Rather than being fatalistic, a Hindu's place in the universe in striving to live according to dharma (see Chapters 2 and 4) means that existing in the Kali Yuga places a greater emphasis on being counter-cultural and reflecting the virtues of Hinduism (see Chapters 2 and 7). Also of interest for students may be the applicability of the descriptions of the Kali Yuga; being recorded in the *Mahabharata*, these descriptions are over two thousand years old, and an interesting activity would be for students to find evidence from newspapers/sites that Hindus might use to show that we are in the Kali Yuga (see Table 3.3) recognizing that there are still thousands of years of decline left.

Chapter 4

The Nature of Humanity

In exploring the nature of humanity within Hindu worldviews, it is artificial to separate it from the previous three chapters and their discussion of dharma, and the cosmology and cosmogony of Hinduism. The various aspects that have already been explored can all be drawn together and expanded to understand the nature of humanity. One Hindu has said:

> Human beings are the latest among living beings in the cycle of evolution. Purpose of life is to continue sustaining the universe and all that is on earth, and to evolve morally.

This suggests that humans have a central place in existence. In exploring the nature of Brahman, one aspect of debate has already been discussed: whether Hinduism is monistic or dualistic. If it is monistic, then the soul that is the central aspect of humanity, and the wider natural world, is part of Brahman and as such everything is Divine. The purpose of a human is then to realize this truth that is obscured by maya (illusion) and attain moksha (liberation) from the fetters of samsara (see below) and realize union with the Divine. Within dualism, the soul and God are believed to be eternally distinct even though both are Brahman. Within this worldview of humanity, the aim is still moksha, but it is the attainment of union with the Divine rather than the realization. This is a very subtle difference and may have little effect on the overall aim and the actions of the individual Hindu, but it is important to recognize the diversity of approach towards the various aspects of the nature of humanity.

The creation of humanity

In exploring the varnashramadharma in Chapter 2, we briefly explored the separation of Purusha into the various varnas. The *Rig Veda* speaks of Purusha:

> A thousand heads hath Purusa, a thousand eyes, a thousand feet. On every side pervading earth he fills a space ten fingers wide. This Purusa is all that yet hath been and all that is to be; The Lord of Immortality which waxes greater still by food. So mighty is his greatness; yea, greater than this is Purusa. All creatures are one-fourth of him, three-fourths eternal life in heaven. (X.90)

Purusha is the cosmic presence, often identified with Brahman, but also with Shiva or Vishnu as the Supreme Being. The *Bhagavad Gita* identifies Purusha as synonymous with Vishnu:

> Sanjay said: Hearing these words of Keshav, Arjun trembled with dread. With palms joined, he bowed before Shree Krishna and spoke in a faltering voice, overwhelmed with fear. Arjun said: O Master of the senses, it is but apt that the universe rejoices in giving You praise and is enamoured by You. Demons flee fearfully from You in all directions and hosts of perfected saints bow to You. O Great One, who are even greater than Brahma, the original creator, why should they not bow to you? O Limitless One, O Lord of the devatas, O Refuge of the universe, You are the imperishable reality beyond both the manifest and the non-manifest. You are the primeval God and the original Divine Personality; You are the sole resting place of this universe. You are both the knower and the object of knowledge; You are the Supreme Abode. O possessor of infinite forms, You alone pervade the entire universe. (11:35–38)

Klostermaier (2007) identifies that

> This purusa begets viraj, the 'widespread,' and both together bring forth purusa, the son, who becomes the sacrificial victim of the great sacrifice of the gods. From this great sacrifice originate the verses of the Vedas, horses, cattle, goats, and sheep. The four castes, also, have their origin in him, the sacrificial victim. (87)

As such, when Purusha is separated, human life is created and is part of the cosmic presence that is Brahman. Within samkhya traditions, purusha and prakriti (matter) combine and the physical world is created. Purusha is thus the atman of a person or a being. The soul of every living thing is identified with the Divine. This is often described in the story of the two birds in the *Mundaka Upanishad*:

> Two inseparable companions of fine plumage perch on the self-same tree. One of the two feeds on the delicious fruit. The other not tasting of it looks on. On the self-same tree, the Jiva drowned as it were and perplexed, grieves owing to helplessness. Hut when he sees the other, the lord who is worshipped by all, and his glory, lie becomes absolved from grief. When the seer sees him of golden line, the creator, lord, Purusha, and the source of (Apara) Brahma, then the knower, having shaken off all deeds of merit and sin, attains supreme equality, being untouched with stain. (Mundaka Upanishad 3.1.1–3)

The suggestion in the passage above is that the jiva, meaning the soul that sees the atman as identical with the body, is 'drowned' or weighed down because of life and the various aspects including karma. Only when the second companion who sees the truth of the atman and Brahman shakes off the effects of karma, and 'attains supreme equality.' In this way, the realization of Brahman is the attainment of moksha (see below).

Often when this is taught within a classroom, the focus is on a univocal understanding of the nature of the relationship between the atman and Brahman. As indicated earlier, the recognition of both monistic and dualistic approaches is important. The aim of life becomes to understand the nature of the reality of the relationship between the atman and Brahman:

This Atman cannot be attained by dint of study or intelligence or much hearing – whom he wishes to attain – by that it can be attained. To him this Atman reveals its true nature. (*Mundaka Upanishad* 3.2.3)

As with all living things, humanity is seen to be composed of the panchamahabhutas (five elements) (see Chapter 3). In the first understanding, these gunas are:

- Space/Ether (akasha)
- Air (vayu)
- Fire (tejas)
- Water (apa)
- Earth (prithvi)

The interaction of each of these elements, along with the atman, is what makes a person unique. Shiv Sharma (2003) outlines that 'for a healthy mind and body all the five elements must remain properly balanced in the body' (93). These panchamahabhutas are kept in balance by yoga (see Chapter 6).

In the more popular understanding of the gunas, they are also a balance of that found within prakriti:

- Sattva (goodness)
- Rajas (passion)
- Tamas (decay)

Initially in perfect balance they work within living beings. Bernard (1999) suggests:

> In the process of cosmic evolution, the three Gunas are never separated; they coexist in everything. Never do they function separately, but one or the other may predominate. They always support one another and intermingle with one another. They are as intimately conjoined as an electron and proton, the constituents of an atom. As the arrangement of atoms accounts for all the elements known to science, so does the arrangement of the Gunas account for all the manifestations of nature. (75)

Lochtefeld (2002) outlines that:

> All things and beings in the world have these three basic qualities, but their nature and tendencies differ according to the differing proportions . . . Although much of Samkhya metaphysics has been long discredited, the notion of all things drawing their tendencies from the differing proportion of these three gunas has become an accepted part of Indian culture. (365)

The gunas work together to develop the progress of a being and their character. If one or more of these is out of balance then the person is similarly affected. Thus, the development of an equilibrium in life, according to the laws of karma (see below), enables a person to keep these gunas in balance. Thus, actions can be seen to be sattvic, rajasic or tamasic and contribute to the well-being of a person. If a person becomes imbalanced with regard to the gunas, then it is possible for the environment and people around them to be similarly affected. It is important to note in this understanding of the nature of things that while prakriti is subject to change, purusha or the atman is unchangeable. This has been described in terms of a flower behind a crystal. While the crystal may appear to take on the colour of the flower, it is in reality unchanged.

The purusartha

In the different interpretations of Hinduism, the aim of life is union with the Divine, also known as moksha. This very much links with the purusartha or the four aims of life: *dharma*, *artha*, *kama* and *moksha*. This chapter will necessarily explore all four of these, but only moksha in detail. However, before doing so, it is important to note Julius Lipner's caution:

> In Brahminic Hinduism the goals of human existence are said to be fourfold. These goals or purusarthas are (i) artha or prosperity, (ii) kama or gratification, (iii) dharma, to be understood here as religious merit, and (iv) moksa or liberation from samsara, the flux of existence. Though one often comes across this division in the literature, there is nothing sacrosanct about it, in that many Hindus today simply do not make much of it, unlike modern Hindu (and non-Hindu) writers on Hinduism! (Lipner, 2010, 194)

This is repeated in the various curricula that can be observed to be taught in schools. Each of these four aims of life is given equal weighting, whereas in reality the focus may be more heavily weighted towards one, and for the most part that may be seen to be moksha. The other three should work together in harmony as suggested in the *Mahabharata*:

> Morality is well practised by the good. Morality, however, is always afflicted by two things, the desire of Profit entertained by those that covet it, and the desire for Pleasure cherished by those that are wedded to it. Whoever without afflicting Morality and Profit, or Morality and Pleasure, or Pleasure and Profit, followeth all three – Morality, Profit and Pleasure – always succeeds in obtaining great happiness. (9.60)

Thus, the three aspects of dharma (translated in the passage as morality), artha (profit) and kama (pleasure) work together in harmony. When artha and kama are explored or pursued independently of dharma, 'they lead to social chaos' (Flood, 1997, 16).

Artha

Although artha is often translated as 'aim' or 'goal' as in the wider concept of purusartha of which this artha forms a part, in this context it refers to worldly prosperity, wealth and possibly power. The accumulation or possession of wealth to an extent is necessary to a Hindu's life, and practice of dharma. Although it is seen as a worthwhile goal of life, it is, in many ways, a means to an end. It enables a person to be in a position to live their dharma and perform their duties. As with the gunas, the pursuit of wealth and power should be kept in balance and not be done in a way that hurts other people or consumes a person's life. In some ways, this 'aim' of human life becomes a basis for the fulfilment of dharma, meaning that with appropriate resources it becomes 'easier' to live according to dharma. On the other hand, it is somewhat anathema to a renunciate life.

Kama

Kama is often translated as 'pleasure' or 'desire' and refers to the idea that life should be enjoyed. The *Kama Sutra* suggests:

> Kama is the enjoyment of appropriate objects by the five senses of hearing, feeling, seeing, tasting, and smelling, assisted by the mind together with the soul. (1.2)

In Western eyes, the concept of Kama focuses specifically on sexual desire and pleasure because of an overfocus on the *Kama Sutra* and the misunderstanding that it is all about sex. Rather, the Kama Sutra, while speaking about sexual activity, has as its major themes 'philosophy and theory of love' (Levy, 2010, xv). As such, the proper focus of kama is any desire or physical pleasure including, but not limited to, music, art, love, sex and natural beauty. An exploration of various elements of the sexual aspect of love will be developed in Chapter 7. Rather than being disruptive to a person's experience, kama is an important aspect of life but should be kept within the bounds of dharma. Thus, when exploring sexual activity, it might be suggested that this is within the context of the grihastha ashrama, where a householder is to be married. The undesirability of certain acts motivated by kama is highlighted in the *Kama Sutra*:

> In a like manner the mighty Kichaka, who tried to seduce Draupadi, and Ravana, who attempted to gain over Sita, were punished for their crimes. These and many others fell by reason of their pleasures. (1.2)

Of note, however, is the prioritization of kama for certain groups including 'the occupation of public women, they should prefer it to the other two' (*Kama Sutra* 1.2) which would not be seen to have application today.

Dharma

Dharma is explored in great detail in Chapter 1, but in many ways is the primary purusartha in relation to artha and kama. The *Kama Sutra* outlines:

> When all the three, viz., Dharma, Artha, and Kama come together, the former is better than the one which follows it, i.e., Dharma is better than Artha, and Artha is better than Kama. (1.2)

Dharma is the frame for all other motivations and actions, and as such lies at the heart of human nature and responsibility. It can be seen to frame all actions, as two Hindus have suggested about the purpose of life:

> Follow Dharma with the aim of moving towards Nirvana that is merging with the creator.
>
> Attaining 'moksha', and enjoying the world that god has created, *but within limits* (emphasis added).

Moksha

Moksha is sometimes translated as 'liberation' or freedom from the cycle of *samsara* (death and rebirth). In relation to moksha as an aim of life, it has been observed that:

> Hindu philosophy regards moksha as the highest purpose of life, achievable through pursuing self-realization and consciousness of unity with the all-pervasive Supreme Being. It is one of those ideas that have remained central to not only all strands of Hinduism, but also the various religious beliefs that emerged from it. It reinforces the belief in an afterlife and how the consequences of right and unrighteous actions in one life are carried forward into another, tying the essence of an individual, the soul, in an endless cycle of rebirth. Attaining a release from this samsara, or cycle of rebirth. Attaining a release from samsara, or cycle of transmigration of the soul based on karma, is moksha, the final liberation. (Ranjan et al., 2017, 420)

Within some forms of Hinduism, there are seen to be two types of moksha.

- *jivanmukti* (liberation in this life)
- *videhamukti* (liberation after death)

Within Hinduism more widely, and certainly within the classroom, it is videhamukti that is more commonly spoken of. Indeed, Klostermaier (2003) suggests that most Hindu 'systems are primarily concerned with teaching paths to liberation from rebirth' (104). In discussing jivanmukti, Klostermaier (1985) suggests that:

> Moksha implies a setting free of hitherto fettered faculties, a removing of obstacles to an unrestricted life, permitting a person to be more truly a person in the full sense. It presupposes an unused human potential of creativity, compassion and understanding which had been blocked and shut out. (66)

This is the idea of realizing one's true nature, and viewing reality as the nature of the relationship between atman and Brahman. In this way, the obfuscation of maya is overcome:

> It may also be noted that each one of us is mukta (self-realised) to some extent; in each one of us there is already some manifestation of self in the form of cognitive potentials and creative activities. The difference across individuals exists only with respect to the level of illumination of the self. The self is like the sun covered by the clouds. More the

self becomes free from illusions, the more illuminating it becomes, like the sun getting free from the clouds. By freeing oneself from all illusions, a person obtains his true self (nij svarup), which is called atman, or paramatman, or brahman, or Shiva, or God. In spiritual philosophy, God and our true self are one. (Mishra, 2013, 34)

This will undoubtedly have an impact on the individual, who will perform actions that reflect this self-realization and union with the Divine.

The videhamukti is liberation from the cycle of samsara or reincarnation at death, though there are alternate understandings not dissimilar to the idea of nibbana and parinibbana within Buddhism. The atman is subject to karma. Karma is the law of cause and effect; that every action (and indeed thought) is positive or negative and leads to an accumulation of karma, that leads to positive or negative births in the future. In some traditions, this is as a natural result of actions, whereas it might be controlled by the Divine. The Brahma-Sutra outlines:

From Him (the Lord) are the fruits of actions; for that is reasonable. (3.2.38)

In living their dharma, a Hindu is seen to be developing positive karma, resulting in a positive reincarnation and eventual liberation (moksha) from the cycle of samsara and realization of, and union with, the Divine. Within Hinduism, there are seen to be three types of karma:

- Sanchita karma is the accumulation of karma over various lifetimes, all of which will be impossible to balance in one lifetime.
- Prarabdha karma is the selection of the sanchita karma that will be experienced in one lifetime.
- Kriyamana karma is that karma which is accumulated in the current lifetime. This will build up the sanchita karma that will be drawn upon in future lifetimes.

As the cycle of samsara is driven by karma, and karma is consistently built through different lifetimes, it could be suggested that the removal of karma to enable liberation is difficult. There are suggestions that there are rebirths into heavens and hells that could reduce sanchita karma, and also animals and children are not subject to karma as they are 'innocent'.

As such, this leads to the positing of three paths that might enable karma to be overcome and liberation from the cycle of samsara to be achieved:

- karma-marga, sometimes called karma yoga, is the path of action.
- bhakti-marga, sometimes called bhakti yoga, is the path of devotion.
- jnana-marga, sometimes called jnana yoga, is the path of knowledge.
- astanga/raja marga, sometimes called astanga yoga, is the path of exercise and meditation.

For some Hindus, these are all parallel paths to moksha, while others would see one as more effective, and all of them as steps on the same path.

Karma yoga

> But those who rejoice in the self, who are illumined and fully satisfied in the self, for them, there is no duty. Such self-realized souls have nothing to gain or lose either in discharging or renouncing their duties. Nor do they need to depend on other living beings to fulfil their self-interest. Therefore, giving up attachment, perform actions as a matter of duty because by working without being attached to the fruits, one attains the Supreme . . . As ignorant people perform their duties with attachment to the results, O scion of Bharat, so should the wise act without attachment, for the sake of leading people on the right path. (*Bhagavad Gita* 3:17–19, 25)

As is evident from the above passage, the path of karma yoga is the path of selfless action. One is performing actions 'without being attached to the fruits', meaning that there is no thought of reward, and that while the body is performing those deeds there is no attachment to them. One Hindu has highlighted this as part of their devotion:

> In Hinduism everyone believes that we should help others. Some else's concern should also be our own. We should live for ourselves but also help others. God gave us two hands; one to help ourselves, and the other to help others.

In some ways, this is the path to moksha suggestive of jivanmukta, where the realization of the Divine means that a person lives selflessly and unattached to anything, a virtue or practice known as *seva*. The framing of the selfless actions to be performed is often seen to be framed by dharma, but can be extended to any act of selflessness.

Bhakti yoga

> If one offers to Me with devotion a leaf, a flower, a fruit, or even water, I delightfully partake of that item offered with love by My devotee in pure consciousness. Whatever you do, whatever you eat, whatever you offer as oblation to the sacred fire, whatever you bestow as a gift, and whatever austerities you perform, O son of Kunti, do them as an offering to Me. By dedicating all your works to Me, you will be freed from the bondage of good and bad results. With your mind attached to Me through renunciation, you will be liberated and will reach Me. I am equally disposed to all living beings; I am neither inimical nor partial to anyone. But the devotees who worship Me with love reside in Me and I reside in them. Even if the vilest sinners worship Me with exclusive devotion, they are to be considered righteous because they have made the proper resolve. Quickly they become virtuous, and attain lasting peace. O son of Kunti, declare it boldly that no devotee of Mine is ever lost. All those who take refuge in Me, whatever their birth, race, gender, or caste, even those whom society scorns, will attain the supreme destination. What then to speak about kings and sages with meritorious deeds? Therefore, having come to this transient and joyless world, engage in devotion unto Me. Always think of Me, be devoted to Me, worship Me, and offer obeisance to Me. Having dedicated your mind and body to Me, you will certainly come to Me. (*Bhagavad Gita* 9:26–34)

Bhakti yoga is a path of loving devotion to a personal deity, to Bhagavan. The deity will be according to the wishes of the devotee and may be Vishnu, Shiva, Ganesh, Rama, Krishna, Saraswati, Durga or many others. One Hindu has highlighted this as a purpose of life:

> To love and serve Lord Krishna and understand that we have a relationship with him.

As indicated above in the passage from the *Bhagavad Gita*, the devotion to a deity would overcome the actions of even 'the vilest of sinners' in the smallest act of devotion, if 'offered with love'. This will form the basis for most of a Hindu's devotional activities (see Chapter 6). There are different types of relationships or love that can be expressed between the deity and the devotee, including that of servant/master (*dasya*), friends (*sakhya*), parent/child (*vatsalya*), child/parent (*santa*), husband/wife (*kanta*) and lovers (*rati*). This shows the depth and breadth of love that can be shown through bhakti yoga. It is important to note that as a part of bhakti, the actions must be motivated by love and devotion. The actions are not performed out of self-interest but out of love for the Divine, in so doing a bhakta can 'know Brahman as of the nature of bliss, infinitude, and unsurpassability' (Grimes, 1996, 84). This is not a one-time event; rather, this is an approach to life, and a path to be followed, and one that is guided by the laws of dharma and the rituals that have been expressed as part of devotion. The *Bhagavata Purana* highlights the importance of the following of correct devotion and ritual:

> For those means and courses of conduct which have been taught (prescribed) by the Lord, for easily attaining realization of the Self even by ignorant persons – Be sure that those are the duties which please him the most and lead easily to self-realization. By betaking one's self to those paths, O king, no person will ever go astray. (This path is so safe and easy that) even if one runs with his eyes closed (i.e. is ignorant of Srutis and Smrtis which are regarded as eyes) will not miss his path (and take the wrong way). (And even if he hurries across the path of devotion, jumping in haste from one step of Bhakti to another out of the nine steps (viz. Sravana 'hearing the Name of the Lord', Kirtana 'glorifying the deeds of the Lord', and others), he would not stumble (into Samsara again or miss the fruit of his devotion). Whatever a person does by his body, speech, mind, cognitive and conative sense-organs, intellect and ego and by the force of nature (as formed by his previous karmas), he should dedicate all such (voluntary and involuntary) acts to the Supreme Lord Narayana. (11.2.34–36)

Though, Gavin Flood (2020) highlights that acts of bhakti can be based on text or acts of spontaneous passionate expression.

Jnana yoga

> In this world, there is nothing as purifying as divine knowledge. One who has attained purity of mind through prolonged practice of Yog, receives such knowledge within

the heart, in due course of time. Those whose faith is deep and who have practiced controlling their mind and senses attain divine knowledge. Through such transcendental knowledge, they quickly attain everlasting supreme peace. But persons who possess neither faith nor knowledge, and who are of a doubting nature, suffer a downfall. For the sceptical souls, there is no happiness either in this world or the next. (*Bhagavad Gita* 4:38–40)

The path of knowledge can be seen as world-renouncing and focuses on the acquisition of wisdom; not just knowledge but the wisdom that comes through an awareness of the world as it really is and the elimination of desire. It is based on a study of the Vedas and the Upanishads (see Chapter 5), and through the asking of questions to attain knowledge of the self and of the Divine. One Hindu has highlighted how humans are uniquely positioned to adopt this practice:

> To be human is the highest achievement of the evolution of all life forms. It gives a chance to ask the questions: who am I? what is existence ? And to pursue this is the purpose of human life.

The devotee is often helped along the path with a *guru* (often translated as teacher). Shankara highlights that:

> The result of the true knowledge of the Self leads to Liberation and so serves a very, very fruitful purpose. Therefore an inquiry about Brahman through an examination of the Vedanta texts dealing with It is worthwhile and should be undertaken. (Vireswarananda, 1936, 23)

As such, Shankara highlights that there are four aspects to the gaining of knowledge:

- *Viveka* (discrimination): the ability to recognize the difference between those things that are permanent and those that are impermanent.
- *Viraga* (dispassion): indifference to the fruits of action.
- *Satsampat* (the six treasures): 'not allowing the mind to externalize and checking the external instruments of the sense organs (*Sama* and *Dama*), not thinking of things of the senses (*Uparati*), ideal forbearance (*Titiksha*), constant practice to fix the mind in God (*Samadhana*), and faith (*Sraddha*)' (Vireswarananda, 1936, 24).
- *Mumukshutvam*: the intense longing for moksha from ignorance.

Linked as this knowledge is with the Vedas, this will also include aspects of Vedic ritual and living according to dharma to realize Brahman.

Raja yoga

> Those who seek the state of Yog should reside in seclusion, constantly engaged in meditation with a controlled mind and body, getting rid of desires and possessions

for enjoyment. To practice Yog, one should make an asan (seat) in a sanctified place, by placing Kush grass, deer skin, and a cloth, one over the other. The asan should be neither too high nor too low. Seated firmly on it, the yogi should strive to purify the mind by focusing it in meditation with one pointed concentration, controlling all thoughts and activities. He must hold the body, neck, and head firmly in a straight line, and gaze at the tip of the nose, without allowing the eyes to wander. Thus, with a serene, fearless, and unwavering mind, and staunch in the vow of celibacy, the vigilant yogi should meditate on Me, having Me alone as the supreme goal. Thus, constantly keeping the mind absorbed in Me, the yogi of disciplined mind attains nirvan, and abides in Me in supreme peace. (*Bhagavad Gita* 6:10–15)

In Western 'outsider' terms, raja yoga is 'yoga', and refers to the actions that might incorporate meditation and various postures and positions. Within Hinduism, it is much more than this (this will be explored in much greater detail in Chapter 6). Within raja yoga, there are many practices including asceticism, *samadhi* (meditation), breathing, *tantra* and yogic positions, all with the express aim of uniting with the Divine, attaining moksha – both jivanmukti and videhamukti. Through raja yoga, 'the yogin in samadhi is liberated and the liberated yogin must continue to practise it . . . the logical outcome of both works is the ongoing need to practise yoga, even for one who is liberated-in-life' (Birch, 2020, 226).

On the other hand, liberation-in-life is described as the outcome of a transformative process that takes place in samadhi. In other words, the liberated yogin emerges from samadhi as an all-powerful god who can know and do anything in the world.

Thoughts for the classroom

There are many aspects of the nature of humanity that can be explored with students. The interrelatedness of humanity with each other, and with the Divine through the story of Purusha, can form the basis of discussions surrounding the divisiveness, acrimony and destruction within the world. Aspects of this will be explored in Chapter 7. The interplay of the various aspects of the purusarthas as the aims of life is similarly ripe for exploration. Consider the sociological perspective of Abraham Maslow (1943). In his seminal paper *A Theory of Human Motivation*, he suggested something not dissimilar in nature; he suggested that a person has certain basic needs: physiological, safety, love and belonging, esteem and self-actualization. This is often portrayed as a pyramid, with the physiological needs being the basis for safety, in turn being the basis for love and belonging and so on. A pyramid may not be the best image for this hierarchy as there is an interplay of the various needs. It does, however, highlight the wisdom of Hinduism in articulating a view of life that is not just about moksha; in order to attain moksha, there needs to be a recognition of the other aspect of life.

In approaching paths to moksha within the classroom, the focus is often on karma yoga as a path to liberation. This may well be necessary, as it is perhaps the most easily accessible and understandable for the majority of Hindus, but to suggest it is the only path would be to ignore the reality of daily living for many Hindus. Indeed, one Hindu has suggested their practice which combines elements of the various paths of yoga:

> I do yoga, chant Vedic Mantra and other prayers, pray in the shrine at home, read one Bhagwat Geeta shlok, and learn Sanskrit. I try to explain principles of life and help others to identify themselves. Also I try to do community service by teaching Yoga, meditation and medical help, wherever possible.

Teaching them separately may be easier, but the interconnectedness of them all is a valuable expression of the lived experience of many Hindus. It should also be noted that sometimes teachers can suggest karma without recognizing the underlying search for the Divine. The activity below could be susceptible to this, and the proper framing within wider beliefs and practices would make it more authentic.

Moksha Chitram is a game that can be used in the classroom to show the interrelatedness and application of moksha, the atman, dharma and karma. This is a traditional Indian game that has been transported to the rest of the world as 'Snakes and Ladders'. By utilizing this game, students can begin to understand the concepts that lie at the heart of samsara. The teacher can design the boards themselves or have students do this. If students are designing the board, the teacher should print out a hundred squares and then:

1. Have students make a list of ten animals from worst to best. This is completely subjective, for example, a snail is better than a slug because it has a house on its back.
2. The students number the squares from 1 to 100 in the format of a snakes and ladders board – this is harder than it looks.
3. Between the numbers one and thirty-five, students should put their animals in certain squares evenly spaced out.
4. Number thirty-seven should be a human. Number 100 should be moksha.
5. Place five ladders on the board of varying lengths; all of the ladders should begin after thirty-seven. This highlights that animals follow their dharma; it is only humans that can gain positive or negative karma. At the bottom of the ladder, put a good action.
6. Place five snakes on the board of varying lengths. All of the snakes' heads should be after thirty-seven but can finish anywhere on the board. Write a negative action at the top of the snake's head.

This game is designed to show you how a Hindu believes in reincarnation and the belief that good and bad karma can affect your future life, and place in the cycle of samsara.

Each roll of the die is a lifetime, and students should write down what happens in each lifetime. The animal that is closest to where they are (looking back) is the life form they are in that life. To play the game, each player:

7. Chooses a counter each and places it at the start position.
8. In turn, the dice is rolled. The one with the highest score goes first and so on.
9. In turn, the dice is rolled to see how many places each player can move forward.
10. If a player lands on a square with a ladder in it, the player has made a good move and has gained good karma. They move up the ladder.
11. If a player lands on a square with a snake's head in it, they have gained bad karma. Therefore, they have to slide down the snake and be reborn as a lower life form.
12. The first one to reach 'Moksha' is the winner, but as in all games of snakes and ladders, and in life, if people play long enough they all win and attain moksha.

Tasks that could be completed as a follow-up include writing a diary of the game with the title 'The Journey of the Atman'. Students should remember to talk about karma and how the atman shifts from one body to another. They might be then prepared to answer a question about how these beliefs in karma and reincarnation might affect the way a Hindu would live their life.

Chapter 5

Sacred Writings

A Hindu is someone who believes in the Vedas. There are 4 Vedas. Rig veda, Sama veda, Yajurveda, Atharvana veda. Upanishads are a summary of Vedas. Epic and Puranas like Ramayana, Mahabharata tells how society should function, humanity and how the characters in these lived up to the values as per Hindu dharma. Hence all these things help me to lead a person's life in the right track.

This description of the scriptures or sacred texts within Hinduism provides a useful introduction to their place in Hinduism and in the life of a Hindu. This is developed further by this statement from a Hindu:

Veda and Upanishads are the ultimate authority of sanatana dharma. Geeta and the Upanishads provide tools for achieving the ultimate goal. Itihasa tells us about our history.

It would appear from these descriptions that the place of texts is fairly settled within Hinduism, but as with most things within Hinduism, once the surface is scratched, there are a multiplicity of approaches that become evident. This chapter will explore the types and uses of the various texts within Hinduism.

Within Hinduism there are seen to be two types of scripture:

- *Sruti*: what is heard or what is revealed. These deal 'with eternal principles' (Prinja, 2003, 129).
- *Smrti*: what is remembered. These deal 'with the practical application of eternal principles' (Prinja, 2003, 129).

For both types of scripture, there are many texts, some of which are outlined in Table 5.1.

While the Vedas are almost universally accepted, other aspects including their interpretation are given various levels of authority. There will be many Hindus who will utilize different texts and not give any thought to others. The 'canon' is not closed within Hinduism; as can be seen in Table 5.1 there are modern teachings that can be seen to take on the function, and in some cases the status, of scripture. For example, the teachings of Chaitanya, or the teachings of Swaminaraya. These are generally linked to a specific tradition within Hinduism. Almost all of the traditions in Hinduism have come from texts such as the Vedas. They teach the values and history of Hinduism through thousands of

Table 5.1 Hindu Scriptures (see Prinja, 2003, 129–130)

	Sruti
Main writings/groups	*Subdivisions*
Rig Veda Yajur Veda Sama Veda Atharva Veda	*Karma Kanda* The main section contains hymns and prayers (*samhitas*) and descriptions of rituals (*brahmanas*). *Jnana Kanda* An ancillary section contains the *Upanishads* (to sit down near) which are conversations between a teacher and their pupils. These provide interpretations of the Vedas. Some of the later parts of the Vedas are known as *Aranyakas* which attempt to explain the meaning or philosophy of the rituals.

	Smrti
Main writings/groups	*Subdivisions*
Upa Vedas	Ajur Veda (medicine) Dhanur Veda (military science) Gandharva Veda (music) Shilpa (mechanics/architecture)
Vedangas	Shiksha (phonetics) Chanda (prosody) Vyakrana (grammar) Nirukta (Vedic glossary) Jyotisha (astronomy) Kalpa (household/religious duties)
Darshanas (philosophy)	Nastika (atheistic) Charvaka (materialism) Astika (theistic)
Dharmashastras (law codes)	Niti shastras (Chanakya, Vidhur, Shukra) 18 Smrtis (e.g. Manu) Kautilya shastra (economics, politics, law)
Puranas	46 Upa Puranas 18 Main Puranas
Epics	Ramayana Mahabharata (including the Bhagavad Gita)
Agamas	Shakta Shaiva Vaishnava
Modern	Swaminarayan – Skikshapatri ISKCON – Teachings of Chaitanya Arya Samaj – Satyarth Praksah

slokas which are still chanted today. While the Vedas and Upanishads contain *slokas*, the Epics and Puranas have stories that teach how society should be constructed and how people should live with values according to Hindu dharma.

While the Vedas are somewhat authoritative, for the day-to-day life of a Hindu, it is the smrti texts that have the most application, as they seek to help Hindus put eternal principles into practice. Das notes that 'For popular purposes in the UK, the Ramayana, the Mahabharata, the Puranas, and the Bhagavad Gita are most commonly used' (2002, 123). Though, as one Hindu has suggested, while they are important, their use will vary:

> Veda, Upanishad, Gita, Ramayan Mahabharat form the foundation of Hindu Dharma. I do believe but have not read them all.

The Vedas

> The Vedas/texts is where we got our 'rules' for when we should do things. For example, what kinds of chants/slokas we do at what events, and what kind religious customs we do when.

As already mentioned, the Vedas can be seen to be the unifying feature of Hinduism. However, it should be noted that sramana groups rejected the Vedas as revelation and, as such became *nastika* (heterodox). Some, such as Buddhism and Jainism, are today seen as different religious traditions outside of Hinduism. It is noted that for all other Hindus, 'the truths of the Vedas were first revealed by God at the beginning of human creation for the benefit of humankind, and they are timeless and eternal truths' (Voiels, 1998, 53). The Vedas are used today mainly for an understanding of ritual and practice, as one Hindu has noted:

> The roots of Hindu heritage are 'Vedas', what should we practice every day, what should be our beliefs, what should we do on a daily basis, what not to do etc. all come from Vedas. Following these is our dharma as Hindus.

The Vedas were originally passed on in an oral tradition, serving the 'function of enabling each of the specialist priests who performed Vedic ritual to learn his role' (Killingley, 2008, 941). The different parts of the Vedas developed over time, and in some traditions the Rig, Yajur and Sama are given priority as the three Vedas, while the Atharva Veda is an addition, though by some seems to be superior, as it 'specialised in rituals for personal ends such as cures, curses, love-charms or acquisition of special powers, which were separate from the ritual performed by the other three classes of priest' (Killingley, 2008, 943). Exploring the different sections of each noted in Table 5.1, there also seems to be a linear development of these.

- The *Samhitas* which are mainly the hymns that are sung during rituals, or prayers/mantras offered to deities. Usually seen to have been composed between 1500 BCE and possibly as late as 900 BCE.
- The *Brahmanas* were built upon the Samhitas and offered explanations, commentary or developments of the rituals. These are believed to have been composed between 900 BCE and 700 BCE. Some are additions after the Samhitas, while others are woven into the hymns.

- The *Aranyakas* (forest treatises) are often included in the designation of the Brahmanas, which are seen to be discussions and interpretations of the rituals in the Samhitas.
- The *Upanishads* are similarly sometimes included as Brahmanas. Usually seen to have been composed between 600 BCE and 300 BCE, these are philosophical commentaries. Doniger (1990) suggests that 'The Upanishads supply the basis of later Hindu philosophy; they alone of the Vedic corpus are widely known and quoted by most well-educated Hindus, and their central ideas have also become a part of the spiritual arsenal of rank-and-file Hindus' (2–3). There are later Upanishads that were composed after the end of the Vedic period, which continued the philosophical and metaphysical development of Hindu ideas.

It is believed that Veda Vyasa (literally Veda Compiler) compiled the Vedas into the four collections. His birth name was Krishna Dvaipayana and he is variously believed to be an incarnation or avatar of Vishnu or Brahma. Drawing upon the oral traditions of the various *rishis*, Vyasa 'classified all the different, random bits of it, decided which portions went together and compiled those into chunks, and then divided those chunks into separate Vedas' (Pai, 2019, 7). The association with Brahma is particularly strong because in murtis

Table 5.2 The Composition of Each of the Four Vedas

	Samhitas	Brahmanas	Aranyakas	Upanishads
Rig Veda	Rig Veda Samhita	Aitareya Brahmana Kausitaka Brahmana	Aitareya Aranyaka Sakhayana Brahmana	Aitareya Upanishad Kausitaka Upnaishad
Sama Veda	Sama Veda Samhita (including a large proportion of the Rig Veda)	Jaiminiya/Talavakara Brahmana Pancavisma Brahmana		Chandogya Upanishad Jaiminiya Upnaishad Kena/Talavakara Upanishad
Yajur Veda *Black Yajurveda*	Taitturya Samhita Kahaka Samhita Maitrayaniya Samhita	Included in the Samhitas	Taitturya Aranyaka	Taitturya Upanishad Maitri Upanishad Katha Upnaishad Maha-naraya Upanishad
White Yajurveda	Vajasaneyi Samhita	Satapatha Brahmana	Brahad Aranyaka (found in the Satapatha Brahmana)	Brahad Aranyaka Upanishad (found in the Satapatha Brahmana) Isa Upanishad
Atharva Veda	Atharva Veda Upanishad (inclosing a small proportion of the Rig Veda)	Gopatha Brahmana		Mundaka Upanishad Prasna Upanishad Mandukya Upanishad

he traditionally holds the four Vedas in one of his hands. Vyasa is also believed to be the author of the *Mahabharata*, and in some traditions is seen as a *Charanjivi* who is believed to be eight beings who are to remain on earth until the end of the Kali Yuga.

A brief summary of the four Vedas suggests their use and composition:

- The Rig Veda is the most important of the Vedas, split into ten books, and as a whole is a collection of 1028 hymns of praise and devotion. These hymns are usually directed to deities.
- The Yajur Veda. In essence, this is a priestly handbook.
- The Sama Veda contains melodies and chants to be used during worship.
- The Atharva Veda contains hymns that fall outside the aspects of the Yajur Veda and touches on aspects of scientific knowledge.

Thoughts for the classroom

It is important to note the fundamental role of the Vedas within contemporary Hinduism. Throughout history, they have been 'appealed to in defence not only of religious orthodoxy'. Today, they are used in ritual, and for some Hindus, it is observed that they pay

> lip service to Vedic authority, they [have] embarked spiritually on a different trajectory from that of Vedic study (the rise of the Swaminarayan faith is a case in point). But in the early nineteenth century, it was the untiring efforts for social and religious reform in Bengal of a remarkable man, Ram Mohan Roy, that gave Vedic religion a new lease of outward-looking life. (Lipner, 2010, 77)

There are rituals from the Vedas that have their parallel in modern Hinduism, and this is an area that can provide a basis for exploration in the classroom. As Pai (2019) points out:

> Agni is still the witness and the accepter of offerings at yagnas conducted as part of Hindu religious ceremonies (if you have ever attended a Hindu wedding, you have been witness to a yagna!), the yagna kunda is still a simple portable container (most people now prefer to stick with a straightforward square), priests are still invited to officiate at important religious events, ancient Vedic mantras (yup, the same songs of praise we talked about earlier) are still chanted at modern-day ceremonies, and very few people (apart from the priests) still understand what is being chanted! (37)

Two such examples include the use of samskaras, of which there are commonly seen to be sixteen:

1. Conception (*garbhahana*): usually on the first day of menstruation for a new bride following her wedding.
2. During the second or third month of pregnancy (*pumsavana*).
3. Between the sixth month of pregnancy (*simanatonnayana*).

4. Birth (*jatakarma*).
5. Naming ceremony (*namakarana*).
6. Child's first outing at approximately four months (*nishkramana*).
7. Child's first solid food (*annaprashana*).
8. Child's first haircut (between one and three years old) (*chudakarana*).
9. Child's ears are pierced (*karnavedha*).
10. Sacred Thread ceremony (*upanayana*).
11. Beginning of a child's formal education (*vidyarambha*).
12. End of studies (*samavartana*).
13. Marriage (*vivaha*).
14. Retirement (*vanaprastha*).
15. Entering the *sanyasa* stage.
16. Death rites (*antyeshti*).

Aspects of these will be explored in Chapter 6 in the section on Life cycle rituals; at this point, it is important to note that when certain rituals are taught, their links to the Vedas are important and should not be missed out. There are further examples, Vedic *yajnas* (sacrifices, devotions) often form part of various rituals at different points in people's lives and worship in the mandir. Klostermaier (1989) highlights the performance of such yajnas at a time of danger:

> In February 1962, Indian newspapers carried numerous articles describing measures to meet a predicted astagraha, an astronomical conjunction of earth, sun, moon, and five planets. The astrologers were unanimous in considering it an extremely evil omen, possibly the harbinger of the end of the world . . . The rich engaged thousands of pandits and Brahmins to organize Vedic yajnas that would go on for weeks, reciting millions of Vedic mantras. The dreaded event passed without a major disaster. (148)

While the Vedas give sense to some of the rituals performed today, it is important to note that not all modern rituals are a replication of Vedic rituals. The Vedas' role in ritual observance is important, but their root for Hindu belief in practice and the history of Hinduism is that which can go some way to unifying Hindus.

Itihasa

Itihasa ('so indeed it was') is a collection of the histories of important events in the history of the universe within Hinduism, and is seen to include the Puranas, the Dharmashastras and the Epics. There is some thought that Itihasa is used only to refer to the Epics; in the sense that one of the criteria for its classification is that the events are written by an eyewitness, for example Veda Vyasa who wrote the *Mahabharata*, and Valmiki who wrote the *Ramayana*. Whereas, the Puranas were written, almost as biographies, though Veda Vyasa is also seen to be a compiler of the Puranas. For the purpose of this book, the various elements that are used in teaching being so similar, the Epics and the Puranas will be treated as a subsection of the Itihasa, though with the caveat that not all agree with this classification.

The Puranas

There are a vast number of Puranas, often each individual Purana is in praise of an individual deity. There are often seen to be eighteen major and eighteen minor Puranas. These, however, differ according to the compiler of the list. Dimmitt and Buitenen (1978) bring together the various lists and suggest a list of twenty that are considered 'major' by some:

- Agni
- Bhagavata
- Bhavisya
- Brahma
- Brahmanda
- Brahmavaivarta
- Garuda
- Harivamsa
- Kurma
- Linga
- Markandeya
- Matsya
- Narada
- Padma
- Skanda
- Siva
- Vamana
- Varaha
- Vaya
- Vishnu (4–5)

Not all of the names of the Puranas are indicative of content; for example the extant *Brahma Purana* has nothing that relates to Brahma, but has content such as 'creation legends, a description of the manvantaras and the history of the solar and lunar dynasties. Much of the rest of it consists of mahatmyas or descriptions of sacred places, particularly in Utkala.' It is perhaps named the Brahma Purana because while the 'introduction states that Lomaharshana narrated this Purana to rishis of the Mainmisha forest . . . it was earlier revealed by the god Brahma to Daksha' (Dalai, 2014, 80).

Other Puranas do focus on the deity that is mentioned in the title, for example the Vishnu and Shiva Puranas, written in praise of the respective deities. There is no inconsistency in the Puranas praising at the same time Vishnu, Shiva or Shakti.

The Puranas contain similar topics which are known as the panchalakshana, and as such are a 'loose guide' to their contents:

- sarga: cosmogony
- pratisarga: cosmogony and cosmology
- vamsa: genealogy of the deities, the sages and kings
- manvantara: the cycles of the universe
- vamsanucaritam: narratives of various dynasties (Bailey, 2001, 438).

Though it is important to recognize that while attempts have been made to establish a general approach or content, the focus is on the individual text. There is a multiplicity of approaches but all of them, while they may be

> bulky, unwieldy, and sometimes stylistically inelegant . . . contain picaresque myths and legends replete with sex, humour, colour, and drama; they include extensive details of rituals, customs, and lifestyle information and multitudes of case studies that reveal how the formative teachings of the culture that the Puranas reflect should be applied in practice. (Bailey, 2001, 139)

In essence, they become a manual of how to implement aspects of the philosophical systems taught in the Vedas. The way that they are described by Hindus today indicates this:

> Puranas are texts of history, sociology, our culture and our faith-based practices.
>
> Puranas and other texts help us to think and find essence of life.
>
> I believe Puranas written several thousands of years back give a lot of solutions and give direction on we should lead our life and give the same to our next generations.

There is some level of crossover with the Epics (see below) in that there are stories told of various deities, especially of the avatars of Vishnu. For example, the love of Radha for Krishna is explored in the *Brahmavaivarta Purana*. In selecting *Mahagatha: 100 Tales from the Puranas*, Stayarth Nayak (2022) asks the question:

> Do you know the story where Brahma and Vishnu race against each other or where Shiva battles Krishna? Where Indra attempts foeticide or where Rama punishes a Shudra? Do you know about Maya Sita or Narada's monkey face? Or why Surya falls from the

sky or why Chandra commits adultery? The Puranas of Hinduism are a universe of wisdom, embodying a fundamental quest for answers that makes them forever relevant. (Author's Note)

While they may not be encyclopaedic in the traditional sense, they are so in the range of topics they include. There are similarly a vast array of stories that are contained in the eighteen major and the eighteen minor Puranas. In the aforementioned book by Nayak, there are one hundred tales selected from a much wider array. Similarly, one website has a myriad of stories under the title of 'Stories from the Puranas' including:

- The Vedic Gods
- Durga's battle with Shumbha
- The Battle of Bana and Krishna
- Trishanku and Vishwamitra
- Who were the first humans created by Brahma?
- Lakshmi and Uchhaisravas
- Shakuntala, Dushyanta and the birth of Bharata
- Nandi, the meditative bull (see Amar Chitra Katha Media, 2022).

Epics

As noted earlier, sometimes the Epics are identified as the only form of Itihasa, mainly because of the identity of their authors: Valmiki for the *Ramayana*, and Veda Vyasa for the *Mahabharata*. As their name in English suggests, another difference is the length. Although the Puranas are of great length, the stories are somewhat shorter, and the 'epic' length of the stories of the Mahabharata and the Ramayana means that they are somewhat distinct. In commenting on the place of the Epics in their lives today, some Hindus commented:

> Epics are a combination of history, exemplifying acts of dharma and adharma.
>
> Ramayana, and Bhagavad-Gita [a part of the Mahabharata] are the most important with the knowledge that Hindu texts are vast and diverse.
>
> It teaches pure history, and it keeps me at peace when looking at it. They are very beneficial to me.

The Mahabharata

The story of the *Mahabharata* is summarized by Chitra Banerjee Divakaruni as she remembers the story from her childhood:

> At the core of the epic lies the fierce rivalry between two branches of the Kuru dynasty, the Pandavas and the Kauravas. The lifelong struggle between the cousins for the

throne of Hastinapur culminates in the bloody battle of Kurukshetra, in which most kings of that period participated and perished. But numerous other characters people the world of the Mahabharat and contribute to its magnetism and continuing relevance. These larger-than-life heroes, epitomizing inspiring virtues and deadly vices, etched many cautionary morals into my child-consciousness. (2008, xiii)

The story is believed to have been narrated by Veda Vyasa in a way that highlighted the truths of the Vedas so that all people would be able to understand. Once he had composed the *Mahabharata*, it is said that he petitioned Brahma to provide him with a scribe. At the suggestion of Brahma, he approached Ganesh as the remover of obstacles. Ganesh agreed on the condition that Veda Vyasa would never pause in the retelling. In this way, Ganesh was ensuring 'that what Vyasa dictated was free of human prejudice' (Ahmed, 2017, 26). The meaning and importance of the *Mahabharata* are multi-faceted. Roopa Pai (2015) outlines:

On one level – the most obvious level - the story of the Mahabharata is the story of a Great War between two sets of cousins – one set noble, righteous, law-abiding and virtuous, the other corrupt, deceitful, crooked and unscrupulous. But on another level, the Mahabharata is about the battles that rage in our own minds and hearts each day, as we struggle to choose between what we know is right and good and difficult, and what we know is not-so-right, not-so-good and definitely way easier. (xix)

The Mahabharata is primarily a message about dharma and fulfilling it even amidst the most difficult of circumstances. However, even the 'righteous' cousins missed the important aspect of dharma: 'The Pandavas followed Krishna's directive to do what was good for the world, but this victory did not change the Pandavas themselves. They did not gain any wisdom. And in the absence of spiritual insight, they gloated over their victory'; had they acted truly according to dharma, they would have 'attained victory over self' (Ahmed, 2017, 427).

One of the reasons that the Mahabharata is so beloved is the promise given in the Swargarohana Parva at the end of the blessings attending those who read the volume:

The Bharata is cleansing and sacred. In the Bharata are diverse topics. The Bharata is worshipped by the very gods. The Bharata is the highest goal. The Bharata, O chief of the Bharatas, is the foremost of all scriptures. One attains to Emancipation through the Bharata. This that I tell thee is certain truth. One that proclaims the merits of this history called the Mahabharata, of the Earth, of the cow, of Sarasvati (the goddess of speech), of Brahmanas, and of Keshava, has never to languish. (6)

One further aspect of the Mahabharata is the focus on Krishna as an avatar of Vishnu. He is beloved by many Hindus around the world (see Introduction and Chapter 2).

The Bhagavad Gita

Within the Bhishma Parva of the *Mahabharata* is the *Bhagavad Gita*, which by itself is one of the most read books within Hinduism today. Briefly, the Gita contains eighteen chapters which recount a conversation between Krishna as charioteer, with the Pandava prince Arjuna. The conversation takes place on the battlefield at Kurukshetra. It concerns itself with aspects of dharma, with Arjuna worrying about the compatibility of his duty as he prepares for battle against his family. Each of the eighteen chapters is qualified in its title with the word 'yoga' meaning 'path', four of which explore the four types outlined in Chapter 4.

It is observed that the Bhagavad Gita may be the most widely read of all Hindu texts, and its influence has been far-reaching in the articulation of Hinduism in the modern world, and that 'in an important sense Hinduism itself has been recreated on the Gita's foundations' (Sharpe, 1985, 175). Whatever the truth of that, the prevalence of the Gita in Hindu circles means that it is worthy of study as a volume in its own right.

The Ramayana

> The *Ramayana*, at its simplest, is about the exile of a righteous prince who performs deeds of spectacular valour. At its most exalted, it stands for the moment at which the Divine, in His play and grace, manifests Himself in this earthly realm. (Jain et al., 2021, 12)

There are various retellings of the *Ramayana*, perhaps the most famous is Valmiki's *Ramayana* recorded by the sage Valmiki, himself a character within the story. The story ostensibly narrates the story of Rama and his wife Sita. The epic is split into different sections, following the various life stages of Rama:

- Bala Kanda (Book of Youth)
- Ayodhya Kanda (Book of Ayodhya)
- Aranya Kanda (Book of Forest)
- Kishkindha Kanda (Book of Kishkinda)
- Sundara Kanda (Book of Beauty)
- Yuddha Kanda (Book of War)
- Uttar Kanda (Last Book)

Rama is exiled from Ayodha, having been denied his kingdom because of a promise made by his father to his step-mother Kaikeyi. Sita follows him into the forest despite his protestations. Sita is taken prisoner by the Raksha Ravana, and is rescued by her husband with the help of many Divine beings such as Hanuman and Jatayu. They return home in happiness, but while many of the narrations in classrooms stop at that part, there is much more to Valmiki's epic, including the exiling of Sita and her living with her two sons in Valmiki's hermitage. In a similar way to the Mahabharata, the *Ramayana* is seen as a distillation of the truths of the Vedas and the Dharmashatras. At many points, there are competing dharmic demands on the various characters and the choices they make help them stand as role models throughout Hinduism.

When explored within the classroom, it is usually done so in relation to Diwali, as well as the victory of good over evil. It is also possible to explore the story as an example of dharmic living. There are many other interpretations of the symbolism associated with the *Ramayana*. For example, Ravana is said to have performed great penance for 10,000 years; at the end of each millennium, he was granted a new head as a boon from Brahma. This devotion led to the promise that no mortal would be able to kill him. On another level, the ten heads of Ravana represent ten negative qualities identified within Hinduism:

1. *kaam* (lust)
2. *krodh* (wrath)
3. *lobh* (greed)
4. *moh* (obsession)
5. *mada* (vanity)
6. *maatsarya* (envy)
7. *ahankaara* (ego)
8. *chitta* (will)
9. *manas* (heart)
10. *buddhi* (intellect)

In another interpretation, Ravana is respected as a devotee of Shiva and also as a learned being. His ten heads symbolize the six dharmashatras and the four Vedas. There are also many other challenging aspects of the narrative. For example, the killing of Valin to gain the assistance of Sugriva raises questions that Valin himself raises:

> You are the handsome, renowned son of a ruler of men. You also have the visible signs associated with righteousness, king. What man, born in a kshatriya family, learned, free of doubts, and bearing signs of righteousness, would perform such a cruel deed? Born in a royal family, reputed to be virtuous, why do you go about with the appearance of decency when you are in fact not decent, Rama? Conciliation, generosity, forbearance, righteousness, truthfulness, steadiness, and courage, as well as punishment of wrongdoers are the virtues of kings, your majesty. (Goldman & Goldman, 2021, 369)

As such, even without further discussion, the Epics would be worthy of focus within the RE classroom. As stories that are used throughout Hinduism in many different ways, these are arguably the scriptures that most Hindus will be most familiar with. They are stories that teach people important moral lessons and how to behave, and show the application of Vedic principles in the lives of the gods and others. These scriptures can often be seen in carvings on temples, comic books or picture stories and thus are accessible to all people whatever their level of literacy. The Ramayana was serialized on television in the 1980s, and when it was shown, 'life in cities, towns and villages came to a standstill. It was estimated that over 80 million people [in India] watched it – in a place where most people don't own televisions' (Dyson, 2009, 16). Within Hinduism, some see these stories as depicting real events; others as allegories. However, they are understood, they are extremely important in the transmission of Hinduism and the way to live.

Thoughts for the classroom

The Itihasa, while seen as histories, are not intended as either biographies or hagiographies but as writings put together to help people understand the life and teachings of important figures. To try to read them as history would perhaps be problematic, but to dismiss them would be similarly problematic. They can be seen as 'alternative histories existing elsewhere in the thoughtworld of Hindu culture, the contents of which – especially the events associated with the lives of individual gods – come to life in recitations and at religious festivals', they are seen, as it were, as 'sacred history' (Bailey, 2008, 642). Their mythical and allegorical dimension does not reduce their importance for Hindu belief and identity.

Within an exploration of the sources for the narratives surrounding the experiences of deities, there are a range of possibilities that arise for their use in the classroom. The stories of the deities are normally narrated in the classroom with little discussion, but in a similar way to the Christian Gospels, the narrations of the life of the Buddha (see Holt, 2023b), along with texts from many religions, there are opportunities for critical reading of such. At no point does this mean that the teacher or pupils seek to criticize the person or role of the deities. The teacher and students can explore their validity and impact for Hindus today. It is possible in analysing the writing of the texts to explore them in terms of understanding both the deities and the communities which produced them. This was explored in greater detail in a discussion of hermeneutics in Chapter 2.

The Puranas form an important link between the Vedas and the modern day. Bailey (2001) has suggested that 'the function of the Puranas was to reprocess and comment upon old knowledge – somehow to anchor the present back in a timeless past of an artificially reconstructed and remotely remembered Vedic culture' (142–143).

One activity that could be used to explore one of the stories in the Puranas or an aspect of a story in the Epics is a fortune line. In a fortune line (see Figure 5.1) twelve events from the story are plotted, and students would be asked to explain how one of the figures would have felt at those points. After plotting a line graph, a second figure could be chosen to compare their feelings at different points, and students could explore reasons for such. After doing so, because the words on the *y* axis are blunt instruments,

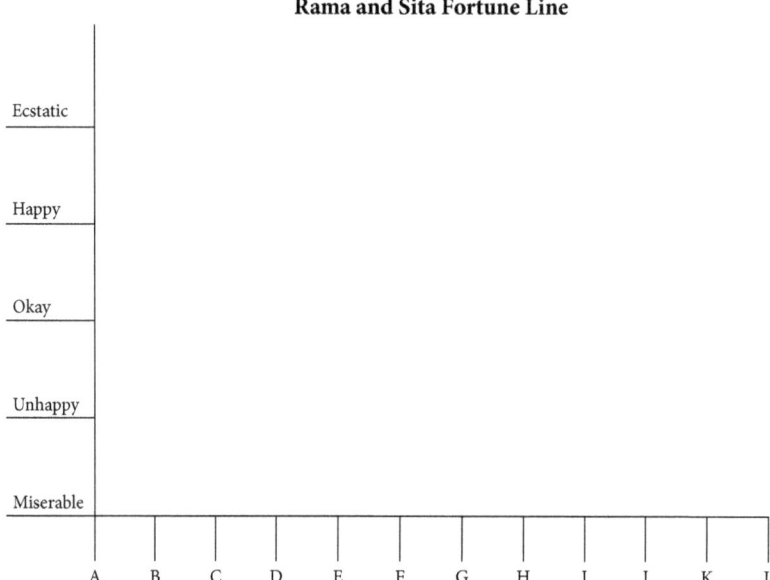

Figure 5.1 Ramayana fortune line

the students could suggest different words that would explain the figures' feelings in a better way. Dependent on age and understanding, the students could be given the events by the teacher or select the events for themselves.

The suggested events for the Ramayana may include:

A. Rama is banished from his kingdom.
B. He sets up home in the forest with his wife Sita, and servant Lakshmana.
C. Rama and Lakshmana go hunting.
D. Sita is kidnapped by the evil king Ravana.
E. Rama and Lakshmana search for Sita with no success.
F. Hanuman offers to help.
G. Hanuman finds Sita.
H. They build a bridge across the sea to Ravana's kingdom.
I. A battle takes place. Rama kills Ravana.
J. Ram and Sita are reunited.
K. Rama tells Sita he cannot take her home with him because people may think she is impure.
L. Sita passes through fire unharmed to prove she is pure, and they return home.

Chapter 6

Expressions of Belief

Within Hinduism, expressions of belief are usually found in the way that a person lives. The chapter above on dharma (see Chapter 1) highlights that a person's outlook on life, informed by the teachings of Hinduism, finds expression in every aspect of a person's life. To separate expressions of belief from a person's life would be anathema to the overall message of Hinduism. Every aspect of a Hindu's life is imbued by dharma and the beliefs that they hold. It is therefore possible to speak of every act that a Hindu performs as a potential expression of belief, though it may not be outwardly observable. Examples of this can be found in Raghunathan and Eswaran's (2012) book, *Ganesha on the Dashboard*; in this, the authors offer a somewhat negative view of the interplay between religion in India and a lack of scientific temper. They suggest on the back cover:

> Take the way we go about buying a new car. We identify an auspicious date and time, then proceed to break a coconut, plonk a plastic deity of Ganesha on the dashboard, and zoom off at great speed, refusing to wear our seatbelts.

The negative tone aside, it highlights the religious in every aspect of life. A recent advertisement of the services offered by a Brahmin in England illustrates the all-encompassing nature of Hinduism in a person's life:

> For All Your Hindu Religious Worship / Ceremonies, Religious Advice, Astrology & Body Geo - Pathic Consultancy and including: Dev Pratishtha, Auspicious Timings, Baby Shower, Baby Name Rashi, Baby Head Shave (Mundan), Janoi, Engagements, Manda Ropan, Satak, Grah Shanti, Weddings, Raandal Mata Ji Puja, Katha, Havan/Homa, Vastu Shanti (New Home Blessings), Car Blessings, Nav-Chandi, Nakshatra Shanti, Abhishek, Havan, Yagna & Yagadi, Funeral, Shraddha (After Funeral Ceremony).
>
> Certified Astrologer For Birth Charts, Muhurat Choghadiya, Match Making, Gem Stone Examinations, Vastu Shastra For Home, Shanti Karma for peace and tranquillity, Astrology for Checking Land, Home, Business.
>
> Geo - Pathic Consultancy For Negative Energy Levels: Consultation For Human Body, According To 7 Body Energy and 2 Hidden Chakras.

This contrasts, very much, with the discussion in the Series Editor's Foreword that outlines 'religion' as a modern and 'settled' term. The neat structures that Western colonialists had constructed based on a Christian lens are not transferred to other religious traditions neatly, no matter how hard people try. Within the classroom, this is one of the problems that a teacher will face when exploring Hinduism. When the GCSE specifications are explored in England, we note that sections such as 'Living the Hindu Life' or 'Practices' deal with topics such as meditation, puja (both of which will be explored in the chapter) and ethics (see Chapter 7) alongside further expressions of belief such as 'festivals' and life cycle rituals.

This is a result of the Department for Education issuing guidance for the reformation of the GCSEs that followed a common structure, and tried to fit everything into a structure that had been inherited from a world religions paradigm. It is incumbent on teachers, who may need to teach within this structure, to highlight the reality of Hindu living compared to that which is found in the specification, and their attendant textbooks. For those teachers who are able to construct an approach to Hinduism not constrained by outside curricula, it will be useful to consider how to approach expressions of belief. This might be better done alongside the beliefs that are expressed. Separating the two is not always the most sensible approach and does not give the idea of a cohesive approach to a person's way of living. Elsewhere (Holt, 2022) I have suggested that one of the five 'bridges' to ensure effective learning within the classroom is through the underpinning of practices with beliefs. Those practices make no sense without an understanding of the attendant beliefs.

Throughout this chapter, the various expressions of worship will be explored from Hinduism, alongside other expressions such as puja or devotion. The various celebrations of festivals will be touched upon, as they are an important expression of Hinduism and community within the UK today. At this stage of the development of a worldviews approach within England, it is important to reflect on how beliefs and practices are intertwined rather than separated.

Darshan

Central to many traditions within Hinduism is bhakti (see Chapter 4) and the idea of a devotional, and personal, loving relationship with the Divine. Within the *Bhagavad Gita*, it is highlighted:

> The Lord said: Those who fix their minds on Me and always engage in My devotion with steadfast faith, I consider them to be the best yogis. (12:2)

Further:

> The devotees who worship Me with love reside in Me and I reside in them. Even if the vilest sinners worship Me with exclusive devotion, they are to be considered righteous because they have made the proper resolve. (*Bhagavad Gita* 9:29–30)

Bhakti, as one of the paths to moksha, is also elucidated in what is known as the bhakti traditions or movements. Evidence of such can be traced back to the fourth century BCE but was especially important between the twelfth and eighteenth centuries, continuing today in individual worship as well as various Shaiva and Vaishnava traditions. There is a corpus of poetry that uses the imagery of love between the deity and the devotee. In general, this type of devotion is helped and supported by sagun, picturing a deity with physical characteristics. There are, however, what are termed nirguna bhakti traditions that express this love and devotion to the formless Divine. Ron Geaves (2008) suggests that nirguna bhaktas 'must be incorporated into the fold of bhakti . . . because of their intense love for a personal but formless divinity, both transcendent and immanent in creation, but, above all found within the heart of the human beings' (95).

Within bhakti, however, it is more often that a representation of the Divine, a murti, is part of worship. Diana Eck (1998) highlights the centrality of darshan (seeing) to the worship of a Hindu:

> Darsan means 'seeing.' In the Hindu ritual tradition it refers especially to religious seeing, or the visual perception of the sacred. When Hindus go to a temple, they do not commonly say, 'I am going to worship,' but rather, 'I am going for darsan.' They go to 'see' the image of the deity be it Krsna or Durga, Siva or Visnu – present in the sanctum of the temple, and they go especially at those times of day when the image is most beautifully adorned with fresh flowers and when the curtain is drawn back so that the image is fully visible. The central act of Hindu worship, from the point of view of the lay person, is to stand in the presence of the deity and to behold the image with one's own eyes, to see and be seen by the deity. Darsan is sometimes translated as the 'auspicious sight' of the divine, and its importance in the Hindu ritual complex reminds us that for Hindus 'worship' is not only a matter of prayers and offerings and the devotional disposition of the heart. Since, in the Hindu understanding, the deity is present in the image, the visual apprehension of the image is charged with religious meaning. Beholding the image is an act of worship, and through the eyes one gains the blessings of the divine. (3)

Darshan is a reciprocal relationship between the deity and the devotee, as the devotee both sees and is seen. This is reminiscent of the teaching about Shiva outlined earlier (see Chapter 2) that those who seek him are sought by him. Darshan is an aspect of worship, or indeed the main focus of devotion, that is integral to understanding a Hindu's religious expression. As discussed earlier (see Chapter 2), throughout history, there has been a paternalistic and incorrect understanding of the focus of worship being representations of the Divine. Viewing through a Christian lens, the attitude towards Hindu murtis has been one that sees them as 'idolatrous', or in the more well-meaning approach mere visual representations in a similar way to a crucifix. Both of these approaches are wrong. Although the objects themselves are not Divine, they are more than representations as they, as Eck suggests above, are imbued with the presence of the Divine. What does this mean for Hindus today? Jeaneane Fowler (1997) outlines the divinity within; she suggests that while:

Photographs project the mind to the reality beyond the print, no one identifies the photographic image as the real person. In the same way it could be said that a *murti* projects the mind of the worshipper to the essence of divinity beyond the immediate emotive representation. Thus, anthropomorphic representations, of deities are by no means the norm in worship – a brass pot, a stone, or a linga of the deity Siva, will symbolize the power of the respective deity. Having said this, a murti is often regarded as a manifestation of the presence of the power of a deity, something of the essence or spirit of the deity which is manifest in the world. (42)

The devotee recognizes a spark of the deity that is either temporarily within the murti, or in the case of murtis within the mandir, they are there more permanently. That these are more than statues is evident when darshan is experienced or observed, and when the treatment of the murtis is explored. The murtis that are installed in the mandir are woken, dressed, fed and given time to rest. The offerings that are left (*prasad*) are considered to be blessed as they have been offered to the Divine, and they are left for the blessing of devotees as they are believed to purify the body, mind and soul and to provide positive karma. The *Bhagavad Gita* records Krishna's recognition of such offerings:

> If one offers to Me with devotion a leaf, a flower, a fruit, or even water, I delightfully partake of that item offered with love by My devotee in pure consciousness. (9.26)

Prior to their day-to-day treatment, the murtis are sculpted in a particular way that has developed over time. Thomas Hopkins (1971) suggests that:

> The actual physical images in wood, stone, or metal were made by craftsmen who produced murtis for all sects on the basis of standard iconographic descriptions. Special texts called *Silpa Sastras* were gradually developed for the use of these craftsmen, and these in time tended further to eliminate variations. (113)

The *Shilpa Shastras* outlined the environment for the creation of the murti, the materials (such as wood, metal and stone) that should be used. One text, the *Brihat Samhita*, suggests that the image 'with its pedestal ought to be as high as the door diminished by an eighth, of these, the idol being of two parts and the pedestal one' (56:11–16). The *Brihat Samhita* continues with measurements for the various body parts of a murti but does recognize there may be differences in decoration, outlining

> An image should be made in such a way that its ornaments, dress, decorations and form conform to the practices prevailing in the country. If it is possessed of the required good features, it will bestow prosperity by its presence. (58:29)

Once sculpted and ready for installation in a mandir, often the final action in the mandir is the painting or opening of the eyes of the murti:

> In the later Hindu tradition, when divine images began to be made, the eyes were the final part of the anthropomorphic image to be carved or set in place. Even after the

breath of life (prana) was established in the image there was the ceremony in which the eyes were ritually opened with a golden needle or with the final stroke of a paintbrush. This is still common practice in the consecration of images, and today shiny oversized enamel eyes may be set in the eye-sockets of the image during this rite. The gaze which falls from the newly-opened eyes of the deity is said to be so powerful that it must first fall upon some pleasing offering, such as sweets, or upon a mirror where it may see its own reflection. More than once has the tale been told of that powerful gaze falling upon some unwitting bystander, who died instantly of its force. (Eck, 1998, 7)

Thus, darshan or the act of seeing and being seen is a significant act for Hindus as they seek to worship the Divine. While the murti is a representation of the deity, it does form a connection between the devotee and the deity. Acts of devotion to the deity are important acts that show the relationship between the two beings, and this is a blessing to the devotee. These murtis are a focus for meditation. The *Vishnu Samhita* outlines the importance of an image for the mind:

Without a form, how can God be mediated upon? If (He is) without any form, where will the mind fix itself? When there is nothing for the mind to attach itself to, it will slip away from meditation or will glide into a state of slumber. Therefore the wise will meditate on some form, remembering, however, that the form is a superimposition and not a reality. (IX:55–57)

The use of the murtis in devotion is most often seen in *puja* (often translated as worship).

Puja

While puja refers to the specific act of devotional worship to the deity within the mandir or in the home, it has begun to be used as a catch-all for various devotional activities which include the following.

Bhajan/Kirtan

Bhajan usually means the congregational singing of hymns of adoration. Kirtan is similar, except that it usually involves the singing of mantras. The hymns and mantras are usually accompanied by musical instruments such as drums and the harmonium. Bhajan often forms an important part of the arti ceremony that takes place after puja, with the use of incense, music and fire devotion becomes a multi-sensory experience. This links very much with the gunas and the panchamahabhutas, and the need for all to be kept in balance.

Darshan

The meaning of darshan is outlined above, and while it can be accompanied by puja and by other acts of devotion, darshan can also be a short visit to the mandir to bow (pranam) and make an offering and prayers. After taking darshan, a worshipper may sip *charanamrita* (water with which the deity was bathed) or receive some prasad.

Pravachan

A 'priest' will deliver a lecture on aspects of scripture that may be from the Vedas, Upanishads or the Puranas. This will be followed by a question and answer session. This enables a Hindu to focus their attention on the Divine, and develop a greater understanding of reality.

Personal study of holy books

Havan (fire sacrifice or sacrificial fire)

Sometimes called *homa* or *agnihotra*, havan is a ritual practice that is often performed at festivals or rites of passage (see below), though for some Hindus, this is a daily observance. Offerings such as grains are given to the fire while mantras are chanted. This is a central practice of the Arya-Samaj tradition.

Meditation

Meditation may be focused on the recitation of a mantra (known as *Japa*) to focus the mind on the Divine. This may be *om namo shivaya* as a focus on Shiva, or *Hare Krishna* as practised by devotees of Krishna. A further popular mantra comes from the Rig Veda and is known as the Gayatri mantra or the Savitri mantra, focused on the Divine feminine:

> *om bhur bhuvah suvah*
> *tat savitur varenyam*
> *bhargo devasya dhimahi*
> *dhiyo yo nah pracodayat.* (Rigveda 3.62.10)

Translated as:

> We meditate on the glory of that Being who has produced this universe; may She enlighten our minds. (Vivekananda, 1989, 211)

A *mala* (string of beads) may enable a devotee to maintain their focus. Meditation purifies the mind and enables a connection with the Divine.

Prayer

Prayers can be formal and include the recitation of traditional prayers, or they can be more personal in the way that they offer adoration and devotion and seek blessings.

Circumambulation

In many mandirs, there is space to enable the circumambulation of the deity, which is a way of offering respect and devotion. Within India, this circumambulation may be of a mandir, a shrine or a town of special importance that may be performed by pilgrims.

Seva

This is devotional service to the deity, whether that might be the washing or clothing of the deity by the priests, for the laity there are many opportunities in the mandir to prepare food for the deity or in cleaning the environment.

Each of these elements of devotion is an important aspect of Hindu worship, and while they may be combined with the more general term of puja, it is important to include them in a discussion of Hindu devotional activities. Some of these are focused on the mandir, while others can be performed anywhere.

Puja generally includes at least sixteen devotional acts; these sixteen steps are seen to be:

1. Invocation of the deity (*avahana*).
2. Offering a seat to the deity (*asana*).
3. Water is offered to wash the deity's feet (*padya*).
4. Water is offered to wash the head and body of the deity.
5. Water is offered to wash the mouth of the deity (*arghya*).
6. The symbolic bathing of the deity (*snana* or *abhisekha*).
7. The deity is dressed (*vastra*).
8. The sacred thread is placed on the deity (*upaveeda* or *mangalsutra*).
9. Placing perfume on the murti (*anulepana* or *gandha*).
10. Placing flowers before or on the murti (*pushpa*).
11. The burning of incense (*dhupa*).
12. An arti lamp is waved before the image (*arti*).
13. Food is offered to the deity (*naivedya*).
14. Devotees bow before the image (*samaskara* or *pranama*). The worshipper and family bow or prostrate themselves before the image to offer homage.
15. Devotees circumambulate the deity (*parikrama* or *pradakshina*).
16. The devotee takes leave of the deity.

This short description perhaps does reflect the vibrancy of such worship. Often in the mandir, this service will be repeated throughout the day, and will be, as the arti and bhajans suggest, a multi-sensory experience for the devotee. This ceremony utilizes all of the *panchamahabhutas*: space/ether, air, earth, fire and water. The ceremony begins with the blowing of a conch shell filled with water (water and air), the earth is represented by the offerings of incense and flowers, and air is represented as a fan is waved. The arti lamp signifies fire, as it is waved slowly in front of the deity, and then offered to the devotees who cup their hands over the flame and then pass their hands over their eyes, forehead and the top of the head.

Puja in the home is an integral part of a Hindu's life, and will often take place early in the morning before the day begins. One Hindu has suggested:

> I do puja every day, and I teach other women in my apartment how to do the poojas and slokas. I also chant some slokas and songs with some women from my apartment on certain days in a week.

All the actions are performed to bring the presence of the deity into the home, and to help the devotee develop a good state of mind, with loving feelings towards the deity and all beings. The following is a description of what puja in the home may look like with the focus on a home shrine.

- Those taking part will bathe and dress in clean clothes. This shows respect and the desire to clean both body and soul.
- The deity is invited to be present in the image by special prayers and ringing the bell.
- The deity is offered a special seat and welcomed like an honoured guest, and a bowl of water is offered to it.
- The deities are given a bath using panchamrit (a mixture of milk, yoghurt, sugar, honey and butter). They are given fresh clothes specially made to fit the image.
- A red paste spot is placed on the image's forehead. This contains sandalwood, which calms the worshipper.
- Flowers are laid before the deity or hung over them as garlands. The flowers represent worldly desires, and the offering of flowers shows the willingness to get rid of one's desires and express love and devotion for the deity.
- Incense sticks are lit to create a fragrant atmosphere. Fragrant oils, representing the destruction of selfish desires, may be burnt.
- A small ghee lamp is lit and waved before the deity.
- Fruits and food are then offered to the deity to thank the deity for everything.
- Then the arti ceremony is performed. A special arti lamp, containing five cotton wool wicks dipped in purified butter, is lit. The number five represents the five elements: earth, air, wind, water and fire.
- This lamp is rotated around the deity while a small bell is rung.
- Blessings are received by the family when they pass their hands over the lamp. This represents the desire to receive knowledge.
- The food offerings are then given out; these are now called prasad, meaning food blessed by deity.

Puja is not just reserved for bhakti traditions; it provides a connection between the devotee and the Divine and is an important part of Hindu expression. While attendance at the mandir may be sporadic, the personal devotion within the home and in personal lives will give expression to the most deeply held beliefs. These 'formal' expressions are supported and enhanced through seemingly almost incidental activities such as touching the head of Saraswati and invoking her blessings, or petitioning Ganesh who may or may not be on the dashboard at the beginning of a journey or an important project. These 'personal' acts of devotion and worship enable a person to express devotion to and receive the blessings of the Divine.

Yoga

The path that becomes known by the shorthand yoga is rajayoga or *hathayoga* (see Chapter 4). The word is usually translated as 'the act of joining' and is linked to the English word 'yoke'. This suggests a linking or joining to the Divine. It is also linked to the idea of balancing the gunas (sattva, rajas and tamas), ensuring that there is an equilibrium and that suffering is not being caused by an imbalance. Yoga is similarly linked to balancing the five elements of matter that make up a person and the universe. This is reflected in the use of mudras (hand and finger movements) in yoga. Sharma (2003) explains that they are easy to practise:

> Five fingers of the hand correspond to five elements as shown hereunder.
>
> 1. Thumb: Agni, fire or heat
> 2. Index finger: Wind and air
> 3. Middle finger: Space (Akash)
> 4. Ring finger: Earth
> 5. Little finger: Water
>
> A person enjoys mental and physical health so long as all five elements remain in requisite proportion in our body. So, for a healthy mind and body all the five elements must remain properly balanced in the body. (93)

For the most part in the West, yoga is identified with physical positions, breathing exercises and meditation. Yoga in the Hindu sense does include all of those things, and its purpose is to attain moksha and union with the Divine, though the *Bhagavad Gita* only prescribes a sitting position. It is part of a wider practice of Hinduism. In the *Yoga Sutras*, Pantanjali outlines the eight limbs of yoga:

> Yama (restraint), niyama (observance), asana (posture), pranayama (regulation of breath), pratyahara (withholding of senses), dharana (fixity), dhyana (meditation and samadhi (perfect concentration) are the eight accessories (means of attaining Yoga). (2:29)

The yamas are the basis of moral living and explored in greater detail in Chapter 7. The remaining seven are what would be traditionally associated. As a path to moksha, yoga is highlighted in various scriptures. The *Vaiseka Sutra* explains:

Pleasure and suffering arise as a result of the drawing together of the sense organs, the mind and objects. When that does not happen because the mind is in the self, there is no pleasure or suffering for one who is embodied. That is yoga. (5.2.15–16)

While the *Katha Upanishad* outlines the equanimity yoga brings:

When the five senses, along with the mind, remain still and the intellect is not active, that is known as the highest state. They consider yoga to be firm restraint of the senses. Then one becomes un-distracted for yoga is the arising and the passing away. (6:10–11)

In the *Bhagavad Gita*, the ultimate purpose of yoga is explained:

Just as a lamp in a windless place does not flicker, so the disciplined mind of a yogi remains steady in meditation on the Supreme. When the mind, restrained from material activities, becomes still by the practice of Yog, then the yogi is able to behold the soul through the purified mind, and he rejoices in the inner joy. In that joyous state of Yog, called samadhi, one experiences supreme boundless divine bliss, and thus situated, one never deviates from the Eternal Truth. Having gained that state, one does not consider any attainment to be greater. Being thus established, one is not shaken even in the midst of the greatest calamity. That state of severance from union with misery is known as Yog. This Yog should be resolutely practiced with determination free from pessimism. (6:19–23)

This last passage explains its purpose in exchanging 'union with misery' with union with the Divine. Yoga will be part of the daily practice of many Hindus, and for some, it will be the central focus of their seeking of moksha. David White (2012) highlights the 'spiritual' goals of yoga, and it can be seen that they all lead to moksha:

1. 'Yoga as an analysis of perception and cognition' (6). This separates reality from sense perceptions and allows the source of suffering to be recognized and overcome.
2. 'Yoga as the raising and expansion of consciousness' (8) suggesting that a person's consciousness can become yoked or united with the Divine. The Mahabharata describes this level of consciousness:

That man who looks upon this world as the result of the combination of the five primal essences, and who behaves himself in this world, keeping this notion foremost, is emancipated. That man who regards pleasure and pain as equal, and gain and loss as on a par, in whose estimation victory and defeat differ not, to whom like and dislike are the same, and who is unchanged under fear and anxiety, is wholly emancipated. (9:289)

3. 'Yoga as a path to omniscience' (White, 2012, 9), meaning a knowledge of that beyond the senses.

4. 'Yoga as a technique for entering into other bodies, generating multiple bodies, and the attainment of other supernatural accomplishments' (11), which is the basis of forms of tantric practice.

In terms of how raja yoga is practised, it is very much linked to the passage of the *Bhagavad Gita* highlighted in Chapter 4, which suggests:

- Making a seat that is neither too high nor low.
- Meditating with one-pointed concentration, controlling all thoughts and activities.
- Hold the body, neck and head in a straight line.
- Hold their gaze on the tip of the nose.
- Meditate on the Divine with the goal of union with the Divine.

The word for seat is *asana*, which is used today in *hathayoga* for a range of poses not suited to sitting meditation. Indeed, hathayoga is seen to have been restricted to ascetics:

> Many of the more complicated postures common today are first found in texts from about the fifteenth century. Hatha yoga, the yoga of force, aimed to manipulate subtle energy channels as a means of uniting deities that practitioners believed resided along the central axis of the body. This was well outside of the Hindu mainstream and seems to have been a practice for males who lived outside of the usual social structures of family and work. (Prill, 2022, 162)

The hathayoga that utilizes postures is seen by many to be a development from asana yoga, and began to become widespread in the Western world in the twentieth century. The desirability of the adaptation of yoga for the Western world is explored below, and although Prill (2022) suggests that it was not hugely significant for Hindu practice, its increasing popularity within wider culture has led to its growth 'in popularity in India and in Hindu diaspora communities' (162). In many ways, there has been an interplay between Hinduism and the West where both have been the recipient of the 'other' in terms of yoga. Indeed, the 'Indian government has celebrated yoga as India's "gift to the world"' (Prill, 2022, 162). One Hindu has commented that this type of yoga is part of their practice:

> I do yoga, chant Vedic Mantra and other prayers, pray in the shrine at home, read one Bhagwat Geeta shlok, and learn Sanskrit.

Thus recognizing and illustrating that postural yoga is no longer restricted to ascetics. It is, however, combined with other aspects of Hindu living.

One aspect of yoga that, while not practised by many, is worthy of note is *Tantra*:

> Tantra is inseparable from yoga. Tantric ritual practices and doctrines always include yogic elements. There are Tantric works on yoga . . . and yogic portions or yogic elements in most Tantric texts. (Padoux, 2017, 39)

Tantra is a practice that is focused on moksha, highlighting different planes of understanding. It recognizes that Shakti, as Brahman, is within everything and as part of a human can be harnessed and used to attain moksha, as well as performing rituals and transformations. The focus of the tantrika is often a mantra, a deity, chakras, mandalas, yantras and other stimuli. These enable the person to utilize the *nadis* (channels, see Chapter 2) to harness shakti and connect with the Divine. Indeed, the focus on the nadi is seen to be the difference between the yoga explored above and Tantric yoga. Tantra can be found across the different traditions of Hinduism, especially those focused on Shiva, Vishnu and Shakti. Continuing the focus on tantra and its practices, Padoux (2017) highlights:

> A practicing Tantrika is nearly always a yogi, for his ascesis (sadhana) most often includes somatopsychic practices that are yogic. Many rites, notably the worship of deities (puja) but also a number of ritual, magical, or spiritual practices, include yogic elements. These practices are usually 'undergirded' by, or even patterned according to, a yogic experience of the body . . . This almost continuous presence of yoga is an important point. (74)

The rituals associated with tantra are often secret and passed on through gurus; recognizing the diversity and multiplicity of tantric practices, it is necessary to highlight that while utilizing the physical body, the focus is on the Divine within. One specific type of meditation is kundalini meditation:

> According to the theory behind Kundalini meditation, life energy lies at the base of your spine (root chakra), coiled like a snake – and that's where its name comes from. In Kundalini meditation, you can work to awaken this energy and achieve enlightenment through a combination of techniques, including:
> - deep breathing
> - mudras (hand movements)
> - mantras (phrases)
> - physical movements-. (Raypole, 2020)

There are many other tantric rituals; some seen to have some immoral aspects, but all seen to enable power and the possibility of liberation in one lifetime.

Discussion of the exploration of yoga in the classroom is found below, but it should be noted that one-dimensional explanations, especially of tantra, should be avoided. It is often easy to present a simplistic view of ritual, but care should be taken to recognize the significance to practitioners and not just accept that which might be found as the first result on a search page.

Festivals

Festivals are perhaps the most observable and popular expressions of Hinduism used in the classroom today. The focus in many classrooms seems to mainly be on Diwali and

Holi; indeed, one Agreed Syllabus seems to address Diwali in each of their suggested units of work, though the syllabus gives freedom as to what festivals are explored (Telford & Wrekin, 2021). There are a myriad of different festivals that can be focused upon in the classroom. Listed below are twenty-two major Hindu festivals (see Table 6.1).

Space does not allow for a full treatment of each of the festivals listed above, nor of the myriad of others not listed, and so this section of the chapter will only give a summary of a small number in terms of how they are celebrated and what they celebrate. Note should be taken that for every festival, depending on the background of who is celebrating it and where, there will be different traditions and also different stories that are remembered. This is an important aspect of Hindu festivals that is often forgotten when we teach the main expression. Thus, Diwali is about Rama and Sita, and is also linked with Krishna killing the demon Narakasur, the birth of Lakshmi, and a celebration of Vamana, an avatar of Vishnu.

Diwali is usually a celebration of Rama's defeat of Ravana and his army, and the return of Rama and Sita to Ayodhya. Celebrations begin two days prior to the day and usually include the cleaning of the home, and the decorating the interior and exterior of homes with saaki, diyas (both types of lamp) and rangoli (a pattern representing happiness and prosperity) signifying it as a festival of light. Often puja will be offered to Lakshmi as the deity of prosperity. There are many resources within the Hindu community that tell the stories celebrated, and also explain the nature of the celebrations. Care should be taken to ensure that both the celebrations and reasons behind them are explored. Books such as *Mr. Men Little Miss Happy Diwali* (Hargreaves, 2020) explain their celebration but not the reasons, and so when used should be accompanied with other explanations from books such as *The Story of Diwali: Rama & Sita* (Anika, 2020).

Holi is a celebration of spring, love and colour, usually focused around the love of Krishna and Radha. Other reasons may be the victory of Narasimha or a celebration of the love of Shiva. Its name comes from Holika, who attempted to burn Pahlada, in so doing she was burnt to death and Prahlada was unharmed. Thus, the celebrations usually begin the night before with the burning of a bonfire. The most recognizable celebration is Rangwali Holi and the throwing of coloured powders or water, followed by celebrations with dancing, food and community. At the end of this chapter is a discussion about cultural appropriation of certain customs, and although Holi is not mentioned in that context, similar questions could be raised as colour runs, and community Holi celebrations can be seen throughout the world. Kolhatkar (2022) addresses this sensitivity by suggesting the appropriateness of attending when invited, but:

> If you are not Indian, don't organize a colour run or a Holi-related festival yourself – unless you're collaborating with an Indian organizer or the local Indian–South Asian community in your city. And, especially, don't try to make money off of it. Instead, consider raising money for immigrant communities or to support Indian-led projects in India. Ultimately, think about what culture means to immigrant communities and adjust your responses to it using the same reverence you might expect for traditions you hold dear.

Table 6.1 A List of Twenty-Two Festivals

Name of festival	Short description	Usual time
Makar Sankranti	A celebration of Surya and new beginnings.	January
Vashant Panchami also known as *Saraswati Puja*	A celebration of Saraswati and the arrival of spring.	Jan/Feb
Mahashivaratri	Celebrating Shiva, and often his marriage to Parvati.	Feb/March
Gaura Purnima	Celebrating the birth of Chaitanya, the founder of Gaudiya Vaishnavism.	March
Holi	Celebrates the love of Radha and Krishna, as well as the victory of Narasimha, or the love of Shiva.	March
Chaitra	A New-Year festival for some Hindus.	March/April
Rama Navami	Celebrates the birth of Rama.	March/April
Hanuman Jayanti	Celebrates the birth of Hanuman.	April
Narasimha Jayanti	Celebrates the birth of Narasimha, an avatar of Vishnu.	April/May
Ganga Puja	Celebration of Ganga (River Ganges)	June
Vaikasi Visakam	Celebrates the birth of Murugan, who is identified with Kartikeya, son of Shiva and Parvati.	June
Ratha Yatra	The chariot festival linked with various deities.	June/July
Raksha Bandhan	When sisters tie silk bracelets on their brothers' wrists.	August
Janmashtami	Celebrates the birth of Krishna.	August/Sept
Ganesh Chaturthi	Celebrates the birth of Ganesh.	August/Sept
Navaratri	The festival of nine nights in honour of the Shakti and various female deities.	Sept/Oct
Durga Puja	Celebration of Durga.	Sept/Oct
Dussehra	The celebration of Rama's victory over Ravana.	October
Lakshmi Puja	Celebration of Lakshmi.	Oct/Nov
Diwali	A festival of lights usually celebrating Rama and Sita's return.	Oct/Nov
Govardhana Puja	Remembering when Krishna uses the hill Govardhana to protect a village.	Oct/Nov

Navaratri is a festival of nine nights, usually focused around Durga as a manifestation of Parvati, but is also a celebration of further avatars of the goddess on each day in turn: Shailaputri, Brahmacharini, Chandraghanta, Kushmanda, Skandamata, Katyayani, Kalaratri, Mahagauri and Siddhidatri. Retellings or re-enactments of the stories of the Divine Mother are shared on each day, often accompanied by fasting, while on the final day (*Vijayadashami*), murtis of the deities are immersed in a river, and often the images of the evil characters are burnt signifying the victory of good over evil. This festival provides an opportunity for exploration of the Divine feminine which is sometimes overlooked in the classroom.

Raksha Bandhan, meaning 'bond of protection' is a festival celebrated by sisters tying an amulet around the wrist of their brother. This is to symbolize protection, and in previous centuries was performed by Brahmins; the fusion of two similar events on the same day means that it is now performed by sisters. In return, the brother gives a gift to his sister. Although having its roots in a more traditional patriarchal society where a brother would be the source of protection for a woman when her father died, and a way of maintaining communication with family, it has taken on a more celebratory role emphasizing ties of kinship in the modern world. Close friends of the opposite sex may also participate in this festival, but it would suggest that there would never be anything but friendship between them.

Mahashivaratri is a festival focused on Shiva, and sometimes remembers the wedding of Parvati and Shiva. Other explanations focus on the remembering of the vent where Brahma and Vishnu tried to find the top and bottom of the Shiva lingum (see Chapter 2). It is a night-time festival known for its solemnity, rather than the exuberant celebrations of many other Hindu festivals. During the festival, devotees will fast, vow to forgive others, tell the truth, practise ahimsa and worship Shiva for twenty-four hours:

> One spends the night reciting the manta of Shiva – *om namah shivaya* – and praying for forgiveness. If the rites are performed faithfully one is rewarded with worldly success and the heavenly realm of Shiva. (Jones & Ryan, 2007, 269)

This provides an alternative purpose of festivals for students as they explore the different celebrations within Hinduism. Also, those chosen for a brief discussion would also allow for an exploration of devotion to Vishnu, Shiva and Shakti; though as noted festivals are not exclusively the purview of one deity.

Life cycle rituals

The *samskaras* are rituals that have traditionally marked various important stages in life. The exact number suggested or mentioned in the Vedas is debated, but there are commonly seen to be 16:

1. Conception (*garbhahana*): usually on the first day of menstruation for a new bride following her wedding.
2. During the second or third month of pregnancy (*pumsavana*) to pray for the optimum physical growth of the unborn child.
3. Between the sixth and eighth months of pregnancy (*simanatonnayana*) to pray for the optimum mental growth of the unborn child.

4. Birth (*jatakarma*) where the ceremony involves a small amount of honey being placed into the baby's mouth, and the name of the Divine being whispered into their ear.
5. Naming ceremony (*namakarana*) which is normally performed eleven days after birth. The name that is chosen is linked to the horoscope of the date of birth.
6. Child's first outing at approximately four months (*nishkramana*) to introduce the newborn child to nature and the Divine that is throughout it.
7. Child's first solid food (*annaprashana*).
8. Child's first haircut (between one and three years old) (*chudakarana*). The shaving of the head symbolizes the removal of bad thoughts.
9. Child's ears are pierced (*karnavedha*) usually performed between three and five years of age.
10. Sacred Thread ceremony (*upanayana*) when the child reaches the age where he would go to school. Upanayana means 'getting closer to someone', in this case the guru to whom the child is introduced. The *yajnopaveet* (Sacred Thread) has three strands representing:
    - *Rishi rin* – the obligation to promote knowledge gained from all sages, scientists and learned people.
    - *Pitri rin* – the obligation to look after parents and elders.
    - *Dev rin* – representing the moral purity expected of someone in the brahmacharya samskara (see Chapter 1).
11. Beginning of child's formal education (*vedarambha*) when learning begins. It usually begins with a recitation of the Gayatri mantra:

    May we attain that excellent glory of Savitar the God:
    So May he stimulate our prayers. (*Rig Veda* 3.62.10)

12. End of studies (*samavartana*) where a person is ready to participate in all aspects of community life.
13. Marriage (*vivaha*) marks the beginning of the grihastha ashrama. There are differences in the various rituals according to tradition and region. Some of the most common aspects of a Hindu wedding include:
    - Varmala: the bridegroom and his parents are welcomed to the home where the wedding is taking place by the parents of the bride. A red mark is placed on their foreheads, and the families are formally introduced to each other. The bride and groom exchange garlands.
    - Madhu parka: the groom is seated on a mandap (decorated altar) and given a ceremonial drink.

- Gau Daan and Kanya Pratigrahan: an exchange of gifts.
- Vivaha-homa. The Purohit lights a sacred fire and recites mantras, and oblations are offered to the fire.
- Paanigrahan: a ceremony of the vows between the bride and groom.
- Shilarohan and Laaja Homa: the bride steps over a stone symbolizing a willingness to overcome any difficulties as she strives to live her dharma. The bride and groom walk round the fire four times, on the first three the bride leads the way, and on the last the groom leads. Their responsibilities are outlined. Barley is poured into the joined hands of the couple, who then throw it into the fire, symbolizing their willingness to work together. The husband applies the sindhoor, or mark of a married woman, to the bride's forehead with red kum kum powder.
- Sapta-Padi: in this part of the ceremony, the couple takes seven steps together, offering a prayer with each step. Each step represents something different: food, strength, prosperity, wisdom, progeny, health and friendship in turn. The seventh step completes the service and a ceremonial knot is tied.
- Surya Darshan/Dhruva Darshan: seeing the sun to be blessed with a creative life; seeing the Pole Star to symbolize steadfastness.
- Ashirvada: the Brahmin and others bless the couple.

14. Retirement (*vanaprastha*) at the beginning of the vanaprastha ashrama, usually in a person's early fifties, they will begin to prepare for spiritual life and withdrawal from the world.

15. Entering the *sanyasa* stage, usually around the age of seventy-five, to renounce all worldly concerns.

16. Death rites (*antyeshti*): the body is washed by people of the same gender before being clothed in white cloth to symbolize peace and purity, with two toes tied together and a tilak being placed on the forehead. Different traditions mean that some women may wear white in mourning, while others wear red. Traditionally the eldest son will light a funeral pyre, but in the UK and other countries crematoriums are used, with cremation generally being the appropriate way to treat the body, in this way 'death represents a return to the five elements that constitute a body' (Olson, 2007, 100). The ashes will usually be scattered, ideally in the Ganges, but often in the UK it will take place in a river.

In today's society, there are different levels of observance of the various samskaras, and it is important for teachers not to establish an orthopraxy, where people can only be considered to be practising Hindus who follow everything exactly. While 'the rites of passage affect the entire person and not just his or her spiritual side' and they shape an individual 'into an adult member of society . . . Contemporary Hindus do not observe all the rites of passage. Generally speaking, some early childhood rites are combined or not observed, while marriage and funeral rites are more widely practiced at the present time' (Olson, 2007, 100). This is a reminder that in a worldviews approach to religions, it is possible to observe cultural, generational, geographical and individual variation in the way that Hinduism is experienced and lived.

Thoughts for the classroom

Within this chapter, time has necessarily been taken to explore the various expressions of Hindu devotion. The expressions chosen have been illustrative and are in no way to be seen as a comprehensive outline of the ways that Hindu beliefs are expressed and lived. One such example that has not been explored is pilgrimage, including the sacred geography of India. This has been alluded to at various points within the book, for example, when speaking of the pithas of Sati (see Chapter 2), or the importance of Mother Ganges in relation to Shiva (see Chapter 2), but space has not allowed a detailed exploration of this, and other aspects of Hindu devotion. Exploring aspects of the four paths to moksha will hopefully enable the reader to utilize the underlying beliefs to begin a much more in-depth study of Hindu practices, both those explored here and those not.

There are many opportunities for using expressions of Hindu belief in the classroom, which provide concrete examples of how beliefs are put into practice. Using the concept of darshan and the idea of seeing and being seen in the context of bhakti will enable students to make links between different aspects of Hinduism, as well as gaining a greater appreciation and understanding of Hindu devotion. When looking at religious beliefs, it is important to build bridges to help students understand what is being taught. Two of these bridges are with their own experiences and with local and national communities (Holt, 2022). The exploration of samskaras enables both of these bridges to be utilized. The completion of a 'Journey of Life' by students to highlight important aspects in their own lives that have happened, and that they hope will happen, will provide a springboard for the exploration of important points in a Hindu's life. This type of activity breaks down illusory barriers of 'them' and 'us' as students recognize the similarities in the life experiences of all people. One tendency that might need to be thought through as a teacher is the representation of Hindu practices and communities. Sometimes it is tempting to use examples from India, for example, a celebration of Holi or a funeral in Varanasi. These will be engaging, but if this is all students see then they build a skewed view of Hinduism. It is much more beneficial for students to see expressions from the local area, either with local voices from the local community or prepared videos by organizations such as TrueTube that highlight the lived reality of Hindus in the UK.

One other aspect that has been discussed in Chapter 2, and also alluded to earlier with respect to Holi, is the issue of cultural appropriation. In this area, it is interesting that when yoga is taught within the classroom, it is generally taught quite briefly, while recognizing that there are different types. This chapter has shown that there is much more to yoga and, dependent on the age and understanding of the students, it is important to make this clear. This book has only been able to scratch the surface of the various types of yoga, but the complexity has been recognized. This, again, draws upon the diversity or messiness of Hinduism as not being able to generalize with any degree of accuracy.

The second way that yoga is 'used' within the classroom is to have children undertake some yoga exercises. This is a controversial aspect of teaching religion and worldviews that I have discussed elsewhere (Holt, 2022) in exploring the suitability of experiential approaches to learning. This is something that a teacher needs to consider carefully before undertaking such approaches. The concerns that people may express are twofold. Firstly, the mundanification of what are 'spiritual' or 'sacred' practices. How does the teacher safeguard against making the sacred mundane, as it does not have the same intents and purposes as within Hinduism? In using yoga as an activity, it could be that it is being cheapened. There are questions that need to be asked as teachers consider activities that might replicate religious experience in a vacuous way. As such, a teacher needs to be very conscious of the reasons why they are doing something, and the aim of the activity. Do the benefits outweigh the potential concerns? Does this activity desanctify some of the religious actions of Hinduism and make them mundane?

The second concern is that students are being asked to 'perform' a Hindu ritual act by engaging in yoga. The purpose of such an activity is to have pupils feel what it is like. As indicated by the previous concern, without the same purpose and belief supporting it, it is impossible to get the same feeling. Within the classroom, there seem to be an inconsistent approach to the re-enactment of, or participation in, ritual acts. For example, the re-enactment of a wedding may be considered fine, where the repeating of ritual actions of prayer would not. Where is the line drawn, and how do teachers know what is appropriate or not?

Hindu yoga is an interesting case, in the sense that in today's world it may be seen to have been secularized. It is not unusual for yoga classes to be held in community centres, workplaces, hospitals and schools. Is yoga a Hindu approach, or has it been appropriated and transformed into something else? Liz Bucar (2022) raises this issue with regard to meditation:

> To me, it seemed clear the techniques were grounded in, as Paul Tillich would say, an ultimate concern . . . By engaging in the techniques, and feeling their benefits, we were implicitly externalising the religious ideas behind them as well . . . I wanted him to acknowledge that we were in an ethical grey area when we offered these techniques to students without mentioning these religious connections. (221)

This is too big a discussion for the scope of this book, but it is something that we, as teachers, need to consider. There is a possibility that there is a difference between yoga as perceived in the world and Hindu yoga. Indeed, Bucar (2022) suggests that there could be a differentiation between the two yogas where one is used for devotion, while the desecularized version is termed 'respite' yoga which is focused on health and wellness.

> The practice Bucar calls respite yoga is all about physical health, stress reduction, and overall well-being. She describes it as 'feel-good yoga, good-vibes-only yoga.' It's the kind of secular practice we expect from a studio or a fitness centre. The benefit of a secular yoga practice is that it can be accessible to more people, regardless of their religious or spiritual leanings. But eliminating the esoteric parts of yoga distils it down to little more than calisthenics and deep breathing. (Jeffries, 2022)

There is a range of literature that suggests that yoga may be a secularization of a Hindu concept and as such care should be taken over its use in the classroom. From a Hindu perspective, it is possible to suggest that secular mindfulness is not Hindu, as its ultimate aim is far removed from the yoga of Hinduism. There are many commentators who would suggest that yoga in the modern world has been stripped of its 'spiritual' or 'religious' roots and commodified:

> Not only is yoga hybridized and westernized through the appropriation and marketization processes, but as a consequence of globalization, it also becomes easternized through juxtaposition with other Asian bodily practices. In this way, yoga becomes part of an eastern package of technologies of the self. (Askegaard & Eckhardt, 2012, 53)

The separation of yoga from its roots is seen by some as a 'whitewashing' and a hybridization with Western New Age ideals, rather than being rooted in the spirituality of Hinduism. Sophia Rose Ariana argues:

> These pressures lead workers, who are also consumers, to seek out paths to health, wellness, and balance, such as yoga, meditation, and other spiritual practices. Through these practices, the business of mysticism and spirituality serves the corporatization of bodies. There are numerous examples of this. American yoga typically negates its Hindu and Jain origins, but refers to it as Eastern, or part of a wisdom tradition. The avoidance of Hindu practices is one of the ways in which yoga is rearticulated as a Western practice and sanitized for a white customers. As one yoga studio owner puts it: 'We don't do chanting because people are not comfortable with it . . . We never use the word "God." We talk about energy, we talk about peace, we talk about mindfulness. We use those New-Agey kind of words.' (2020, 149–150)

Rather than seeking liberation and union, a person practising secular yoga is only seeking health or momentary escape. Thus, teachers may feel it appropriate to use forms of yoga recognizing that it is not Hindu but has been appropriated in a secular way for the modern world.

Part 2

Contemporary Issues

Chapter 7

The Ethical Dimension

When considering the ethical dimension of Hinduism, there is a temptation to treat it in a similar way that may be found in other religions. For some, or many, Hindus, there may be a focus on karma in an individual's life as a reason to live in an ethical way, especially as these are expressions of dharma. There is, however, a focus on the development of character or of virtues which underpin a Hindu ethical outlook. The purpose is the process of becoming so that moksha can be attained within Hinduism. The ethical dimension is intertwined with the Hindu view of the world and of existence more generally. Thus, within Hinduism, there can be different motivations behind ethical actions, but all ethical actions can be seen to be outworkings of the worldview of Hinduism.

Throughout this chapter, we will explore various ethical guidelines such as the five yamas and their links to the niyamas. These will include virtues of *ahimsa* (non-violence), *satya* (truthfulness), *asteya* (not stealing), *brahmacharya* (chastity) and *aparigraha* (non-attachment), and how these may find expression in the lives of Hindus today, building on the introduction in Chapter 1. It bears repeating that these are not checklists to be ticked off; they are but guiding principles. Other aspects of ethical issues will be explored as appropriate.

Ahimsa

> Ahimsa is the highest dharma,
> Ahimsa is the highest self-control,
> Ahimsa is the greatest gift,
> Ahimsa is the best practice,
> Ahimsa is the highest sacrifice,
> Ahimsa is the finest strength,
> Ahimsa is the greatest friend,
> Ahimsa is the greatest happiness,
> Ahimsa is the highest truth,
> and Ahimsa is the greatest teaching. (Mahabharata 13.117.37–38)

Perhaps because of the influence of Gandhi, ahimsa (non-harm/non-violence) is perhaps the aspect of Hindu living that is most well-known outside of Hinduism. Gandhi expressed his approach to ahimsa in his interactions with colonial powers in seeking Indian rights in South Africa, and then in seeking independence for India. The story of Gandhi has filled books and inspired films, but a couple of examples of his expression of ahimsa will assist in understanding its practice and ideal in Hindu living. It should be noted that Gandhi's personal living has been subject to recent interrogation, and the inappropriateness of some of his actions. These will not be explored here, it is ahimsa that is the focus in this section. This should not be taken as condoning all of Gandhi's actions, rather that in his approach to the governments of the time, his is an example that provides important insights. This is also not to suggest that Gandhi is the only example of ahimsa, rather he is a familiar figure who can help students understand its various nuances. He is not the source of the teaching, rather he expressed how it could be lived in the modern world.

Gandhi describes ahimsa both positively and negatively:

> In its negative form it means not injuring any living being whether by body or mind. It may not, therefore, hurt the person of any wrong-doer, or bear any ill-will to him and so cause him mental suffering . . . In its positive form, Ahimsa means the largest love, the greatest charity. If I am a follower of Ahimsa, I must love my enemy. I must apply the same rules to the wrong-doer who is my enemy or a stranger to me, as I would to my wrong-doing father or son. This active Ahimsa necessarily includes truth and fearlessness. As man cannot deceive the loved one, he does not fear or frighten him or her. Gift of life is the greatest of all gifts; a man who gives it in reality, disarms all hostility. (1922, 283–284)

Ahimsa can be taught in a purely negative way; in the sense that Hindus, through living ahimsa, are not to harm any other living being. Similarly, there could be an approach to ahimsa that separates beings and things within the natural world so that there are levels of ahimsa. This may be true in people's minds, but the virtue of ahimsa is one that can become intuitive and a part of their character, indeed Gandhi himself described ahimsa as 'part of my life' (1922, 282).

An early example of Gandhi's application of ahimsa comes during his time in South Africa. In working for the rights of Indians within South African society, he was met with much opposition; on occasion he was beaten for his efforts. He describes one such event in 1897:

> A mob followed us. With every step we advanced, it grew larger and larger. The gathering was enormous when we reached West Street. A man of powerful build took hold of Mr. Laughton and tore him away from me. He was not therefore in a position to come up with me. The crowd began to abuse me and. shower upon me stones and whatever else they could lay their hands on. They, threw down my turban. Meanwhile a burly fellow came up. to me, slapped me in the face and then kicked me. I was about to fall down unconscious when I held on to the railings of a house nearby. I took breath for a while and when the fainting was over proceeded on my way. I had almost given up the hope of reaching home alive. But I remember well that even then my heart did not arraign my assailants. (1956, 45)

He was asked to identify his assailants so that they could be prosecuted. He demurred because, as he said in the last part of his recounting, 'my heart did not arraign my assailants'. This is an expression of positive ahimsa; his view of the 'other' was one of love and therefore he sought no repercussions for those who attacked him. To an extent, however, this could be used to justify the allowance of violence towards a person. It becomes the 'victim's' responsibility to not retaliate, and possibly for the aggressor to receive no punishment or consequence. This passive ahimsa is rejected by Gandhi; rather, he see the act of love as a force to be reckoned with and one which can transform society. He suggested:

> [Ahimsa] does not mean helping the evil-doer to continue the wrong or tolerating it by passive acquiescence. On the contrary, love, the state of ahimsa, requires you to resist the wrong doer. (1968, 126–127)

In South Africa and afterwards, he developed a philosophy and approach that he termed *satyagraha*. Gandhi describes this:

> Truth (satya) implies love, and firmness (agraha) engenders and therefore serves as a synonym for force. I thus began to call the Indian movement Satyagraha, that is to say, the Force which is born of Truth and Love or non-violence, and gave up the use of the phrase 'passive resistance', in connection with it, so much so that even in English writing we often avoided it and used instead the word 'satyagraha' itself or some other equivalent English phrase. (2006, 65)

This is perhaps best evidenced in Gandhi's relationship with the British, as the colonial power in India. The Salt March or Salt Satyagraha was an act of satyagraha led by Gandhi in 1930 (from 12 March to 5 April), where an ever-increasing group from Sabarmati Ashram to Dandi, a distance of 240 miles. As context, there had been a law or salt tax passed in 1882 that forbade Indians from collecting or making salt; they were to buy salt that had been mined in Britain. By 19,1930, the salt tax represented 8.2 per cent of the revenue collected in India. In an act of civil disobedience, Gandhi walked across India, and at the beach in Dandi Gandhi made salt through the evaporation of the salt water on 6 April. He had thus broken the law. Thousands of people followed his example, and Gandhi continued down the coast holding meetings and collecting salt. On 5 May 1930, Gandhi was arrested and imprisoned. His actions, and the actions of many Indians in the months that followed, did not have an immediate effect on the British. But the satyagraha continued, and over 60,000 people were arrested. The headlines around the world highlighted the injustice of the British laws and actions and caused the British to reconsider their approach. John Court Curry, a British police officer, reported experiencing 'nausea every time he had to deal with Congress demonstrations in 1930'. The peaceful resistance had a great impact on him:

> Curry and British policymakers in London and Delhi realized that terrorism was easier to control than nonviolent resistance. Curry experienced no ambivalence in his work to

suppress terrorist organizations in India. It was suppressing nonviolent resistance which made him sick and led to his resignation. (Johnson, 2006, 33)

In January 1931, Gandhi was released from prison, and as a result of the protests, he was able to secure a place at the negotiating table that was debating the freedom and future of India (see Bondurant, 1959).

In some ways, satyagraha is a large and 'flashy' expression of ahimsa that reflects an approach to life, and is the 'ultimate' expression of ahimsa. For many Hindus, the application of ahimsa is found in the daily acts of living. A person's dharma (see Chapter 1) establishes phases of a person's life, and while civil disobedience motivated by love will form part of that dharma, there are smaller aspects of a person's life that work together to build ahimsa as a part of life and living. This lies behind the philosophy of a UK/India-based charity *Go Dharmic*. Examples of their initiatives that they invite people to get involved with range from those that ask for an individual commitment to those that require a larger group. These include:

- *Shape a Future*. This concludes the goal to build libraries and opportunities include donating funds, setting up a library in a school, or volunteering at a Go Dharmic-supported school.
- *Feed Everyone*. This can include financial donations, or volunteering to help with the distribution to those in need, especially the homeless.
- *Give Oxygen India*. This project requests financial donations so that oxygen tanks can get to those who need them in India, as well as temporary hospitals, and other medical items.
- *Go Plant Based*. A campaign to encourage people to go vegan to prevent harm to animals and to protect the environment.
- *Save and Switch*. Raises awareness about the cost of power and encourages people to switch to renewable sources of energy.
- *Go Organic*. A campaign for people to buy organic products.
- *Mini Minds*. Co-ordinates people to teach yoga and mindfulness in schools.

Ahimsa, as a reflection of love, finds expression in the actions of people. Whether that is the telling of truth or the treating of others with compassion. Aspects of these virtues will be explored below, but they should always be against the background of ahimsa. Possibly the two most common expressions of ahimsa that a person might observe within Hinduism are with regard to environmental issues and vegetarianism.

The environment

Possibly the greatest problem in the world today is that of the many threats to the environment. In an exploration of the nature of the Divine (see above Chapter 2) and also of ahimsa, it would appear that the combined nature of created beings and living things as being imbued with the Divine, and the virtue of not harming living things coalesce in an environmentalism of Hinduism. Srinivasan Gandhi (2018) suggests:

> Pancha Mahabhutas (The five great elements) create a web of life that is shown forth in the structure and interconnectedness of the cosmos and the human body. Hinduism teaches that the five great elements (space, air, fire, water and earth) that constitute the environment are all derived from prakriti, the primal energy. Each of these elements has its own life and form; together the elements are interconnected and interdependent. The Upanishads explains the interdependence of these elements in relation to Brahman, the supreme reality, from which they arise: 'From Brahman arises space, from space arises air, from air arises fire, from fire arises water, and from water arises earth.'

There is an interconnectedness within the universe that gives all beings a responsibility for its maintenance. When a person considers that prakriti can be found throughout creation, that the earth is represented by the deity Bhumi, or that Ganga herself is manifested in the River Ganges, it becomes evident that a proper treatment of the natural world is an expression of devotion.

The overuse of the world's resources means that a person is acting out of greed, and is forgetting the interconnectedness of all things. ISKCON (1994) highlights that the bad or thoughtless treatment of the world and its resources would accrue negative karma:

> The Vedic scriptures state, 'Human prosperity flourishes by natural gifts and not by industrial development. If human civilisation has sufficient grains, cotton, minerals, jewels and water, why should we hanker after terrible industrial enterprises so that the few can live lavishly at the cost of the many?' The scriptures further explain that such artificial endeavours are a result of godlessness whereby man remains ignorant of any higher supervision. According to the law of karma, (action and reaction), the more we selfishly exploit the earth's resources, the more we become victimised by scarcity, pollution and catastrophe.

There are organizations such as *Go Dharmic* who suggest ways in which Hindus, and everyone, can treat the environment better. One such example is the campaign *Go Green*, which links with other campaigns:

> Go Organic
> Give it a Grow
> Go Plant-Based
> Go Fuel Free
> Save and Switch

They suggest further that:

> Apart from working through our campaigns, we also try and inculcate green values in our other campaigns.
> *Feed Everyone*

Under this campaign, we are working relentlessly to provide food to the homeless and vulnerable people across the globe! To ensure environmental safety while we do this, we

A. Provide plant-based meals
B. Use biodegradable boxes to serve these meals
C. Avoid using plastic in packaging

Good Karma Store

The Good Karma Store is our initiative to reuse and upscale fashion. With so much wastage and pollution caused by the Textile Industry, it's time that we consciously select how we deal with clothing (Go Dharmic, n.d.b)

When exploring environmental issues in schools, an exploration of Hinduism and Hindu teachings would provide a different perspective to that offered by the Abrahamic religions and the idea of being given stewardship. Hinduism, while some may disagree, could be seen as a somewhat animistic worldview where everything contains the Divine. As such, it provides an important reflection on the sacredness of the world. The actions that result from these beliefs have a different, but equally effective, impact on striving to 'save the planet'.

Vegetarianism

Somewhat linked with the issue of environmentalism but also an issue on its own is vegetarianism. The same principles apply in exploring issues of vegetarianism as with the ideas linked to the environment. Based on the principle of ahimsa or non-harm, it would seem to follow that Hindus would avoid harming animals, and as such, vegetarianism, or veganism, would be a logical outworking of the principle. The *Bhagavad Gita* seems to extol the virtue of not eating meat:

> He who desires to augment his own flesh by eating the flesh of other creatures, lives in misery in whatever species he may take his [next] birth. (Mahabharata 13.115.47)

> The sins generated by violence curtail the life of the perpetrator. Therefore, even those who are anxious for their own welfare should abstain from meat-eating. (Mahabharata 13.115.33)

There is, however, evidence in history and in the Vedas of animal sacrifice, and the desirability of the eating of that which had been offered in sacrifice. Although that may have been the case, most Hindus would recognize that was a lesser sacrifice, and that abstention from such is of greater merit. Indeed, the Bhagavata Purana describes the use of animals in these rites as 'sham sacrifices' (5.26.5).

Although there seems to be the view within Hinduism that the use of animals for meat should be avoided, as it can be viewed as an act of *himsa* (harm), it would appear that there are differences of practice. The Pew Research Center (2021) report *Religion in India: Tolerance and Segregation* canvassed attitudes towards the eating of meat among Hindus in India. The report's findings suggest that:

- 44 per cent of Hindus in India are vegetarian.
- 16 per cent have no restrictions on eating meat.
- 39 per cent have some restrictions such as only eating it on certain days, or only eating certain meats.

An interesting nuance of the report about Indian attitudes is that 'Hindus who express a favourable view of the Bharatiya Janata Party (BJP) are more likely than others to be vegetarians (49 per cent vs. 35 per cent)' (Pew Research Center, 2021, 187). Linked with the discussion in the Series Editor's Foreword and in Chapter 9, this might suggest that vegetarianism is a part of an increasing reification of Hindu belief and practice. There are examples of Hindu organizations assuming an approach to animal life that intertwines ahimsa with animal rights. Go Dharmic mentioned above has a series of campaigns including *Go Plant Based* and *Compassion for Animals*. In this campaign, they suggest that people could:

> Educate our children to treat animals with love, care and respect.
> Avoid using any textiles made up of an animal's body
> Take care of the stray animals in our surroundings such as cats, dogs, cows, etc.
> Avoid eating non-vegetarian food items such as meat, beef, sea food, etc.
> Form animal welfare groups to take care and keep a check on stray animals.
> If any animal is suffering from any sort of disease or injury, contact the veterinary doctor to rescue the ailment. (Go Dharmic, n.d.a)

This highlights actions individual Hindus can take in protecting and caring for animals in a way that is not restricted to vegetarianism.

There is no equivalent data set for attitudes towards vegetarianism within the UK, and it is hard to predict with any certainty. For some Hindus in the UK, it will be an expression of a distinctive Hindu identity to be vegetarian, whereas for others, cultural assimilation may take precedence. Some British Hindus shared mixed views on whether vegetarianism is a part of Hindu life. On the one hand:

> It's very favourable to a Hindu part of life.
> Ahimsa (nonviolence) is a part of our dharma. As we are given free-will, if one wants to kill animals and eat meat, that would be one's personal choice. Vegetarianism is thus a moral imperative. The meat-eaters will face the consequences of this action at some time (karma phala). I believe that most meat eaters have not understood their action thus.

While others see it as a personal choice:

> While many Hindus including me are vegetarian, a large number of Hindus are not. Food is more to do with what is available locally rather than any religious basis. In India, people from coastal areas eat fish, people from mountains eat meat.
>
> Vegetarianism is not a part of Hindu life. It is preferred but not essential. Basic thought was that our thinking gets affected by what we eat. Therefore, simple food was always preferred to avoid any unnecessary excitement and negative emotions caused by our eating habits.

Of interest is the identification of vegetarianism with caste:

> Vegetarian is not part of Hindu life. In Hindu life we have different categories like brahmins, Kshatriyas, Vaishyas and Shudras. Some of these categories (especially) do not eat meat but others do.

It would appear, then, that the traditional view of Hindus as vegetarians may not be applicable in all cases. This will be affected by local circumstance, family background and interpretation of texts. This is, again, an important aspect of an education that reflects on worldviews. While teachers, and even religious people, might try to establish an orthodoxy or even orthopraxy, the lived reality of individuals is a complex interplay of factors, that in this case may lead to vegetarianism or not.

One seeming non-negotiable aspect of meat eating is the sacred nature of the cow, and the avoidance of eating beef. Indeed, the Pew Research Center (2021) identified that 'most Hindus say a person cannot be Hindu if they eat beef', the percentage is 72 per cent (187). The cow is seen to be sacred, though it may not have always been so. The cow is a symbol of the earth and sustenance and its life-giving nature. Its importance may have its background in the role of Krishna as a cowherd and a protector of the cow. Thus, cows have a pre-eminent place in Hinduism. They are not, as is sometimes erroneously suggested, worshipped; rather, they are respected. Gandhi (1955) suggested it as a defining characteristic:

> Cow protection is the dearest possession of the Hindu heart. No one who does not believe in cow protection can possibly be a Hindu. It is a noble belief. Cow worship means to me worship of innocence. For me, the cow is the personification of innocence. Cow protection means the protection of the weak and the helpless. As professor Vaswani truly remarks, cow protection means brotherhood between man and beast. It is a noble sentiment that must grow by patient toil and tapasya. (178)

There are many elements of ahimsa that seemingly find expression in the lives of Hindus today, and the exploration of ahimsa within the classroom will help students understand the demands of Hinduism as a way of life today. There are further expressions such as the desirability of war and the use of weapons of mass destruction that could be similarly explored in relation to ahimsa. In some ways, there are so many applications of ahimsa that can be found in life. It is also perhaps the greatest irony that, with the centrality of ahimsa, on the testing of a nuclear bomb, Robert Oppenheimer is reported to have quoted from the *Bhagavad Gita*:

> I am become death, the destroyer of worlds. (11:32)

Satya

Satya means truth, and is one of the grounds for all behaviour. The Mahabharata teaches:

> To speak the truth is meritorious. There is nothing higher than truth. Everything is upheld by truth, and everything rests upon truth. (Shanti Parva CCCLIX)

Making truth the ground for behaviour means that it is more than telling the truth, though it does include that it has an impact on a person's thoughts, words and deeds. Truthfulness in action means that a person's dharma and actions are in complete harmony, meaning that they are living all of the other virtues associated with Hinduism. In relationships with others, truthfulness is treating other people with dana (compassion). Being true to oneself and others means that others are treated with dignity. The *Rig Veda* teaches:

> Bounteous is he who gives unto the beggar who comes to him in want of food, and the feeble, Success attends him in the shout of battle. He makes a friend of him in future troubles, No friend is he who to his friend and comrade who comes imploring food, will offer nothing. (10.117)

Truth means living a coherent life, where one's actions reflect the beliefs that are held.

Asteya

Asteya means not stealing, and as such can similarly be seen as fundamental to Hindu ethics, taking that which is not one's own is wrong. This is not limited to actions; a person should not even think about taking something that does not belong to them. Asteya can extend to different aspects of a person's life, perhaps in accepting something that has not been earned. It could also be phrased positively as being generous with one's own resources.

Brahmacharya

Brahmacharya means 'pure conduct' or 'conduct leading to Brahma'. Although it can mean any aspect of life, it is mainly associated with self-restraint, particularly with regard to sexual activity. For those who become ascetics or sannyasin, absolute celibacy in thought and action is prescribed. One might ask that for a Hindu who has not become a renunciate how can brahmacharya be practised:

The result was that in the Grihasthashrama, Brahmacharya meant moderation, a wise rational, restrained use of the sex energy for the purpose of procreation. Moderation, and chastity or fidelity to one's married partner, were laid down. It was enjoined upon the married person not to cast any impure look upon any person other than one's lawfully wedded wife or lawfully wedded husband. (Sivananda, 1997, 127)

Thus, for people before marriage, it is absolute celibacy, while it is fidelity after marriage to one's spouse. It would therefore seem that marriage, as part of the grihastha ashrama, is the ideal for those outside of the renunciate life.

Same-sex relationships

Sometimes when using terms such as chastity and fidelity, there may be an assumption of a heteronormative approach to life. It should be sufficient to outline sexual conduct that the same principles apply regardless of sexuality. However, it is however still important in the teaching of religions, worldviews and ethical systems to mention of approaches to same-sex relationships and LGBTQ+ issues. The earlier discussion of kama (see Chapter 4) outlined the importance of pleasure, including sexual pleasure, as an aim of life. In exploring this, there seemed to be no mention of the type of relationship being expressed, just as long as it was not harmful. However, there is ambiguity in the contemporary Hindu world. In India, same-sex sexual relationships were banned by law until 2018, and although it could be argued that India is a secular nation, it is possible to posit the influence of the beliefs of its legislators on laws within society. For some Hindus, the idea of same-sex relationships is seen to go against the dharma of a householder, where a couple is unable to naturally conceive a child. Prijna, writing in 1996 in the UK, suggested:

> Sexual power is one of the precious gifts of God and should be used properly. It is necessary to conserve and make healthy use of sex in a natural way. Sexual activity between persons of the same sex does not create progeny; it is therefore considered to be an improper use of a God-given gift and hence it is discouraged. Indulging in homosexuality is harmful to all parties and is now known to cause the spread of diseases like AIDS. It is also against nature and the natural order of things. (169)

However, for many Hindus, this would be seen as the influence of a colonial lens. The suggestion might be that prior to colonization, Indian and Hindu attitudes towards sexuality were broad and accepting, and that 'a homophobia of virulent proportions came into being in India in the late nineteenth and early twentieth centuries and continues to flourish today' (Vanita & Kidwai, 2000, 200). Wilhelm (2003) suggests that homosexual people are a part of the group referred to in the Vedas as the 'third sex'. Wilhelm outlines:

> Ancient Hindu teachings describe homosexuality as a 'third sex' (tritiya-prakriti), an inborn nature combining both male and female properties. Homosexuals and

transgenders were recognized for their unique nature and incorporated into Vedic society accordingly. They were not punished or persecuted under ancient Hindu law and elaborate descriptions of homosexuality can be found in the Kama Shastra (Hindu scriptures describing the art of lovemaking). (646)

Thus, in Wilhelm's (and others') suggestion, any negative attitudes towards same-sex relationships have been filtered through a colonial lens that came to be accepted as a norm within the Hinduism that came through the other side. Nehru, following independence, is an example of this:

> Nehru attempts to halt the publishing of photographs that depict sculptures showing homosexual relations, claiming that such vices are due to Western influence. In fact, it is his own perception of vice that has been influenced by the West. (Wilhelm, 2003, 280)

It is evident that there are different attitudes within Hinduism regarding same-sex relationships. Again, there is an opportunity to explore the worldviews of those outlining different views. On the one hand, it is argued that those opposed to same-sex relationships are influenced by nineteenth-century British attitudes. On the other hand, are contemporary readings influenced by the society of the early twenty-first century? This links with the study of hermeneutics and the use of texts in exploring issues.

Transgender

With regard to transgender and its acceptance within Hinduism, there appears to be support in aspects of the sacred texts. For example, in the *Laws of Manu*, it speaks of the possible results of conception:

> A male child is produced by a greater quantity of male seed, a female child by the prevalence of the female; if (both are) equal, a hermaphrodite or a boy and a girl. (*Manusmrti* 3:49)

The suggestion here is that a person can be both a boy and a girl. This is not a perfect reference to issues of transgender, as while some trans people will use non-gendered pronouns suggesting a third gender, for many trans people, the focus will be on their identity as men and women. In considering the place and acceptance of the third gender, Amara Das Wilhelm (2003) argues:

> Because the Dharma Shastra considers the third sex to be an inborn nature rather than an acquired vice, no verses punish third-gender citizens for their characteristic behaviour. No laws penalize third-gender men for refusing to marry women or conceive children (quite the contrary) and no laws punish crossdressing, male prostitution, private homosexual behaviour, etc. (131)

The possibility of gender fluidity is at least suggested; and this is confirmed in other stories from sacred texts. One such example is that of Sikhandi in the *Mahabharata*.

Sikhandi was born as a daughter to King Drupada, the father of Draupadi, the woman in the story who would become wife to the five Pandava brothers. Sikhandi decided to leave the palace and fast until she died, but encountered the yaksha Stunakarna who agreed to switch genders with her, so that she could kill Bhishma who she had vowed to kill because of his treatment of her in her previous incarnation as Amba. Devdutt Pattanaik (2002) uses the story of Sikhandi and others such as Avikshita, a prince who believed himself to be a woman, Malli who was also Mallinatha, Sudyumna, and many more to suggest the allowance of transgender within Hinduism.

One group still in existence today is those known as hijra, which are sometimes translated as eunuch but would be better classified as transgender, being known in India as intersex or the third gender. They occupy a tenuous place in society, with many placing them on the margins, while they also perform certain rituals and weddings, and are seen to bestow blessings. This ambiguity is highlighted by Rhude (2018):

> The Supreme Court of India stated, 'it is the right of every human being to choose their gender,' and that recognition of the group, 'is not a social or medical issue, but a human rights issue.' They directed the government to open education and job opportunities to all third gender groups. While progress has been slow, in 2015 the first hijra mayor in India was elected in the city of Raigarh, and in 2017 the city of Kochi hired 23 hijra to work for their public transit system. Still progress is slow, and most third gender people remain in poverty, even as they continue to bless Hindu families with prosperity. (2)

The place of the hijra in Indian society may be indicative of a wider view on transgender issues in the Hindu community. Although it is allowed, through the cultural inheritance of colonialism and more conservative values, this may lead to some attitudes that fall short of acceptance.

Aparigraha

Meaning non-attachment, non-possessiveness or 'not being acquisitive' (Jones & Ryan, 2007, 509), this applies mainly to those sannyasi who have adopted an ascetic lifestyle, but when linked with artha (see Chapter 4) is an important aspect of Hindu living. The suggestion is that material wealth is important only insofar as it allows a person to live their dharma. Therefore, greed and grasping are anathema to Hindu principles. This may have an impact on Hindu attitudes to social justice as explored earlier with regard to the positive side of ahimsa. It is about helping those who have not.

The role of women

Throughout the previous chapters, there have been references to the nature and role of women within Hinduism. Perhaps more than any of the larger six religions, there is a greater emphasis placed upon the Divine feminine within Hinduism. The place of Shakti and other female deities (whether expressions of Shakti or independent deities) could be used to suggest elements of radical feminism, or at least a significantly positive view of women, their nature and role. Hiltebeitl and Erndl (2000) have suggested:

> By virtue of their common feminine nature, women are in some contexts regarded as special manifestations of the Goddess, sharing in her powers. Thus, the Goddess can perhaps be viewed as a mythic model for Hindu women. Western religious traditions, on the other hand, while not totally devoid of feminine imagery, lack any true parallel to the Hindu Goddess. (11)

This correlation can be seen to be both true and untrue in Hindu traditions. For some Hindus, the place of the goddess can lead to a strong feminist tradition, while for others, it may be that the goddess is a special case for women to emulate, but she does not necessarily automatically provide positive responses to women. Erndl shares two experiences in her academic career that illustrate this interesting dichotomy. On one occasion, a professor remarked in response to suggesting a link between the goddess and women, 'Ah, yes. We like them as goddesses, but not as people.' Whereas speaking of the beauty of an individual, a 'woman smiled knowingly at me and said, "And why not? She has the shakti [power, energy] of the Goddess. She is the Goddess herself"' (Hiltebeitl & Erndl, 2000, 12). There are views everywhere in between, and beyond, these two expressions.

There are warning voices within Hinduism about the use of shakti as evidence for, or a way to elevate the status of women. While recognizing that 'When a community's object of worship and veneration is female, it is logical to expect that women in general benefit by sharing that elevated status'. Rajeswari Sunder Rajan (1998) argues that it 'is problematic at the present historical juncture both for its assumption of an undifferentiated "woman-power", as well as for its promotion of a certain radicalised Hinduism' (34–35). One does not automatically follow the other, and when it is seen to, then people should be careful about the conclusions and implications that are drawn. Rita Gross (2000) suggests that whether the goddess is a feminist depends on the attitudes and responses of her devotees, and in some ways, this uses a Feuerbachian mirror to suggest that the nature of a deity is in how they are viewed and used by the believer.

The status of the feminine is raised with representation in the Divine, but care should be taken not to idealize women to the extent that all are judged against this standard and expectation. Indeed, Gross (2000) suggests that the range of goddesses could be used to reinforce patriarchy rather than challenge a patriarchal system:

> by feeding women divine images of either decent goddesses who are submissively married or frighteningly out-of-control unmarried goddesses. The message would be clear: since independence makes females blood-thirsty and dangerous, women will imitate Sita rather than Kali. (105)

It is this, perhaps, that has led to a range of feminist re-imaginings of some of the Puranic stories. In Chapter 2, various retellings of the Ramayana were referred to. The closing events surround the innocence of Sita and her 'entrance into the earth' (Goldman & Goldman, 2021, 843). This was in response to Valmiki's declaration to Rama that Sita was innocent and had always been faithful. As a sign of this virtue, Sita said:

> As I have never even thought of any man other than Raghava, so may Madhavi, the goddess of the earth, open wide for me. (Goldman & Goldman, 2021, 843)

While she entered the earth seated upon a throne, this was still used as a test to prove Sita. In Chitra Banerjee Divakaruni's (2019) retelling, Sita is much more an agent of herself, rather than susceptible to the will of Rama. The closing events, when Rama is asking Sita to prove her virtue again so that he can take her back into the palace after her hermitage, are very much in her hands. She replies to this request:

> O king of Ayodha, you know I'm innocent, and yet, unfairly, you're asking me to step into the fire. You offer me a tempting prize indeed – to live in happiness with you and my children. But I must refuse. Because if I do what you demand, society will use my action forever after to judge other women. Even when they aren't guilty, the burden of proving their innocence will fall on them. And society will say, why not? Even Queen Sita went through it. I can't do that to them . . . And that is way, O king Ram, I must reject your kind offer to allow me to prove my innocence again. Because this is one of those moments when a woman must stand up and say, *No more!* (356–357)

It is hard to not read this passage without seeing an underlying condemnation of a society and history that has perhaps used Sita in this way. This retelling places her in the seat of power, to stand up for herself and all women.

There can be seen in the Divine feminine both positive and negative aspects when viewing the role of women. In recent years, there has been a much more a greater emphasis on using the concept and deity of Shakti to reclaim the power of a woman. Much has been achieved, but there is still much to do.

One area where the importance and dignity of women has been reclaimed is with the controversial practice of *sati*. While at times sati has been a part of Indian society, it was a very small part and was not practised widely. Nor does it have any basis in Hindu teachings. Brian Pennington (2022) has suggested that Hindu texts have debated the practice but at no point did it become widespread. However, so abhorrent was it to most people that it is an element of Indian society that has been magnified out of all proportion and has been focused on inordinately. Sati was the practice of a widow placing herself on the funeral pyre of her husband. Through a colonial lens, the British may suggest that as part of the 'civilization' of India they introduced laws that banned sati and infanticide. But neither of these practices are seen to be Hindu, and as Pennington (2022) suggests:

> [The] discussion of the history and practice of sati, therefore, should make it clear that the most responsible and accurate simple answer to the question 'Did women have to jump into the fire when their husbands dies?' is 'Except in truly exceptional circumstances, no.' It should also indicate that the continuing interest in this question says more about the preconceived ideas of non-Hindus than about Hinduism itself. (226–227)

Why, then, is it included in a discussion of the role of women in Hinduism? It is because the stereotype perpetuates. Even if people recognize that Hindus do not practice it, it is with the proviso that they 'no longer' practice it, suggesting that in the past it was a widespread practice. This is not the case and should be challenged by the teacher (see Chapter 9 for further information).

With an increasing focus on the importance of women in Hinduism, and modern feminist reinterpretations, there does need to be a recognition that not everything has always reflected a positive view of women in relation to men. In exploring the concept of dharma earlier (see Chapter 1), it was noted that there were different ashramas, and that for women, the traditional roles were defined in relation to men. There have also been practices that are now seen to be cultural accretions, suggesting that women at certain times are unclean and impure. With regard to menstruation there are contrasting approaches. On the one hand, a girl's first period is marked by a samskara and is seen to be an important step in life. On the other hand, there are reports in history and in contemporary society of those who are menstruating being denied access to mandirs. Dunnavant and Roberts (2013) suggest that the isolation and impurity of menstruating women is an accepted part of Hinduism.

> According to traditional Hindu belief, it is the menstruating woman herself that is polluted. As such, menstruating women are isolated as untouchables. They can do no work, must not comb their hair, bathe, or touch water or fire sources. In addition to being prohibited from engaging in sexual contact, menstruating Hindu women are also restricted from sharing spaces in all forms with others. (123)

This sharing of spaces extends to their interaction with deities. In defence of the separation of those who are menstruating, Sridhar (2020) suggests different reasons why it is beneficial, summarized as:

- Menstruation as Ashaucha: meaning a period of ritual impurity
- Menstruation as a period of tapas (austerity and self-purification)
- Menstruation as a period of rest
- Menstruation as a sacred celebration.

This does not negate the movement for the removal of such restrictions, and the ruling of the Indian Supreme Court that restrictions on worship are unlawful. Though when this law is enforced, there are some Hindus who protest vehemently against the impurity of such actions.

The role of women within Hinduism is an area that is ripe for exploration in the classroom. There are cultural accretions throughout the ages that have been accepted as religious rules. The question arises as to whether they are cultural accretions or reflective of the attitudes of the time that are being challenged through the cultural lens of today. There is undoubtedly the basis for radical feminism; it will be interesting for students to see whether those beliefs are being lived out and expressed in society today.

Thoughts for the classroom

In this chapter. we have only touched on elements of some ethical issues. There are many issues in the modern world that have not been explored, issues such as abortion and euthanasia. This does not mean that others are not important, but that the ones that are included are indicative of the way that Hindus strive to make ethical decisions. Their approaches to ethics are drawn from the underpinning beliefs that are described in the rest of the book. What is notable, however, is the issue of interpretation. In most of the issues explored, there is scope for personal decision-making, and this must be based on a person's interpretation of how best to show wisdom and compassion. Within vegetarianism and same-sex relationships, we have seen that there are views on both sides, and they raise issues for conceptions of authority and interpretation. It is important in exploring many ethical issues to recognize the differing worldviews and cultural contexts among Hindus around the globe. Some 'traditional' Hindus who like the status quo use interpretive lenses from that cultural perspective, whereas younger Hindus view Hinduism through their own lenses. Maybe within Hinduism, there is room for both approaches, but the importance of recognizing the deeply held views of others is paramount in gaining understanding.

Chapter 8

Authority and Diversity in Hinduism

At the end of the Introduction to this book, we listed a number of Hindu traditions that are to be found within the UK and throughout the world. In some ways, these only scratch the surface as there are many 'non-sectarian' groups. Up until this point, there has been exploration of Hinduism in general with specific mention of Vaishnavism, Shaivism and Shaktism. It is important to note that this threefold presentation is not the whole story. In this chapter, we will explore a different traditions that can be found in the UK and around the world. As this task is undertaken, it is important to note the concept of authority in each and whether that authority can be extended beyond that particular tradition. It is interesting that there are many teachings and beliefs that go across the various expressions of Hinduism, and the approach of this book in articulating some of the central concepts of the sanatana dharma has been to draw from different traditions and none, with the understanding that they can help articulate what certain things may mean for many Hindus. It will not be possible to identify every tradition or individual worldview that expresses Hinduism in this chapter, but hopefully, in identifying some of the larger groups, a better understanding of the diversity within Hinduism can be developed.

Before exploring three traditions to be found within the UK and beyond, it is important to note two things:

1. The history, presence and development of Hinduism within the UK will be explored in much greater detail in Chapter 9.
2. In light of the Series Introduction alongside the Introduction to this book (see above) to outline the various traditions is to miss the rich diversity of individual worldviews that will be a panoply of different approaches to, and across, Hinduism. There will be individuals who utilize selected aspects of more recognized organized worldviews. The presentation below is not to negate this worldviews approach, but the delineations do exist and it will be useful to establish them to enable a context to the worldviews of individuals.

Highlighting point 2 above, it is essential within Hinduism to note that the idea of a 'group' or 'tradition' may be anathema to some, and that the organization of certain groups may be seen as a more modern development, perhaps in response to its engagement with religions such as Christianity that have established organizational structures.

In terms of authority and community within the UK, perhaps the starting point might be the different umbrella organizations which include:

- National Council of Hindu Temples (NCHT): Established in 1978, it is 'an umbrella group of Hindu Temples in the UK. It connects a network of over 200 Temples in the UK' (National Council of Hindu Temples, 2021).
- Hindu Council UK (HCUK): founded in 1994 to combine 'all the Hindu faith denominations, whilst representing various Hindu communities and Hindus from different parts of the world settled in the United Kingdom. It's main purpose was to give the UK Hindus an effective voice on policy matters with the Government of the day' (Hindu Council UK, 2022).
- Hindu Forum of Britain: 'it is the largest umbrella body for British Hindus with more than 300 member organisations from around the country. HFB is the first port of call from the central government and the most reported Hindu organisation in the British media' (Hindu Forum of Britain, n.d.)
- Insight UK: 'INSIGHT UK is a social movement of the British Hindu and British Indian (BHI) communities. We work on the issues affecting BHI communities through awareness, advocacy and campaign' (Insight UK, 2023).

Zavos (2012) has suggested that while these groups bring Hindus together, they also have certain perspectives on Hinduism that they represent, and that they are not unbiased groups:

> These umbrella-style organisations project themselves as public authorities on Hindu-ness and as the voice of a community of people with, as Ruth Kelly says, common aspirations and contributions to make to national life. Such organisations, then, exert a powerful influence on the way in which Hindu-ness is shaped in Britain; in turn, I argue, these organisations are influenced by political contexts in which they have emerged and gained legitimacy. (71)

Zavos further identifies the influence of ISKCON (see below) on the organization of the NCHT and HCUK with the former focused on providing support for mandirs in the community, HCUK was more focused on policy and government relations. HFB was organized in response to persecution of Hindus to unify the voice of Hindus. It is interesting to note that in discussing where authority lies in Hinduism, the majority of Hindus suggested that it is a concept that does not have applicability:

> There is no single authority but there are groups like Hindu Forum of Britain or Hindu Swayamsevak Sangh (UK) that are able to mobilise Hindus well.

Suggesting that the organizations are about community and mobilization rather than establishing orthodoxy or orthopraxy.

> This is not an organised religion like Christianity or Islam with some pope or mullah having authority or power. In fact it is not even a 'religion' in the normal sense of the

word. There are leaders of sampradaya who may be the ones to approach for some issues.

With this as a background, this chapter will explore two different sampradayas or traditions, but this not to suggest that this is the limit of expressions found within the UK. There are many more to be found. The two chosen are the International Society of Krishna Consciousness (ISKCON) and Swaminarayan, which develop existing understandings raised by broader and more individual expressions of Hinduism. Each, in their own way, has shown a development of Hinduism for the modern world. They also claim large membership in the UK and, as such are fairly vocal in the Hindu groups around the country.

ISKCON

The International Society for Krishna Consciousness is at the same time a new religious movement and an old religious tradition. With its roots in the Gaudiya Vaishnava tradition that began in India in the sixteenth century, ISKCON was established by Bhaktivedanta Swami Prabhupada as the Hare Krishna Movement (by which name it is sometimes known today). It is so named because of its focus on the Hare Krishna mantra and its recitation in worship:

Hare Krishna Hare Krishna
Krishna Krishna Hare Hare
Hare Rama Hare Rama
Rama Rama Hare Hare

The focus, as is the focus of ISKCON, is on Krishna. The mantra is seen to be in praise of Krishna as the Supreme manifestation of the Divine. The word 'Hari' or 'Hare' has many meanings when attached to being a name of Vishnu; it can mean:

- One who takes away (sins).
- One who removes all obstacles from the path to liberation.
- Lord of nature.

It can also be the 'vocative form of "Hara," which refers to Mother Hara, or Sri Radha' (Rosen, 2006, 244) who is Krishna's consort. The chanting of the mantra is seen to connect the devotee in bhakti worship, or loving devotion with Lord Krishna. Prabhupada (2005) outlined that chanting Hare Krishna:

is the sublime method for reviving our transcendental consciousness, or Krishna consciousness. As living spiritual souls, we are all originally Krishna conscious entities, but due to our association with matter from time immemorial, our consciousness is now polluted by the material atmosphere, called maya, or illusion.

Since the 1960s, the chanting of Hare Krishna has perhaps been ISKCON's most identifiable practice, being performed as kirtan in devotional services, but also in public places. It was not uncommon to see saffron-robed devotees in cities walking along and chanting the Hare Krishna mantra. Zeller (n.d.) outlines this practice as devotional and also as a way of proselytizing:

> During the late 1960s and 1970s, sankirtan bestowed a lasting image on ISKCON, as devotees became known for performing sankirtan in airports and other conspicuous public places, sometimes without regard for the inconvenience they caused. Since that time, ISKCON has shied away from the most confrontational forms of sankirtan, though devotees still engage in the practice throughout the world.

ISKCON, as outlined earlier, traces its beginning to Prabhupada, who brought his devotion to Krishna to the West, in particular to New York in 1965 at the age of seventy. As a swami in India, he had been responsible for spreading of Gaudiya Vaishnavism. He 'traced his lineage to the ecstatic mystic Sri Chaitanya (traditionally 1486–1534), considered by the tradition to be the embodiment of the Godhead', an embodiment of Krishna. For this tradition, 'Krishna is the supreme deity, not merely an incarnation of Vishnu' (Schweig, 2012, 23). His full name and titles, as expressed by followers, give an understanding of his role: A. C. Bhaktivedanta Swami Prabhupada.

- A.C. stands for Abhay (fearless) Charan (feet), the name given to him by his parents 'which indicates that the Lord's feet grant fearlessness'.
- In 1933 when he was initiated his guru 'added aravinda (lotus) to his name, since the Lord's feet are compared to the lotus'.
- '"Bhaktivedanta" (bhakti, or devotion, and Vedanta, or culmination of Vedic knowledge) is an honorary title awarded to him in 1939 by elders in the tradition, in tribute to his piety and scholarship.'
- '"Prabhupada" (the feet of the master), the respectful address used by his followers from mid-1968 onward and reserved for only the most accomplished gurus in the line' (Schweig, 2012, 22).

He was able to develop a following which has flourished into a community with over 800 centres and millions of followers around the world. In its early days, its profile was raised by interactions with the Beatles, and in particular George Harrison. In 1973, Harrison bought what is today known as the Bhaktivedanta Manor in Watford for ISKCON, as the movement was outgrowing its centre in London.

As inheritors of Gaudiya Vaishnava traditions, many of the rites are similar to rituals practised in wider Hinduism. There are seen to be two stages to initiation, including:

1. The person desiring initiation must answer a series of questions before being approved by the guru. This first stage (harinamadiksa) is followed by a yajna, fire sacrifice where the person adopts the vows to eschew gambling, the eating of meat, sexual misconduct and intoxicants as well as the willingness to chant the Hare

Krishna mantra (bestowing of the holy name of Krishna), functions as initial entrance into the movement. The initiate must first answer a series of creedal questions, and after receiving approval from the guru, may engage in the ceremony of initiation. A new name is given which is followed by 'Dasa' (for men) or 'Dasi' (for women) which means 'servant of'.

2. During the second part of the initiation rite 'new initiates become equivalent to Brahmins, the highest caste of Hinduism, receiving knowledge of the sacred gayatri mantra and a sacred thread marking them as twice-born. At this point, devotees gain the ritual status of priests, and can therefore engage in all forms of temple worship' (Zeller, n.d.).

Both aspects of the initiation can be seen to be open to all, and break down the traditional Brahmanical system. Thus, the authority of the rituals and rites becomes more egalitarian. Within these rites, along with the kirtan of the Hare Krishna mantra, there are arti ceremonies (see Chapter 6) in front of Krishna and Radha, as well as japa, which is the recitation of the names of Krishna. All of these rites are indicative of a bhakti tradition that seeks union with Krishna as the Supreme Godhead.

Prior to Prabhupada's death, he established the Governing Body Commission (GBC) in 1970. He outlined his reasons in a letter:

> I am getting old, 75 years old, therefore at any time I may be out of the scene, therefore I think it is necessary to give instruction to my disciples how they shall manage the whole institution. They are already managing individual centres represented by one president, one secretary and one treasurer, and in my opinion they are doing nice. But we want still more improvement in the standard of Temple management, propaganda for Krishna consciousness, distribution of books and literatures, opening of new centres and educating devotees to the right standard. (Ekstrand & Bryant, 2004, 205)

This led to an increasingly centralized structure that has since developed into a group of forty-eight who meet annually and operate on a system of consensus.

Within the UK there are approximately 15,000 members, but of these only about eighty are temple members. There is a difference

> between congregational members, who live in their own homes and have jobs outside the movement, and temple members – or clergy – who live in ISKCON temples and work full time for the movement. Congregational members may or may not be initiated into ISKCON. (Inform, 2019)

Within the UK, outside of its devotional activities, ISKCON has been at the forefront of presenting Hinduism to the community through educational efforts such as the publication of *The Heart of Hinduism* (Das, 2002), and the sponsoring of schools through the Avanti Trust which, as of 2023, included:

- Avanti Court Primary, Redbridge
- Avanti Fields, Leicester
- Avanti Gardens, Bristol
- Avanti House Primary, Stanmore
- Avanti House Secondary, Stanmore
- Avanti Meadows, Bishops Stortford
- Avanti Grange, Bishops Stortford
- Avanti Park, Frome
- Krishna Avanti, Croydon
- Krishna Avanti, Harrow
- Krishna Avanti, Leicester

In tandem with the umbrella groups, ISKCON has been at the forefront of establishing a unified understanding of Hinduism. In many ways, ISKCON has been successful in integrating Hinduism into the West, though there have been many difficulties and controversies along the way. The centralized approach to activities and beliefs is perhaps symptomatic of the globalization of a belief system that, in the past, had been less regulated.

Swaminarayan

The Swaminarayan Sampradaya is a Vaishnava tradition based on devotion to its founder Swaminarayan (1781–1830), who is seen by some as an avatar of Vishnu, while others see him as the 'single manifestation of Purushottam, the supreme person, and, as such, is superior in power and efficacy to all other manifestations of god, including Rama and Krishna' (Williams, 2019, 85). Indeed, Swaminarayan identified himself as Bhagwan, for example in the *Vachanamrut*:

> Therefore, Bhagvan is eternally sakar. In addition, He is the creator, sustainer, and destroyer of countless brahmands; He is forever present in His Akshardham; He is the lord of all; and He is pratyaksha here before your eyes (Gadhada III. 35:12. (Swaminarayan, 2010, 772)

Born Ghanshyam Pande, Swaminarayan began his travels at the age of eleven following the death of his parents. Taking the name Nilkanth Varni, he travelled across India and Nepal asking the questions:

- What is Jiva?
- What is Ishvara?
- What is Maya?

- What is Brahman?
- What is Parabrahman?

He was seeking an ashram, a place to learn. There are many stories associated with his childhood, his travels and studies. Some of these are associated with his command of the Vedas, and of astanga yoga and its eight limbs. In 1800 he was initiated as a sannyasin and given the names Sahajanand Swami and Narayan Muni by Swami Ramanand, who subsequently appointed him as his successor as leader of the Uddhav Sampradaya at the age of twenty-one. The Uddhav Sampradaya would develop into Swaminarayan Sampradaya. Shortly after the death of Swami Ramanand, on 31 December 1801 at Faneni, Gujarat, Swami Sahajanand introduced the Swaminarayan mantra:

> Today, I introduce you to a new mahamantra. It is a mantra that contains the essence of all other mantras. By chanting this mantra, one can overcome any sort of physical, mental, or environmental calamity. It will ward away evil spirits, remove superstitious beliefs, and give all who chant it the courage to face the difficulties in their lives. It possesses the power to liberate jivas from the cycle of birth and death. It is the only mantra which can fulfil all of your mind's wishes and desires. From this moment onwards, you will only recite the Swaminarayan mahamantra during your mala, jap, puja, and other daily activities. (Trivedi, 2015, 194–195)

The impact of reciting the mantra 'Swaminarayan' is narrated in the response of Shitaldas, who comes to seek darshan of Swami Ramanand, only to be disappointed on learning that he had died and he would only be seeing Swami Sahajanand. On reciting the mantra, it is said that he entered a deep meditative trance and

> He had a vision – Darshan – of Shriji Maharaj in Akshardham. He saw that Ramanand Swami was attending on Maharaj. He said to Ramanand Swami, 'I was regarding you as God'. 'NO', replied Ramanand Swami, 'God is sitting before me'. Shitaldas returned from the trance and narrated this story to all those present in the conference. (Shree Swaminarayan Temple – Bhuj, n.d.)

The audience repeated the mantra on hearing this story, and it is reported that they entered this trance. Thus, the Swaminarayan mantra is a central part of devotion within the sampradaya.

There were many developments in Swaminarayan Hinduism that sought to reform some of the practices that had become part of society. He recognized that a linear approach to the four ashramas would not be suitable for people and that a person should 'select in accordance with his natural inclinations the path of the householder, who conducts the affairs of family life and business, or the path of the ascetic who renounces the world' (Williams, 2019, 164). What was most important for Swaminarayan was the devotion and discipline to the dharma. It has been suggested that Swaminarayan's approach means that 'The ascetic fights against temptation and vice from behind the barricades erected as part of renunciation; the householder must fight the same battle from an exposed position' (Williams, 2019, 164). Sadhus or ascetics were to adopt vows that enabled them to renounce the world:

1. Nishkam (Non-lust) meaning celibacy.
2. Nirlobh (Non-greed).
3. Nisneh (Non-attachment).
4. Niswad (Non-taste) Not to indulge in food for the sake of taste.
5. Nirman (Non-ego).

Swaminarayan also encouraged all of his followers to eschew meat, alcohol, drugs, adultery, suicide, animal sacrifices, criminal activities and various tantric rites. Swaminarayan is a bhakti tradition that develops a personal devotional relationship between Swaminarayan and his devotees. The focus of worship in the mandirs is the murtis of Swaminarayan, Radha Krishna, Lakshmi Narayan and Nar Narayan. Darshan, arti and circumambulation of the murti lie at the heart of devotion, the circumambulation being symbolic of the desire to keep Swaminarayan at the centre of their lives.

There are differences in the two main expressions of Swaminarayan Hinduism. For example, in Bochasanwasi Akshar Purushottam Swaminarayan Sanstha (BAPS), the murtis installed in the mandirs will also include those of the Gunatit Guru (perfect devotee) lineage, where Swaminarayan is believed to have remained on earth. His successors in BAPS are:

- Aksharbrahman Gunatitanand Swami (1784–1867)
- Bhagatji Maharaj (1829–1897)
- Shastriji Maharaj (1865–1951)
- Yogiji Maharaj (1892–1971)
- Pramukh Swami Maharaj (1921–2016)
- Mahant Swami Maharaj (1933–)

This lineage is perhaps the main difference between the two main forms of Swaminarayan. Prior to his death, Swaminarayan established two branches or gadi known as the Nar Narayan Dev Gadi and Laxmi Narayan Dev Gadi. Each was based at a particular mandir and had responsibility for specific geographic areas. The Nar Narayan Dev Gadi was based in Ahmedabad, while the Laxmi Narayan Dev Gadi was based in Vadtal. Each was to be led by one of Swaminarayan's nephews. Ayodhyaprasadji was to become acharya at Ahmedabad, while Raghuvirji would become acharya at the Vadtal diocese. This established two seats that would be overseen by acharyas from the family of Swaminarayan. This was established in a document written by Swaminarayan in 1827, the Desh Vibhag Lekh. In this, and also in the Shikshapatri, he outlines their succession and roles:

> I have enthroned both of them with a view to protect and preserve our religion. They shall initiate those disciples who are desirous of salvation. (Mukti.) They shall maintain discipline among the disciples and see that they (disciples) follow the precepts accordingly and perform their religious duties within their precincts. They shall honour the saints and shall study the Vedas and Shastras with reverence. They shall perform with proper rites and ceremonies, the worship of Shri Laxmi–Narayan and other icons of Lord Shri Krishna, installed by Me in big Temples . . . The wives of these Acharyas with the concurrence of their husbands shall initiate and give Mantra of lord Shri Krishna to females only but never to any male. (128–131, 133)

Their roles further include initiating devotees and sadhus, installing deities, approving scriptures and acting as the guru and leader of the community.

Within BAPS, while accepting the appointment of Swaminarayan's nephews as administrative leaders, it was with Shastriji Maharaj that the split with the two administrative centres happened. Shastriji, having received his teaching from Bhagatji, who in turn received it from Aksharbrahman, highlighted the continuity of spiritual leadership. The nephews were to be administrators while the Gunatit Guru would provide spiritual leadership.

> Followers of Ahmedabad and Vadtal dioceses teach that the name Swaminarayan represents one entity, Purushottam. BAPS members indicate that the name represents two entities; 'Swami' stands for akshar represented by Gunatitanand and his successors, and 'Narayan' stands for Purushottam or Sahajanand. Although they write the name as one, BAPS members affirm their allegiance to both when they chant the mantra 'Swaminarayan'. (Williams, 2019, 93)

This split in Swaminarayan Hinduism is evident in the UK today. The most well-known Hindu mandir (see Chapter 9) is in Neasden and is a BAPS mandir. In Manchester, there is a BAPS mandir in Ashton-under-Lyne and an Ahmedabad mandir in Oldham less than four miles away. In the UK, the main BAPS centres are:

- Neasden, London
- Leicester
- Birmingham
- Chigwell
- Coventry
- Havant
- Leeds
- Loughborough
- Luton
- Ashton-under-Lyne, Manchester

- Nottingham
- Preston
- Southend-on-Sea
- Wellingborough

Whereas, for those attached to the Ahmedabad Swaminarayan Centre, the locations are:

- Bolton
- Brighton
- Cardiff
- London
- Crawley
- Harrow
- Leicester
- Oldham
- Stanmore

There is no sharing of devotion or worship; the two communities are separate. While there are many beliefs and practices that they hold in common, there are distinct differences that mean that they co-exist but do not come together.

Thoughts for the classroom

It is evident from the discussion above that issues of authority within Hinduism are complex and perhaps becoming more so as traditions clash with modernity. Whereas in the past differences were seemingly welcomed, there are strict demarcations and attempts to define Hinduism. This chapter has only explored two such expressions, but it is noteworthy that both are flourishing within the UK. However, the question of whether the diversity of Hinduism is welcomed within the UK remains. There are groups who are trying to represent Hinduism with one voice, and individual traditions that have strict boundaries. There are many other groups that have not been explored in this chapter and that have a presence in the UK:

- The Chinmaya Mission: an organization founded by Swami Chinmayananda Saraswati following Vedanta philosophy.
- Ramakrishna Mission: based on the teachings of Ramakrishna's chief disciple, developed by Swami Vivekananda.
- Sai Organisation: based on the teachings of Sathya Sai Baba.

On the other hand, there are many 'non-sectarian' mandirs that embrace diversity in terms of devotion and interpretation. Consider the mandir that has murtis of Shiva, Rama,

Hanuman, Krishna, Ganesh, and Guru Nanak. There still seems to be an appetite among some Hindus for a broad tent approach to religious belief and practice.

The issue of whether there should even be the concept of authority within Hinduism is inextricably linked with the issue of diversity. What is normative Hinduism? Elements of diversity in the community, and particularly in the UK, will be explored in the next chapter. It does, however, raise questions for the way that we teach Hinduism. Is the concretization of Hinduism a positive thing, where there is orthodoxy and orthopraxy that seek to exclude some practices? But, if there are no boundaries, how is it possible to explain what Hinduism is? Returning to the issue of worldviews, is this something that needs to be applied as a lens to recognize the lived reality of Hinduism in the UK today?

Chapter 9

Hinduism and Contemporary Britain

Throughout the previous chapters, there have been many examples expressed of how Hinduism is lived in Britain today. This is an important aspect in striving to teach Hinduism in the classroom. Chapter 8 explored some of the traditions that can be found within the United Kingdom. It is interesting that as each of these has developed, it is against the background of Western modernism and post-modernism.

Although Hindus have been a presence in the UK since the nineteenth century, a fact that is inextricably linked with the Empire, the growing Hindu population of the UK is only 'relatively recent' and dates from after the Second World War:

> Hindus from India began arriving in 1947 at the time of Indian independence and partition, while others were actively recruited by the British government to fill skills shortages. A second group consists of East African Asians, expelled from Idi Amin's Uganda in the 1960s and 1970s. More recent immigrants have come as refugees from Sri Lanka's bitter civil war. The Hindu population in the UK is predominantly urban, with by far the largest numbers living in London. (Fredman, 2022, 119)

In the early part of the twentieth century, Burghart (1987) notes that 'the only active Hindu religious presence was the Ramakrishna Mission led by the Bengali monk Swami Avyaktananda, who arrived in Britain in 1934' (6). There was not a Hindu community to speak of. In the decline of Empire following the Second World War and into the 1960s and 70s, opportunities arose for people to migrate to the UK from the former colonies. In moving to the UK, it is possible to see that for some early migrants, it was discouraged. On travelling to England to study, it is recorded of Gandhi:

> Meanwhile, the Modh Banias of Bombay heard about the projected trip. They convened a meeting of the clan and summoned Mohandas to attend. No Modh Bania had ever been to England, the elders argued their religion forbade voyages abroad because Hinduism could not be practised there. Gandhi told them he would go nevertheless. At this, the headman ostracized Mohandas. 'This boy shall be treated as an outcast from today', the elder declared. (Fischer, 1997, 36)

Gandhi, himself, did not see it as problematic:

> I do not think it is at all against our religion so than! to go to England. I intend going there for further studies. And I have already solemnly promised to my mother to abstain from three things you fear most. I am sure the vow will keep me safe. (1982, 52)

This seems to echo the experience of Madho Singh II, the Maharaja of Jaipur. Having been invited to Edward II's coronation in London in 1902, he was concerned with his ability to be observant and ritually pure. Burghart (1987) reports:

> To him Great Britain was a remote, barbarous country, situated in the northwestern sector of the inauspicious 'Black Sea'. Madho Singh could not sustain his sacred person in such an alien environment. And such as journey would put his subjects at risk, for in the course of his coronation the people of Jaipur had been ritually constituted within the body of the king. (1)

He found a way around his concerns so that he could attend; his solution involved a ritually pure ship with water from the Ganges and soil from India, so he could travel to London while remaining in India. This has to be contrasted with Hindu teachers who in the late nineteenth and early twentieth centuries had travelled to Britain and other countries considering

> such ritual prohibitions to be part of a superstitious Hindu legacy that had no place in the modern world. Reformers such as Swami Vivekananda, Ram Mohan Roy and Sri Aurobindo all travelled to the West, including the UK, to bring Hindu spiritual values to a materialist West. (Tomalin & Singh, 2018, 11)

For others, it was different; one Hindu suggested that his family's migration was driven by curiosity, and after that, it just happened:

> In 1964 it was a little bit of adventure and a little bit of inquisitiveness. Some of my friends made an application to the High Commission and got the employment voucher. In 1963 the British passed legislation to stop, then only those with work permits could go, there was a rush, I made an application and was granted that. Then it was 3 months within which we had to decide . . . it was a week left whether to go or not to go. I thought I'll go and see. I left my wife and daughter and when I was disappointed I wanted to return. My wife said, be there for 6 months, then we will decide. She joined me . . . and said we will see another year or so, it went on like that. (Oxford Centre for Hindu Studies, 2004a, 4)

One respondent to the *British Hinduism Oral History Project* (Oxford Centre for Hindu Studies, 2004b) outlined that over time their family was able to settle, and the question of a return to India was negated because of the assimilation that they were able to achieve in wider society:

> And I could say with proud, that we are a part of a British citizen. And I think, we have supported our economic as well, by going in various business factories, hardworking nature, our children are doing very well in the colleges, schools as well, getting good results. And I must say that, we are hardworking people and now we are well settled here. Now, when I am asking my children that I want to move there or this, they says, 'no, we cannot go anywhere from here.' They like here. So that is how my life and our life is here.

This leads us to the place of Hindus today in the UK. In the 2021 Census, there were one million people who identified as Hindu in the Census of England and Wales, up from 816,633 in 2011, which in itself was a rise from 558,342 in 2001. Hinduism is growing as a religion, and there are rising numbers of second- and third-generation Hindus in the UK. The need to recognize a Hinduism that may have been adapted for living in the UK is important. In 2011, the Office for National Statistics (ONS) reported the birth country for those identifying as religious. For Hindus, there were 272,000 born in the UK, with 545,000 born outside of the UK. There can be seen to be generational comfort for Hindus in Britain. Many Hindus report the positive aspects of being able to live as a Hindu in Britain today:

> It's a free country to practice the faith peacefully where there is no harm to others.

> Britain is one of the ideal places to live for Hindus due to rule of law, freedom to practice religion, meritocracy and opportunities for Education.

> We can follow our principles without any having interference.

> Freedom of expression, freedom to practice the religion, easy availability of vegetarian food. Established mandirs and communities.

Assimilation or retrenchment

Within the sociology of religion, the linked concepts of retrenchment and assimilation are present. On the one hand, there is a 'strain toward greater assimilation and respectability', and on the other, a strain 'towards greater separateness, peculiarity, and militance'. Armand Mauss (1994, 5) further suggests that:

> Along the continuum between total assimilation and total repression or destruction is a narrow segment on either side of the centre; and it is within this narrower range of socially tolerable variation that movements must maintain themselves, pendulumlike, to survive.

In many ways, this might be the experience of Hindus within Britain since the mid-to-late twentieth century. This can also be related to the experience of many immigrant communities over the past couple of centuries. In terms of the Hindus in Britain, there might be seen to be a general desire to fit into society. There was a tenuousness to the position of Hindus in British society; this tenuousness was also reflected in the gurdwaras which were generally to be found in converted homes.

As time went on, and there began to be an increased confidence in the Hindu community, there was greater push for the 'establishment' to accommodate the needs of Hindus, rather than Hindus accommodating to the establishment. This is, perhaps, an indication of the more secure feeling of being a part of British society. It could also be that the next phase of Hindu immigrants were coming into a country where the Hindu presence was more settled, and so did not feel the need to hide any aspects of their identity. Rather than this generation being more religious, it is fairer to say that the groundwork had been laid so that there was an environment that was more conducive to expressing faith as a minority. The increasing numbers of purpose-built mandirs are also evidence of a more secure British society for Hindus. Though it should be noted that in 1949 the first building for a Hindu community was established as a result of 'a bequest from an Englishman'. This bequest 'enabled the mission to buy a property and establish a monastic community in Britain. This . . . community . . . located in Muswell Hill in north London, provided the first public place of worship for Hindus in Britain' (Burghart, 1987, 6–7).

In 2018, Emma Tomalin and Jasjit Singh published a report for Historic England entitled *A Survey of Hindu Buildings in England*. This report found that there were 187 Hindu mandirs in England of various types. In terms of affiliation, Tomalin and Singh (2018) reported seven types:

1. Sanatana: universal, open for all Hindus
2. Regional
3. Sampradaya-led ('sectarian')
4. Guru/Swami-led
5. Caste-focused
6. Ashrams
7. Independent (4–5)

While in terms of the type of building, they reported six different types:

1. House Temples
2. Borrowed/hired periodically for meetings
3. Purchased residential reuse and adaptation
4. Purchased other reuse and adaptation
5. Purpose built
6. Reuse/adaptation and purpose built (5)

The importance of a mandir as more than a place of worship was highlighted when discussing the functions that these buildings were put to. It is important to note that a building could perform one or more of these functions:

1. A home for the deities (murtis).
2. A space for Hindu religious practice and the celebration of Hindu festivals.
3. A place where the Hindu priest(s) live in order to be able to carry out the demanding duty of caring for the murtis.
4. A location where cultural activities for Hindus are carried out, including dancing, music and languages.

5. They sometimes incorporate community centres, schools, welfare and advice centres, and centres for caste-based or regional organizations.
6. Sports centres.
7. Halls and kitchens to hire for weddings and other large events (5)

It is to be expected that the number of mandirs will have increased since the publication of this report. Notable is that the development of mandirs over the years has reflected the increasing presence of Hindus and Hinduism within the UK. Initially beginning with gatherings and worship in people's homes, there followed the development of converted buildings as mandirs, and more recently the building of purpose-built mandirs. One such example is the BAPS Swaminarayan Mandir in Ashton-u-Lyne, close to Manchester. In this community, worship began in people's homes in 1971, and then in 1980 a mandir was opened in a converted office building in Ashton. In 2021, the new purpose-built mandir (see Figure 9.1) was opened to serve the needs of the growing BAPS Swaminarayan community in the North West of England.

This same type of experience is replicated in the history of the Gita Bhavan Mandir (see Figure 9.2) in Withington, Manchester. In describing the history of the community and the mandir, its website describes:

> The Hindu cultural society started with five families in 1987, meeting once a month in a church hall. The present site was bought in 1987, the vendor sold it . . . Manchester city council helped us to restore the building to its present standard with a substantial grant. (Gita Bhavan Hindu Temple, 2021)

Possibly the most well-known Hindu mandir in the UK is the BAPS Swaminarayan mandir in Neasden, East London (see Figure 9.3).

This is often used for school visits, and there are worksheets as well as a timetable that goes alongside each visit (see Table 9.1).

It is important to note that in exploring Hindu mandirs in the UK, there are various different types and approaches to their use. As indicated earlier, Tomalin and Singh (2018) noted that there are regional differences (by regional, this is often referring to regions of India), as well as 'sectarian' mandirs. Eleanor Nesbitt (2006) emphasizes this point:

> Hindus' sacred space is likely to need contextualising and decoding, not only in terms of 'Hinduness' but also of the ethnicity (Gujarati, Punjabi, etc.) of those involved and their *sampradaya* ('a tradition focused on a deity, often regional in character, into which a disciple is initiated by a guru. Furthermore, each guru is seen to be within a line of gurus . . . originating with the founding father'). Examples of well-established sampradayas in the United Kingdom include the International Society for Krishna Consciousness (ISKCON) and 'the Swaminarayan religion'. In order to understand Hindu organisations and religious buildings in the United Kingdom, and the Hindu tradition as a whole, one must pay attention to the significant role of *sampradayas*. (196)

Figure 9.1 BAPS Swaminarayan Mandir in Ashton-u-Lyne (Courtesy of James Holt).

Figure 9.2 Gita Bhavan Hindu Mandir, Withington (Courtesy of James Holt).

Figure 9.3 BAPS Swaminarayan Mandir, Neasden (Courtesy of Lee-Anne Brakeswood).

In discussing the importance of mandirs in Britain today, some Hindus responded in a variety of ways:

> Temple helps bring peace to the mind and redirects you to life's purpose. The word man means mind and dir means peace.
>
> For ceremonies, to give thanks. A place to focus on the Divine.
>
> Focal point for community to gather and practice dharmic rituals as well as festivals.
>
> It gives me great sense of peace, community spirit and happiness.

In exploring the different designs and functions of these Hindu buildings, students will be able to see the eclectic nature of Hinduism. This is an important aspect of teaching Hinduism beyond the places of a Hindu majority around the world. Students need to be aware of the reality of Hinduism in Britain today, and while temples around the world

Table 9.1 Schedule of School Visit (Shri Swaminarayan Mandir London, 2023)

What	Where	How Long (approx.)
Welcome and Introductory Address	Reception	10 mins
Short presentation on Hinduism	Assembly Hall	30 mins
'History of the Mandir' video	Assembly Hall	15 mins
'Understanding Hinduism' exhibition (if specified)	Exhibition	30 mins
Darshan (viewing of the sacred images)	Upper Sanctum	15 mins
Arti Ceremony at 11.45 a.m. (if applicable) Note seating arrangements especially	Upper Sanctum	20 mins
Q&A	Assembly Hall or Foyer	15 mins
Souvenir Shop	Foyer	15 mins
TOTAL 2.5 hours		

are stunning, and the portrayal of oversized murtis is awe-inspiring, this is not the lived experience of many Hindus in Britain today. For some Hindus, the community aspect of Hinduism is central, while for others, it is a very individual practice. Indeed, Nesbitt (2006) notes that with an increasing comfort in the UK, many of the younger generation are perhaps ambivalent about mandir worship for political reasons:

> Younger Hindus express concern at the domination of temples by members of an older generation (often in their seventies), who are reluctant to involve younger people as office-bearers, and the unedifying 'politics' and factional in-fighting that are particularly apparent when a temple committee is being elected. (198)

This diversity should be recognized alongside the 'essential' aspects of Hindu belief and practice. Not all Hindus go to retreats, and many Hindu mandirs are used to provide services for the local community. Indeed, there appears to be a growing reliance on a virtual community that meets the needs of Hindus:

> Increasingly, too, Hindus' sacred space is virtual space. A Google search on 30 April 2005 for 'online puja' scored about 173,000 hits of relevant websites. These are of two types. The first offer online puja, whereby the specified deity appears on the screen together with instructions (e.g. the devotee at the keyboard clicks to ring an audible virtual bell as the singing of the appropriate verses comes through the speakers). The second type of websites offer the devotee facilities for ordering worship on his/her behalf in designated temples in India. This development has been characterised as creating 'a global Hindu identity', 'cyberdarshan' and 'recreat[ing] sacred geography in

cyberspace'. While Hinduism's roots are ancient, the Internet is providing a new platform to unite a diaspora, relay a sacred image and enable adherents to go on a pilgrimage from the comfort of their home computer. (Nesbitt, 2006, 204)

The allowance of private and public devotion within Hinduism means that for many Hindus, while mandirs may meet a need, for others they are not the necessity they were in previous years in the development of Hinduism in the UK.

Challenges in Britain for Hindus

While Hindus speak very positively about life in Britain and the modern world, there is a feeling among some that aspects of society are purposefully stacked against Hindus. In some instances there is a purposeful victimization of them. Consider these comments from Hindus in Britain:

> While most of the British society has excellent opinion about Hindus and are warm and welcoming, there is section of mainstream media which for reasons not clear, are always keen to portray Hindus and India in a negative light.
>
> Prejudice against Hindus in spite of being a large peace loving community that contributes enormously to the country. Hinduphobia especially in media.
>
> Risk of being targeted by other communities who openly threaten Hindus. There have been incidents reported correctly and incorrectly.
>
> Subjected to neglect by the Establishment and the media, and to subtle sometimes explicit vilification . . . Absence of Chaplains for Hindus, Chaplaincy Rooms, Hindu Vegetarian Meals in the NHS, and other institutions, need to rectify the Religious Education section of the Education-Curriculum to make it fact-based and sufficient.

This view would seem to be supported by two reports written to explore the representation of Hinduism, and the prejudice that Hindu's face. In Charlotte Littlewood's (2023) report, *Anti-Hindu Hate in Schools*, the key findings were:

- 51 per cent of parents of Hindu pupils surveyed report that their child has experienced anti-Hindu hate in schools, whilst fewer than 1 per cent of schools with Indian pupils queried by FOI reported any anti-Hindu-related incidents in the last five years.
- Teaching on Hinduism has been reported by some participants of this study as fostering religious discrimination towards Hindu pupils.
- 19 per cent of Hindu parents surveyed believe schools are able to identify anti-Hindu hate.
- 15 per cent of Hindu parents surveyed believe schools adequately address anti-Hindu-related incidents (1).

Echoing Insight UK's (2021) report findings referred to in the Introduction that:

- 98 per cent of survey respondents say the study of Hinduism in RE is of low quality and deficient.
- 75 per cent of respondents feel that Hinduism is not taught in a positive light.
- 86 per cent of the respondents is either dissatisfied or very dissatisfied with the teaching of Hinduism in schools within the UK.
- 76 per cent of primary school parents are unhappy about RE teachers' knowledge of Hinduism.
- 81 per cent of Key Stage 3 and 87 per cent of Key Stage 4 parents are discontented about RE teachers' knowledge of Hinduism.
- There is growing evidence of inaccurate resources used by classroom teachers for teaching Hinduism (5).

Hinduism in the school curriculum

A lot of the inaccuracies suggested surround the representation of Hinduism in schools as polytheistic, 'idolatrous', caste-based, practising sati and other misconceptions based on beliefs and practices. Littlewood (2023) gives one example of a Hindu parent describing their child's experience in school:

> You don't know about your own religion, you have so many gods. Your religion is idol worship (even though they were corrected to say deity worship, and they continued to insist that it's the same). When teachers say these things, they undermine the students and make a mockery of them. (14)

Both reports suggest that a national entitlement for RE is one way that this can begin to be addressed. While this might have an impact, the important, but not simple, solution is the increase of subject knowledge training and development with regard to Hinduism, alongside the greater links being made by schools with local Hindus and Hindu communities. Training for teachers is limited and patchy, but there is a growing awareness of the need to gain more authentic experiences of life as a Hindu in Britain. This is one of the purposes of this book, so that teachers can begin to engage with Hinduism through the lens of a worldviews approach. One of the points that cannot be emphasized enough is that there is not just one Hinduism, it is messy. There are many different ways to be Hindu. This has been acknowledged throughout this book, and it is important for Hindus to similarly recognize this point. There are, for example, many different interpretations of the Divine, there are different reasons to celebrate Diwali. The moment that one expression or belief is described as normative without recognition that there are other interpretations means that Hindu diversity is ignored, and one approach is reified. In the Series Editor's Foreword we noted that some Hindus would like this concretization, but that has never been what Hinduism is.

There is a way for Hinduism to be taught that walks a fine line and recognizes the inherited challenges that are faced in its representation in the twenty-first century. Recognizing that issues such as caste and sati are in the public zeitgeist when speaking of Hinduism, it may be necessary in the short term to talk about these issues. The teacher needs to be prepared to answer misconceptions that students have based on erroneous media portrayals or an received teachings from family members and wider society. Consider the child who has watched *Indiana Jones and the Temple of Doom*; they will come away with a particular view of aspects of Hindu worship and deities. By speaking about the 'received wisdom', the teacher is able to challenge the representations encountered and understandings that are in society.

The teacher should be prepared for an accurate and authentic discussion of misconceptions as they arise. One of the issues that may arise for students if this is not done is that they may feel that some issues are taboo, and also that when issues are quickly passed over then there may be something to hide. This is a similar approach when teaching about issues of Islamophobia and links with violent extremism. We may not want to teach about them because they are not 'mainstream' teachings or practices, but if they are not addressed as they arise, then students will get their information elsewhere. This is not to suggest that they are taught at the expense of the central beliefs and practices of Hinduism, nor should they be the focus of curriculum questions, but they should be addressed as appropriate. I have argued elsewhere that when such topics are covered, it 'should be done thoughtfully and not to sensationalise the subject matter. These are lived religions that demand thoughtful consideration' (Holt, 2019, 16).

One further aspect that will help the teacher be prepared to address some of the misconceptions about Hinduism is the complex interplay between religion and culture. In many, if not all, religious traditions, there is the idea of purely religious ideas and teachings that lie at the heart, or even on the periphery, of the religion. There is also the recognition that elements of religion are influenced by the culture of the society within which the religion is found. In Buddhism, for example, there are specific beliefs and practices associated with Japanese Buddhism and Tibetan Buddhism; they are seen to be different cultural expressions of a central truth (Holt, 2023b). Within the modern world, aspects of Republicanism have been seen to provide the context for, and influence the presentation of, some forms of Christianity. This has been the same throughout history, and sometimes the separation of culture and religion is very difficult, as they have formed a symbiotic relationship. This process is described by Peter Berger (1969) who suggests that social institutions such as the law, education, family, language, rules and values are not only the product of human inventiveness but also are the very things that shape human experience. The dialectical process of constructing and being constructed by society proceeds in a particular way – externalization, objectification and internalization:

> Externalization is the ongoing outpouring of human being into the world, both in the physical and the mental activity of men. Objectivation is the attainment by the products of this activity (again both physical and mental) of a reality that confronts its original producers as a facticity external to and other than themselves. Internalization is the reappropriation by men of this same reality, transforming it once again from structures of the objective world into structures of the subjective consciousness. (4)

The recognition that the expression of Hinduism that is found today may be different from that which may have been understood in previous ages. For example, in the past some Hindus may have seen caste as part of a Hindu way of life (see Chapter 4) or, in the past and even today, believe in many different deities. These may have been cultural accretions, but this discussion will help situate beliefs and recognize the various influences that have an impact on the construction of a worldview today, and in the past.

Knowledge, however, is not enough. Although she wrote in 1993, what Barbara Wintersgill wrote has relevance for the teacher of religion and worldviews today:

> How religious and secular philosophies are presented to pupils is critical, if the elusive qualities of 'tolerance and respect' are to be developed, and in this context the method of teaching is as important as the content, if not more so. *Religious traditions in the hands of an unsympathetic teacher, even if a certain amount of subject knowledge has been acquired, is likely to have the reverse effect. Too often, inappropriate teaching methods foster ridicule, disinterestedness and early dismissal of the claims of religions to be taken seriously.* (44, emphasis added)

As well as knowing about Hinduism, teachers need to understand it and recognize its value in the lives of individuals today. There are many ways that this can be developed for the teacher and within the classroom. The most effective way is, as already mentioned, an engagement with Hindus and local Hindu communities. Jackson et al. (2010) suggested this as one of their key recommendations:

> School leaders and RE teachers should develop community partnerships between the school and local faith communities, particularly those with an orientation towards social action, so that pupils can learn about the role of religions in society. (13)

Where this may not be possible, then the engagement with authentic voices in preparation and teaching is paramount. The experience of Hindus in the local and national community is the first port of call for a teacher. There can be a tendency to show the 'flashy' elements of Hinduism, perhaps as practised in India. Consider the following:

> The teacher may show a Hindu funeral taking place in Varanasi. This shows a body being wrapped in cloth, carried through the streets and then placed on a large funeral pyre. The ashes are then scattered in the Ganges. This is not wrong, but it gives the impression that Hinduism is a religion that happens elsewhere. Much more useful in the RE classroom is the 'Being Hindu' documentary from the BBC that shows a

funeral in the UK at the local crematorium. It makes the religion less alien. It may be possible to compare the practices and see what is similar between the two, but when we focus purely on the 'overseas' nature of a religion it is possible that religion is seen to be other. The utilisation of authentic voices from the local community or from the UK is effective. It enables students to see the reality of lived religion in the UK. (Holt, 2023c, 282)

The way that is accomplished will differ according to school context. There may be opportunities for visits to local mandirs, and discussions with Hindus, whether in the classroom or in the mandir. Other opportunities might be through live interviews through video call, or through a video conversation, or possibly a film from websites such as TrueTube. The interaction breaks down barriers and also helps humanize the 'abstract' religious person. If diversity and accuracy are to be brought into the classroom, and the recognition of individual worldviews, then the authentic voice is an important way that this will be accomplished.

Anti-Hindu prejudice

One of the issues that seems to have become more visible in recent years is the articulation of anti-Hindu prejudice and discrimination within the UK and wider society. In the aforementioned report *Anti-Hindu Hate in Schools* by Charlotte Littlewood (2023), it is reported that '51% per cent of parents of Hindu pupils surveyed report that their child has experienced anti-Hindu hate in schools' (1). In this report, a definition of anti-Hindu hate, or Hinduphobia, is given:

> Hinduphobia is a set of antagonistic, destructive, and derogatory attitudes and behaviours towards Sanatana Dharma (Hinduism) and Hindus that may manifest as prejudice, fear, or hatred.
>
> Hinduphobic rhetoric reduces the entirety of Sanatana Dharma to a rigid, oppressive, and regressive tradition. Prosocial and reflexive aspects of Hindu traditions are ignored or attributed to outside, non-Hindu influences. This discourse actively erases and denies the persecution of Hindus while disproportionately painting Hindus as violent. These stereotypes are used to justify the dissolution, external reformation, and demonization of the range of indigenous Indic knowledge traditions known as Sanatana Dharma.
>
> The complete range of Hindu phobic acts extends from microaggressions to genocide. Hinduphobic projects include the destruction and desecration of Hindu sacred spaces; aggressive and forced proselytization of Hindu populations; targeted violence towards Hindu people, community institutions, and organizations; and ethnic cleansing and genocide. (7–8)

Not all of these actions are to be found within schools, or even within the UK, but this is a definition that outlines the problems experienced by Hindus worldwide. The question seems to be whether anti-Hindu prejudice is on the rise or whether it is only now being reported.

As the riots in Leicester in 2022 showed, there is a conflation in the media, and in the minds of the wider public, including some areas of the Hindu community, that conflates Hinduism with Indian politics and more specifically with the work of the Rashtriya Swayamsevak Sangh (RSS). Founded in the 1920s, Littlewood (2022) outlines:

> The RSS was founded in the wake of riots between Hindus and Muslims across northern India. In its mission statement, founder K.B. Hedgewar wrote: 'The Hindu culture is the life-breath of Hindustan . . . we should first nourish the Hindu culture. It is the duty of every Hindu to do his best to consolidate the Hindu society.' In 1927, RSS co-founder – Dr. B.S. Moonje - described the RSS as an institution which could produce 'the military regeneration of the Hindus' and unify the people in line with 'the idea of fascism' (5).

The idea of Hindu nationalism, especially with regard to India, which is a secular nation, has risen in recent years. There are, for some, close links between the RSS and the Bharatiya Janata Party (BJP), one of the main political parties in India, and the party led by Prime Minister Narendra Modi. Recognizing the close links between the BJP and RSS, Padmaja Nair (2009) in a research paper for the UK Government outlines that the two are not synonymous:

> The BJP was formed to advance the political ambitions of some RSS members and has acquired access to power at the national level through its coalition strategy. Today it has an ideological but somewhat fractious relationship with the RSS: the latter seeks political power to push its agenda of cultural nationalism, whereas the BJP is willing to dilute some aspects of that doctrine to widen its political support base and has become less dependent on RSS members. (1)

This Hindu nationalism, sometimes termed Hindutva, has begun to establish a Hindu orthodoxy alongside a more muscular understanding of Hindu figures and teachings. This has been evidenced through the rise of figures such as 'Angry Hanuman' (see Chapter 2) and the portrayal of the main figures in *Adipurush* in a violent manner. The use of an image described as Angry Hanuman is described as a recasting of masculinity and muscular Hinduism:

> The angry masculinisation of Hanuman is not contesting gender injustice or waging a war against rapists and the abusive kin of women . . . [It is used by those who] need an angry avenger, not one who is as Tulsidas said 'gyan gun sagar' (a sea of wisdom and goodness). (Pande, 2018)

This approach and synthesis of Indian politics with Hinduism seem to have at least the tacit approval of Modi (Misquith, 2018). This conflation of Hinduism and India in the eyes of opponents may well have brought some of the issues to the fore. Indeed, Littlewood (2023) identifies that one feature of anti-Hindu prejudice may be the identification of Hindu ideas with Indian politics, suggesting that it is possible to oppose the BJP and RSS, but that should not be used as justification for prejudice and discrimination against Hindus and Hinduism. This idea of Hindutva and the politicization of Hinduism may lie behind some of the anti-Hindu prejudice; it was erroneously identified as a motivator in the 2022 Leicester riots. This should not be the case, and teachers need to be especially careful to separate the two ideologies.

One issue for teachers and Hindus is that the politics of India, and the religious tensions within that society, do spill over into UK society. Colin Bloom (2023) in his report, *Does government 'do God?' An independent review into how government engages with faith,* outlines that:

> In contrast to earlier generations of British Hindus, it appears a small minority are now becoming more passionate about their identification with Hindu political interests in India. While this has rarely led to obvious coercive or violent activity, some British Hindus have expressed frustration with Hindu nationalist involvement in UK politics, which can create division within Indian communities in the UK.
>
> While many faith communities are likely to be interested in regional and geopolitical disputes outside of the UK, government should be attentive to the possibility of nationalist movements exploiting religious rhetoric to incite prejudicial views that may destabilise British society. (120–21)

The examples that he provides seem to be historical and geographical tensions between Muslims and Hindus, and Sikhs and Hindus. Littewood (2023) uses examples to highlight the danger of the identification of Hinduism with Indian politics:

> Other students tried to bully my daughter that she is Hindu – saying 'why you people break our mosque, why you people attack us?' So we changed the school.
>
> Child has faced bullying from other children on many occasions specifically after PM Modi's rise in India and after article 370 [the autonomy of Jammu and Kashmir] was revoked. (15)

Although Littlewood (2022) suggests that there was no link between Hindu nationalism and the Leicester riots, the opposite seems to be the perception of the actions by the Hindus and Muslims involved. As with the exploration of any actions of religious people, there is a need to consider the contributing aspects of worldviews such as culture, experience and politics, rather than erroneously attributing it to one factor, that in these cases are wrong.

This is not, in any way, to frame the anti-Hindu prejudice as a response to Hindu nationalism, rather it is utilized here to recognize that some of the tensions may be political and the teacher should be sensitive in recognizing the complexity of geo-political relations. The anti-Hindu prejudice that caricatures, denigrates, misrepresents Hindu beliefs, teachings and practices in any way should be challenged within the classroom.

This means that the thoughts expressed in the last section, that teachers of Hinduism in schools should be prepared and knowledgeable, is key in addressing and not perpetuating this prejudice. Anti-Hindu prejudice is evident within society, whether it is through the microaggressions shown through a paternalistic attitude, or more physical in nature; it is something that needs addressing so that Hindus can feel they have a place and a voice within British society.

Thoughts for the classroom

Two of the stated aims of RE are:

> To prepare pupils to be informed, respectful members of society who celebrate diversity and strive to understand others.

> To encourage students to develop knowledge of the beliefs and practices of religions and worldviews, and informed opinions and an awareness of the implications of religion and worldviews for the individual, the community and the environment. (Holt, 2022, 17)

It would appear that this is not always realized in terms of the Hindu experience in the UK. Many schools may have Holi celebrations, or make diva lamps, but these are contrasted with a static and sometimes erroneous presentation of Hinduism within the classroom. Indeed, the Holi celebrations could be seen by some to be superficial cultural appropriations, that exoticize Hinduism, and focus on its colour and excitement, detached from the beliefs that such celebrations celebrate. The richness and diversity of Hinduism, especially in Britain, lies at the heart of teaching Hinduism in the classroom.

Throughout this chapter, we have explored the place of Hindus in Britain. Sometimes the focus is on developing Hindu identity so that the beliefs, teachings and practices are not watered down. On the other hand, Hindus are aware of an increasing awareness of their place within and from wider society. As Hinduism has developed, there has been a need for Hindus to find greater representation of the needs of their communities and the individuals therein. Some of this has been able to happen through the development of representative voices within society, and these are also voices that can be used in the classroom. There does need to be care taken by the teachers in the representation of Hinduism. As noted in the Series Editor's Foreword, there is a growing tendency to reify Hinduism; to articulate Hinduism through one lens. In the Introduction, we also mentioned that the great diversity of Hinduism seems to have narrowed since its original definition. Whichever voice we represent in the classroom, either in the resources we provide or the people we listen to, it should be recognized that this is one expression of Hinduism. This is one of the benefits of a worldviews approach; the prisms through which people experience and articulate their religion are recognized.

Hindus in the public eye have raised the awareness of the wider society of Hinduism and Hindu principles. Examples include:

- Rishi Sunak, UK Prime Minister.
- Meera Syal, comedian, writer, actor and presenter.
- Romesh Ranganathan, comedian.
- George Harrison, a member of the Beatles.
- Russell Brand, actor, comedian and presenter.
- Krishnan Guru Murthy, journalist.
- Baroness Isha Prashar, crossbench peer.
- Naga Munchetty, journalist and presenter.

Outside the UK, examples might extend to:

- Sachin Tendulkar, Indian cricketer, widely seen as the greatest batsman in history.
- Priyanka Chopra Jonas, actress.

The most important examples that we use in the classroom are those from our local area. The diversity of the Hindu experience in the UK is significant and should find expression in our classrooms. Unfortunately, this has not always been the case.

Hinduism is a religion that transforms the individual as they understand the nature of existence. Sometimes in our writing and teaching, we forget that everything in Hinduism has its root in this teaching. Nothing in the Hindu worldview makes sense without an understanding of dharma, the nature of the Divine and the purpose of existence. It is my hope that as we explore Hinduism as a lived religion, it will become more than a list of observable phenomena but that it will reflect the reality of Hindu life. It is only then that the richness and diversity of Hinduism can be understood by those we teach.

Glossary

Word	Definition
Advaita	Advaita Vedanta is monistic in the sense that Brahman is the ultimate reality and that the atman is a part of Brahman.
ahimsa	One of the five yamas: non-violence
Antayarami	The concept within Hinduism that the Divine is within the heart, within the individual.
aparigraha	One of the five yamas: non-attachment.
artha	Prosperity. One of the four aims of life.
arti	Part of puja, the use of light or fire to venerate and to bring the blessings of the deity.
ashramas	Stages of life that enable a person to understand and live their personal dharma.
astanga yoga	Sometimes called raja marga. The path of exercise and meditation.
asteya	One of the five yamas: not stealing.
atman	The soul. In monism it is the same as Brahman; in dualism it is similar to but separate.
Aum/Om	The sacred syllable that is symbolic of Brahman.
avatar	The incarnation of a deity into an earthly form.
Bhagavad Gita	A section of the Mahabharata which recounts a conversation between Krishna as a charioteer with the Pandava prince Arjuna.
Bhagavan	Often used interchangeably with God, but it is used to define the Divine who is transcendent and outside of time and the universe.
bhajan/kirtan	'Adoration'. Congregational singing of hymns of adoration.
bhakti	Devotional worship/love to a deity.
bhakti yoga/ bhakti marga	The path of devotion.
bhuvana-jnana	The aspect of cosmology that explores the metaphysical nature of the world.
Brahmacharya	One of the five yamas: chastity.
brahmacharya	The student ashrama.
Brahman	Concept of the Divine suggesting that Brahman is everywhere and in every living thing.
Brahmin	One of the varnas. Those responsible for rituals, often termed 'priests'.
brahmanda	The cosmic egg, seen by some as the source from which all existence and life arose.

Darshanas	'Ways of seeing', often described as philosophical or theological schools.
darshan	'Seeing'. To stand in the presence of a deity and to see and be seen. It is a reciprocal relationship between the deity and devotee.
Dashavataras	The main avatars of Vishnu, usually numbered as ten.
dharma	Often translated as religion or duty. Best left untranslated as it refers to the many different responsibilities and duties within the life of a Hindu.
dharmashastras	Writings that extended the dharmasutras into codes of law, including the Manusmrti, the Yajnavalkya smrti, the Naradasmrti and the Vishnusmrti
Dharmasutras	Writings that are rules of conduct for various social groups, moral duties, rights and obligations.
Dvaita Vedanta	Within Dvaita Vedanta, there are seen to be three parts to reality: Brahman, chit (souls) and achit (the universe).
Epics	Sometimes seen as the only form of Itihasa. Often the most 'popular' of the sacred texts within Hinduism, and include the Ramayana and the Mahabharata.
Grihastha	The householder ashrama.
gunas	Qualities or forces of behaviour. All seem to work together to give experience: sattva (goodness), rajas (passion) and tamas (decay).
Hanuman Chalisa	A hymn of praise and supplication directed to Hanuman.
Harappan Civilization	Also known as the 'Indus Valley Civilization' referring to the civilization of the Indus Valley between 3300 BCE and 1750 BCE.
Havan	Fire sacrifice or sacrificial fire. A specific ritual in worship/devotion.
Hindu	A word derived from the word 'sindhu' meaning river. Initially used as a geographical indicator, Hindu has come to refer to individuals who follow Hinduism or Sanatana Dharma.
Hinduism	A system of religion structured initially by colonialists to refer to the varied religions of India. Now often used as the default description of the religion of Hindus, although some prefer Sanatana Dharma.
Ishvara	Often an accessible form of the Divine with attributes.
ISKCON	International Society for Krishna Consciousness.
Itihasa	'So indeed it was.' A collection of histories of important events in the history of the universe. Often used as the umbrella term for the Epic and the Puranas.
jagadutpatti	The aspect of cosmogony that explores the origin of the world.
jati	Within each varna, there are many jatis which are subdivisions based on various professions.
jiva	Often synonymous with atman, the soul.
jivanmukti	Liberation in this life.
jnana yoga/ jnana marga	The path of knowledge.
kama	Gratification/ pleasure. One of the four aims of life.

Glossary

karma	Karma is the law of cause and effect; that every action (and indeed thought) is positive or negative and leads to an accumulation of karma, which leads to positive or negative births in the future.
karma yoga/ karma marga	The path of action.
kriyamana karma	The karma accumulated in the current lifetime.
kshatriya	One of the varnas. Rulers or warriors.
Mahabharata	One of the Epics believed to be narrated by Veda Vyasa. Tells the story of a great war between two sets of cousins: the Pandavas and the Kauravas. The Bhagavad Gita is a part of the wider story and includes a great focus on Krishna.
mandir	Often translated as 'temple'; a place of worship for Hindus.
maya	Illusion
Mimamsa	One of the six astika darshanas. Sometimes known as purva (earlier) Mimamsa as it focuses on the earlier Vedic texts.
mleccha	An ancient term used to refer to 'foreigners' or non-Hindus when Hindu was a geographical term.
moksha	Liberation from samsara. One of the four aims of life.
moksha chitram	A game reflecting beliefs in samsara, a precursor to snakes and ladders.
mukta	A person who is self-realized.
mumukshutvam	The intense longing for moksha from ignorance.
murti	Physical image of a manifestation of the Divine.
nastika	Forms of Hinduism which are no longer found in the Hindu tradition that generally reject the idea of a Supreme Being, including Jainism and Buddhism.
nirguna	The idea that the Divine is without qualities.
Nyaya	One of the six astika darshanas outlining four ways by which knowledge is gained.
panchamahabhutas	The five primordial elements: space, air, fire, water, earth.
pithas	Seats, usually of the Divine feminine, where the goddess is particularly worshipped. Some pithas are associated with body parts of Sati.
Prakriti	The primary substance, the original substance or force. Sometimes translated as 'matter'.
Pravachan	A leader in the mandir will deliver a lecture on the Vedas.
puja	'Worship'. Often used as a catch-all for various devotional activities, but can be the specific act of devotional worship to the deity.
Puranas	A subsection of Itihasa. Texts that are in praise of, and tell the story of, individual deities.
Purusartha	The four aims of life: dharma, artha, kama and moksha.
Purusha	The cosmic presence, often identified with the Supreme Being, whether that is Brahman, Vishnu or others. Other times Purusha is seen as the first human.

rajas	Passion. One of the three gunas.
Ramayana	One of the Epics. The story of Rama, an avatar of Vishnu, and his wife Sita. One of the most popular texts/stories in Hinduism.
rta	Cosmic order, or the regulating force of the universe. It has three aspects: continuous movement or change, a system based on the interdependence of parts and the inherent order of interdependence and movemenet.
sadharana dharma	universal dharma, sometimes termed universal morality, are the aspects of dharma that apply to all.
saguna	The idea that the Divine possesses attributes such as form, personhood and activity.
samkhya	One of the six astika darshanas outlining the dual nature of prakriti and purusha.
samsara	The cycle of birth, life, death and reincarnation.
samskaras	Rituals or rites that mark certain points in a person's life. They are commonly seen to be sixteen.
Sanatana Dharma	Often translated as 'Eternal Law' or 'Eternal Religion'. Often used in preference to Hinduism to describe the religious system.
sanchita karma	The accumulation of karma over various lifetimes.
sannyasin	The ashrama of renunciation.
sattva	Goodness. One of the three gunas.
satya	One of the five yamas: truthfulness
satyagraha	A philosophy and approach developed by Gandhi, combining truth with love and firmness/force.
seva	Devotional service to the deity.
Shaivites	A group within Hinduism that focuses on the worship of Shiva, sometimes as the Supreme Being.
Shakti	The Goddess, the Divine feminine.
Shaktism	A form/forms of Hinduism that worship the divine in the form of the Divine Mother.
Shilpa Shastras	Writings that outline the environment and method for creating a murti.
Shruti	Scriptures that are heard or revealed.
shudra	One of the varnas. Usually seen as those with manual tasks.
Smarta	A form of Hinduism that focuses its worship on five deities: Ganesha, Shakti, Shiva, Surya, Vishnu. Often described as non-sectarian.
shruti	Scriptures that are remembered.
stridharma	Historically used to refer to the personal dharma of women, first as a daughter, then a wife and mother, and finally as a widow.
svadharma	Personal dharma, is that aspect of dharma that is particular to the individual.
Syndicated Hinduism	A phrase used to describe the systematization of Hindu belief and practice over the last two or three centuries.
tamas	Decay. One of the three gunas.

Tantra	A practice focused on moksha, highlighting different planes of understanding. The rituals are often secret and passed on through gurus.
Trimurti	The representation of the Divine incorporating Brahma as the creator, Vishnu as the preserver, and Shiva as the destroyer.
Upanishads	Texts that are seen as ancillary sections of the Vedas. Literally meaning 'to sit down near' and are conversations between a teacher and their pupils. These provide interpretations of the Vedas.
Vaikuntha	The abode of Vishnu.
Vaisheshika	One of the six astika darshanas outlining two ways by which knowledge is gained.
Vaishnanva	A group within Hinduism that focuses on the worship of Vishnu or his avatars, sometimes as the Supreme Being.
vaishya	One of the varnas. Often seen to be merchants.
Vanaprastha	The retirement ashrama.
varna	The varnas are the divisions within society that are often misreported as castes (see below). Varnas were seen to be an organization of society based on its needs, and also the aptitudes of its people.
varnashramadharma	Focused on the dharma or responsibilities of those within a particular varna.
Vedanta	One of the six astika darshanas. Vedanta is also known as Uttara Mimamsa, which deals with one eternal principle, that of Brahman or the supreme spirit. The three main traditions of Vedanta are Advaita Vedanta, Visistadvaita Vedanta and Dvaita Vedanta.
Vedas	Sacred writings composed of poems and rituals. There are four Vedas: Rig Veda, Sama Veda, Yajurveda and Atharvana Veda. Often seen as a unifying feature of Hinduism.
Vedic period	Refers to the history of India from approximately 1750 BCE to 500 BCE, wherein the Vedas are seen to be composed.
videhamukti	Liberation after death.
viraga	Dispassion. Part of the path of knowledge.
Visistadvaita Vedanta	Visistadvaita Vedanta is seen to be based on the teachings of Ramanuja. This is seen as a qualified non-dualism, meaning that it recognizes Brahman as the ultimate reality, but it is expressed and manifested in diversity.
Viveka	Discriminaton in path of knowledge. The ability to recognize the difference between the permanent and impermanent.
yamas	The yamas are the basis of moral living.
yoga	One of the six astika darshanas. In Western 'outsider' terms, raja yoga is 'yoga', and refers to the actions that might incorporate meditation and various postures and positions. Within Hinduism, it is much more than this with many practices.
yuga	An age. There are seen to be four yugas: Satya/Krita, Treta, Dvapara, Kali. Each reduces in length and decreases in morality.

Reference List

Achuthananda, S. (2018). *The Ascent of Vishnu and the Fall of Brahma (The Galaxy of Hindu Gods Book 2)*. Queensland: Relianz.

Achuthananda, S. (2019). *Rama and the Early Avatars of Vishnu: Plus Ramayana Abridged (The Galaxy of Hindu Gods Book 3)*. Queensland: Relianz.

Addo, R. (2021, February 17). *'It's Disrespectful to Our Religion': Rihanna Is Accused of 'Cultural Appropriation' for Wearing a Pendant of Hindu God Ganesha in Topless Photo.* Retrieved from Mail Online: https://www.dailymail.co.uk/tvshowbiz/article-9270335/Rihanna-accused-cultural-appropriation-wearing-Hindu-pendant-topless-photo.html

Adi Shankara. (2010). *Manisha Pancakam*. Retrieved from ArshaBodha.org: https://arshabodha.org/wp-content/uploads/abc/teachings/adiShankara/ManishaPanchakam.pdf

Ahmed, B., Das, R., Gupta, M., Jain, H., Natesh, S., & Rao, R. (Eds.). (2017). *The Illustrated Mahabharata: The Definitive Guide to India's Greatest Epic*. London: Dorling KIndersley.

Al-Biruni. (1910). *Alberuni's India. An Account of the Religion, Philosophy, Literature, Geography, Chronology, Astronomy, Customs, Laws and Astrology of India About A.D. 1030* (Vol. 1). (E. Sachau, Trans.). London: Kegan, Paul, Trench, Trubner & Co.

Amar Chitra Katha Media. (2022). *Stories from the Puranas*. Retrieved from Amar Chitra Katha: https://www.amarchitrakatha.com/mythology-category/stories-from-the-puranas/

Ammerman, N. T. (2021). *Studying Lived Religion: Contexts and Practices*. New York: New York University Press.

Anika, J. (2020). *The Story of Diwali: Rama & Sita*. Mumbai: Little Book Wallah.

Arjana, S. R. (2020). *Buying Buddha, Selling Rumi: Orientalism and the Mystical Marketplace*. London: Oneworld Academic.

Arni, S. (2011). *Sita's Ramayana*. Toronto: Groundwood Books.

Askegaard, S., & Eckhardt, G. (2012). Glocal yoga: Re-appropriation in the Indian Consumptionscape. *Marketing Theory, 12*(1), 45–60.

Aurobindo. (2000). *The Adoration of the Divine Mother*. Retrieved from Savitri. A Legend and a Symbol: http://savitrithepoem.com/b3c2.html

Bailey, G. (2001). The Puranas. A Study in the Development of Hinduism. In A. Sharma (Ed.), *The Study of Hinduism* (pp. 437–443). Columbia: University of South Carolina Press.

Bailey, G. (2008). Brahma. In D. Cush, C. Robinson, & M. York (Eds.), *Encyclopedia of Hindusim* (p. 112). Abingdon: Routledge.

Bassuk, D. (1987). *Incarnation in Hinduism and Christianity: Library of Philosophy and Religion*. London: Palgrave Macmillan.

Berger, P. (1969). *The Sacred Canopy: Elements of a Sociological Theory of Religion*. New York: Anchor.

Bernard, T. (1999). *Hindu philosophy*. Delhi: Motilal Barnarsidass.

Bhargava, A. (2000). Introduction. Retrieved from Sitayanam... A Woman's Journey of Strength: http://www.sitayanam.com/

Bhatt, N. R. (2008). *Shaivism in the light of epics, Puranas and Agamas*. Varanasi: Indica.

Birch, J. (2020). The Quest for Liberation-in-Life: A Survey of Early Works on Haṭha- and Rājayoga. In G. Flood (Ed.), *The Oxford History of Hinduism: Hindu Practice* (pp. 200–42). Oxford: Oxford University Press.

Bloom, C. (2023). *Does Government 'Do God?' An Independent Review into How Government Engages with Faith*. London: Department for Levelling Up, Housing and Communities.

Bondurant, J. (1959). *Conquest of Violence: The Gandhian Philosophy of Conflict*. Bombay: Oxford University Press.

Bowie, R. A., Panjwani, F., & Clemmey, K. (2020). *Texts and Teachers: Opening the Door to Hermeneutical RE*. Canterbury: National Institute of Christian Education.

Brahmanda Purana. (1958). (G. Tagare, Trans.). New Delhi: Motilal Banarsidass.

Britain, H. O. (2012). Zavos, John. In J. Zavos, P. Kanungo, D. Reddy, M. Warrier, & R. Williams (Eds.), *Public Hinduisms* (pp. 70–89). New Delhi: Sage.

Brockington, J. (2008). Hanuman. In D. Cush, C. Robinson, & M. York (Eds.), *Encyclopedia of Hinduism* (pp. 284–5). Abingdon: Routledge.

Brooks, D. R. (1992). *Auspicious Wisdom: The Texts and Traditions of Srividya Shakta Tantrism in South India*. Albany: State University of New York Press.

Bucar, L. (2022). *Stealing My Religion: Not Just Any Cultural Appropriation*. Cambridge: Harvard University Press.

Burghart, R. (Ed.). (1987). *Hinduism in Great Britain: The Perpetuation of Religion in an Alien Milieu*. London: Tavistock.

Cassidy, R. (2022, November 16). *Whitstable Shop Accused of 'Sacrilege' After Selling £40 Ganesh Swimsuit*. Retrieved from Kent Online: https://www.kentonline.co.uk/whitstable/news/shop-accused-of-sacrilege-over-40-swimsuit-277193/

Chakravorty, S. (2019). *The Truth About Us*. Gurugram: Hachette India.

Chitgopekar, N. (2022). *Shakti. An Exploration of the Divine Feminine*. London: Dorling Kindersley.

Clooney, F. X. (2001). *Hindu God, Christian God: How Reason Helps Break Down the Boundaries Between Religions*. Oxford: Oxford University Press.

Commission on RE. (2018). *Religion and Worldviews: The Way Forward. A National Plan for RE*. London: Commission on RE.

Cooling, T. (2002). Commitment and Indoctrination: A dilemma for Religious Education? In L. Broadbent, & A. Brown (Eds.), *Issues in Religious Education* (pp. 44–55). New York: Routledge.

Cooling, T., Bowie, B., & Panjwani, F. (2020). *Worldviews in Religious Education*. London: Theos.

Coomaraswamy, A. (1957). *The Dance of Siva: Fourteen Indian Essays*. New York: Sunwise Turn.

Crenshaw, K. (1989). Demarginalizing the Intersection of Race and Sex: A Black Feminist Critique of Antidiscrimination Doctrine, Feminist Theory and Antiracist Politics. *University of Chicago Legal Forum*. University of Chicago Law School, 139–168.

Dalal, R. (2014). *Hinduism: An Alphabetical Guide*. London: Penguin.

Das, R. (2002). *The Heart of Hinduism: A Comprehensive Guide ofr Teachers and Professionals*. Aldenham: ISKCON.

de Bruijn, J. (2012). *Hindu*. Retrieved from Encyclopaedia Iranica: https://www.iranicaonline.org/articles/hindu

Dharni, A. (2020, November 12). *Outrage As Cardi B Poses As Goddess Durga To Launch Her Sneaker Business*. Retrieved from India Times: https://www.indiatimes.com/trending/social-relevance/cardi-b-sneaker-ad-goddess-durga-527391.html

Dimmitt, C., & Buitenen, J. (1978). *Classical Hindu Mythology: A Reader in the Sanskrit Puranas*. Philadelphia: Temple University Press.

Divakaruni, C. B. (2008). *The Palace of Illusions*. London: Picador.

Divakaruni, C. B. (2019). *The Forest of Enchantments*. Uttar Pradesh: Harper Collins.

Doniger, W. (1990). *Textual Sources for the Study of Hinduism*. Chicago: University of Chicago Press.

Doniger, W. (1991). Hinduism by Any Other Name. *The Wilson Quarterly, 15*(3), 35–41.

Doniger, W. (Ed.). (1999). *Merriam-Webster's Encyclopedia of World Religions*. Springfield: Merriam-Webster.

Doniger, W. (2009). *The Hindus: An Alternative History*. Oxford: Oxford Univeristy Press.

Doniger, W., & Hawley, J., eds. (1999). *Merriam-Webster's encyclopedia of world religions*. Springfield: Merriam-Webster.

Dunnavant, N. C., & Roberts, T.-A. (2013). Restriction and renewal, pollution and power, constraint and community: The paradoxes of religious women's experiences of menstruation. *Sex Roles: A Journal of Research, 68*(1–2), 121–131.

Durkheim, E. (2001). *The Elementary Forms of Religious Life*. New York: Oxford University Press.

Dutt, M. N. (Ed.). (1896). *Vishnu Puranam*. Calcutta: Elysium Press.

Dyson, J. (2009). What's the Use of Stories? Exploring the Place of Personal Stories and Grand Narratives in RE (and Life in General). *REsource, 32*(1), 14–17.

Eck, D. (1998). *Darsan*. New York: Columbia University Press.

Ekstrand, M., & Bryant, E. H. (2004). *The Hare Krishna Movement: The Postcharismatic Fate of a Religious Transplant*. New York: Columbia University Press.

Ferrari, F. (2008). Saktism. In D. Cush, C. Robinson, & M. York (Eds.), *Encybcopedia of Hinduism* (pp. 733–42). Abingdon: Routledge.

Fischer, L. (1997). *The Life of Mahatma Gandhi*. London: Harper Collins.

Flood, G. (1996). *An Introduction to Hinduism*. Cambridge: Cambridge University Press.

Flood, G. (1997). The Meaning and Context of the Purusarthas. In J. Lipner (Ed.), *The Fruits of Our Desiring: An Enquiry Into the Ethics of the Bhagavadgita for Our Times* (pp. 11–27). Calgary: Bayeux Arts.

Flood, G. (2003). The Saiva Traditions. In G. Flood (Ed.), *The Blackwell Companion to Hinduism* (pp. 200–8). Oxford: Blackwell.

Flood, G. (2020). *The Oxford History of Hinduism: Hindu Practice*. Oxford: Oxford University Press.

Fowler, J. (1997). *Hinduism. Beliefs and Practices*. Brighton: Sussex Academic Press.

Fredman, S. (2022). *Discrimination Law* (Third Edition). Oxford: Oxford University Press.

Frykenberg, R. (2005). The Emergence of Modern 'Hinduism' as a Concept as an Institution: A Reappraisal with Special Reference to South India. In G.-D. Sontheimer, & H. Kulke (Eds.), *Hinduism Reconsidered* (pp. 82–107). New Delhi: Manohar.

Gambhirananda, S. (2009). *Brahma Suira Bhasya of Sri Sri Sankarcarya: Tenth Impression*. Kolkata: Advaita Asrama.

Gandhi, M. (1922). *Speeches and Writings of M. K. Gandhi* (Third Edition). Madras: G. A. Natesan & Co.

Gandhi, M. (1956) *The Gandhi Reader: A Sourcebook of His Life and Writings* (H. A. Jack, Ed.). New York: Grove Press.

Gandhi, M (1968) *The Voice of Truth*. Ahmedabad: Navajivan Publishing House.

Gandhi, M. (1982). *M. K. Gandhi: An Autobiography or The Story of My Experiments with Truth* (M. Desai, Trans.). London: Penguin.

Gandhi, M. K. (1955). *My Religion*. Ahmedabad: Navajivan Publishing House.

Gandhi, M. K. (2006). *Satyagraha in South Africa*. Ahmedabad: Navajivan.

Gandhi, S. (2018). *Hinduism And Brotherhood*. Chennai: Notion Press.

Geaves, R. (2008). Bhakti Movement. In D. Cush, C. Robinson, & M. York (Eds.), *Encyclopedia of HInduism* (pp. 89–96). Abingdon: Routledge.

Gita Bhavan Hindu Temple. (2021). *Temple History...* Retrieved from Gita Bhavan Hindu Temple: https://www.gitabhavan.co.uk/about

Go Dharmic. (n.d.a). *Compassion for Animals*. Retrieved from Go Dharmic: https://godharmic.com/campaigns/compassion-for-animals

Go Dharmic. (n.d.b). *Go Green*. Retrieved from Go Dharmic: https://godharmic.com/campaigns/go-green

Godwin, J. (2011). *Atlantis and the Cycles of Time: Prophecies, Traditions, and Occult Revelations*. Rochester: Inner Traditions.

Gokul, V. (2018, October 10). *Vishnu Avatars and Evolution*. Retrieved from Medium: https://medium.com/@staynatural/vishnu-avatars-and-evolution-8cb6c069105c

Goldman, R. P., & Goldman, S. S. (2021). *The Ramayana of Valmiki: The Complete English Translation*. Princeton: Princeton University Press.

Grimes, J. A. (1996). *A Concise Dictionary of Indian Philosophy: Sanskrit Terms Defined in English*. Albany: State University of New York Press.

Gross, R. (2000). Is the Goddess a Feminist? In A. Hiltebeitl, & K. Erndl (Eds.), *Is the Goddess a Feminist? The Politics of South Asian Goddesses* (pp. 189–197). New York: New York University Press.

Hallet, G. (1967). *Wittgenstein's Definition of Meaning as Use*. New York: Fordham University Press.

Handa, R. (2008). Idolatry. In D. Cush, C. Robisnon, & M. York (Eds.), *Encyclopedia of Hinduism* (pp. 359–60). Abingdon: Routledge.

Hanuman Chalisa. (2020). Mumbai: Sanage Publishing House.

Hargreaves, A. (2020). *Mr. Men Little Miss Happy Diwali*. London: Egmont.

Hay, D. (2000). The Religious Experience and Education Project: Experiential Learning in Religious Education. In M. Grimmitt (Ed.), *Pedagogies of Religious Education: Case Studies in the Research and Development of Good Pedagogic Practice in RE* (pp. 70–87). Great Wakering: McCrimmons.

Hiltebeitel, A. (2002). Hinduism. In J. Kitagawa (Ed.), *The Religious Traditions of Asia: Religion, History, and Culture* (pp. 3–40). London: Routledge Curzon.

Hiltebeitel, A., & Erndl, K. (Eds.). (2000). *Is the Goddess a Feminist? The Politics of South Asian Goddesses*. New York: New York University Press.

Hindu Council UK. (2022). *Hindu Council UK*. Retrieved from Hindu Council UK: https://hinducounciluk.org.uk/

Hindu Forum of Britain. (n.d.). *Hindu Forum of Britain*. Retrieved from Hindu Forum of Britain: https://www.hfb.org.uk/

Holt, J. D. (2019). *Beyond the Big Six Religions: Expanding the Boundaries in the Teaching of Religions and Worldviews*. Chester: University of Chester Press.

Holt, J. D. (2022). *Religious Education in the Secondary School: An Introduction to Teaching, Learning and the World Religions*. Abingdon: Routledge.

Holt, J. D. (2023a). *Understanding Buddhism: A Guide for Teachers*. London: Bloomsbury.

Holt, J. D. (2023b). *Understanding Sikhism: A Guide for Teachers*. London: Bloomsbury.

Holt, J. D. (2023c). Religious Education. In N. Majid (Ed.), *Essential Subject Knowledge for Primary Teaching* (pp. 271–90). London: Learning Matters.

Homan, R. (2000). Don't Let the Murti Get Dirty: The Uses and Abuses of Religious "Artefacts". *British Journal of Religious Education*, 23(1), 27–37.

Hopkins, T. (1971). *The Hindu Religious Tradition*. Belmont: Wadsworth Publishing Company.

Inform. (2019, July 3). *Factsheet: ISKCON and the Hare Krishna movement*. Retrieved from Religion Media Centre: https://religionmediacentre.org.uk/factsheets/iskcon-factsheet/

Insight UK. (2021). *A Report on the State of Hinduism in Religious Education in UK Schools*. London: Insight UK.

Insight UK. (2023). *About Us*. Retrieved from Insight UK: https://insightuk.org/about-us

ISKCON. (1994). *Hinduism and the Environment*. Retrieved from Heart of Hinduism: https://iskconeducationalservices.org/HoH/further-information-and-teaching-resources-secondary/fact-sheets/hinduism-and-the-environment/

Jackson, R. (1997). *Religious Education: An Interpretive Approach*. London: Hodder.

Jackson, R., Ipgrave, J., Hayward, M., Hopkins, P., Fancourt, N., Robbins, M., . . . McKenna, U. (2010). *Materials Used to Teach About World Religions in Schools in England*. Warwick: University of Warwick.

Jacobs, S. (2008). Images and Iconography. In D. Cush, C. Robinson, & M. York (Eds.), *Encyclopedia of Hinduism* (pp. 364–6). Abingdon: Routledge.

Jain, K. (2021, November 2). *Modi's Diwali Extravaganza Shows Why We Need to Tell the Many Stories of Rama*. Retrieved from Religion News Service: https://religionnews.com/2021/11/02/modis-diwali-extravaganza-shows-why-we-need-to-tell-the-many-stories-of-rama/

Jayaram, V. (n.d.). *The Meaning and Significance of Heart in Hinduism*. Retrieved from hinduwebsite.com: https://www.hinduwebsite.com/hinduism/essays/the-meaning-and-significance-of-heart-in-hinduism.asp

Jeffries, T. (2022, October 3). *Is Your Yoga Practice Stealing From Religion?* Retrieved from Yoga Journal: https://www.yogajournal.com/yoga-101/yoga-religious-appropriation/

Johnson, R. L. (2006). *Gandhi's Experiments with Truth: Essential Writings by and About Mahatma Gandhi*. Lanham: Lexington Books.

Jones, C., & Ryan, J. (2007). *Encyclopedia of Hinduism*. New York: Infobase Publishing.

Josephson, J. A. (2012). *The Invention of Religion in Japan*. Chicago: University of Chicago Press.

Kapur, D. C. (2014). *Ramayan 3392 AD*. Bangalore: Graphic India.

Killingley, D. (2008). Veda. In D. Cush, C. Robinson, & M. York (Eds.), *Encyclopedia of Hinduism* (pp. 940–8). Abingdon: Routledge.

King, R. (1999). *Orientalism and Religion Postcolonial Theory, India and 'the Mystic East'*. New York: Routledge.

Kingsley, D. (1986). *Hindu Goddesses: Visions of the Divine Feminine in the Hindu Religious Tradition*. Berkeley: University of California Press.

Klostermaier, K. (1985). Moksa and Critical Theory. *Philosophy East and West*, 35(1), 61–71.

Klostermaier, K. (1989). *A Survey of Hinduism*. Albany: State University of New York Press.
Klostermaier, K. (2003). *A Concise Encyclopedia of Hinduism*. Oxford: OneWorld.
Klostermaier, K. (2007). *A Survey of Hinduism*. Albany: State Univeristy of New York Press .
Klostermaier, K. (2008). Cosmology. In D. Cush, C. Robinson, & M. York (Eds.), *Encyclopedia of Hinduism* (pp. 151–155). Abingdon: Routledge.
Knott, K. (2016). *Hinduism: A Very Short Introduction*. Oxford: Oxford University Press.
Kolhatkar, S. (2022, March 17). *How to Celebrate Holi Without Culturally Appropriating It*. Retrieved from Yes: https://www.yesmagazine.org/opinion/2022/03/17/holi-celebrate-cultural-appropriation
Kozlowski, F., & Jackson, C. (2013). *Driven by the Divine: A Seven-Year Journey with Shivalinga Swamy and Vinnuacharya*. Bloomington: Balboa Press.
Kramrisch, S. (1981). *Manifestations of Shiva*. Philadelphia: Philadelphia Museum of Art.
Kumar, P. (2008). Vaisnavism. In D. Cush, C. Robinson, & M. York (Eds.), *Encyclopedia of Hinduism* (pp. 919–28). Abingdon: Routledge.
Kurma Puranas (1 & 2). (1981). (G. Tagare, Trans.). New Delhi: Motilal Banarsidass.
Labh, S. (2022, August 30). *The 10 Avatars of Lord Vishnu and Darwin's Theory of Evolution*. Retrieved from Medium: https://piggsboson.medium.com/the-10-avatars-of-lord-vishnu-and-darwins-theory-of-evolution-839b3f903cbd
Lakhani, J. (2007, May 14). *Caste & Conversion: Jay Lakhani*. Retrieved from Hindu Janajagruti Samiti: https://www.hindujagruti.org/news/2128.html
Lakhani, S. (2005). *Hinduism for Schools*. London: Vivekananda Centre.
Larson, G. J. (1979). *Classical Samkhya*. New Delhi: Motilal Banarsidass.
Larson, G. J. (2011). Hindu Cosmogony/Cosmology. In J. W. Haag, G. R. Peterson, & M. L. Spezio (Eds.), *The Routledge Companion to Religion and Science* (pp. 113–123). Abingdon: Routledge.
Levy, J. (2010). *Kama Sense Marketing: A Love Affair with Your Customers*. New York: iUniverse.
Lipner, J. (2010). *Hindus Their Religious Beliefs and Practices* (Second Edition). Abingdon: Routledge.
Littewood, C. (2022). *Research Brief: Hindu-Muslim Civil Unrest in Leicester "Hindutva" and the Creation of a False Narrative*. London: Henry Jackson Society.
Littlewood, C. (2023). *Research Brief: Anti-Hindu Hate in Schools*. London: The Henry Jackson Society.
Lochtefeld, J. G. (2002). *The Illustrated Encyclopedia of Hinduism: A–M, Vol. 1*. New York: Rosen Publishing.
Lopez, D. (1995). *Curators of the Buddha: The Study of Buddhism Under Colonialism*. Chicago: University of Chicago Press.
Lorenzen, D. (1999). Who Invented Hinduism?. *Comparative Studies in Society and History*, 41(4), 630–59.
Lutgendorf, P. (2007). *Hanuman's Tale The Messages of a Divine Monkey*. Oxford: Oxford University Press.
Madhava Acharaya. (1882). *Sarva-Darsana-Samgraha or the Review of the DIfferent Systems of Hindu Philosophy* (E. Cowell, & A. Gough, Trans.). London: Trubner & Co.
Maguire, G. (1995). *Wicked: The Life and Times of the Wicked Witch of the West*. London: Headline.
Mahadevan, M. S. (2005). *Hanuman's Adventures in the Nether World*. New Delhi: Katha.
Mair, M. (1989). *Between Psychology and Psychotherapy: A Poetics of Experience*. New York: Routledge.

Mallinson, J., & Singleton, M. (Eds.). (2017). *Roots of Yoga*. London: Penguin.

Marx, K., & Engels, F. (1975). *Collected Works of Karl Marx and Frederick Engels. Volume 3 1843–1844*. London: Lawrence & Wishart Ltd.

Maslow, A. H. (2943). A Theory of Human Motivation. *Psychological Review, 50*(4), 370–96.

Masuzawa, T. (2005). *The Invention of World Religions*. London: University of Chicago Press.

Matilal, B. K. (1997). *Logic language and reality Indian philosophy and contemporary issues*. Delhi: Motilal Publishers.

Mauss, A. (1994a). The Mormon Struggle with Assimilation and Identity: Trends and Developments Since Midcentury. *Dialogue: A Journal of Mormon Thought, 27*, 129–49.

May, T., & Lee, S.-H. (2020, July 11). *Hindu God in a Music Video? A K-Pop Band Runs Afoul of Fans*. Retrieved from New York Times: https://www.nytimes.com/2020/07/11/world/asia/blackpink-ganesha-kpop-cultural-appropriation.html

Mayeda, S. (1979). *A thousand teachings: The Upadesasasahasri of Sankara*. Tokyo: University of Tokyo Press.

McDaniel, J. (1989). *The Madness of the Saints: Ecstatic Religion in Bengal*. Chicago: University of Chicago Press.

McGuire, M. (2008). *Lived Religion. Faith and Practice in Everyday Life*. Oxford: Oxford University press.

Michaels, A. (2004). *Hinduism: Past and Present*. Princeton: Princeton University Press.

Miller, J. (2003). Using the Visual Arts in Religious Education: An Analysis and Critical Evaluation. *British Journal of Religious Education, 25*(3), 200–13.

Mishra, P. K. (2013, November 20). *A temple for god of cricket Sachin Tendulkar in Bihar*. Retrieved from Hindustan Times: https://www.hindustantimes.com/india-news

Mishra, R. (2013). Moksha and the Hindu Worldview. *Psychology and Developing Societies, 25*(1), 21–42.

Misquith, C. (2018, May 5). *Modi Hails Mangaluru-based Artiste's Angry Hanuman*. Retrieved from Times of India: https://timesofindia.indiatimes.com/city/mangaluru/modi-hails-mangaluru-based-artistes-angry-hanuman/articleshow/64044914.cms

Mujmadar, A. (2019). *Sitayana*. New Delhi: Penguin.

Mukundananda, S. (2014). *Bhagavad Gita 2:31*. Retrieved from Bhagavad Gita The Song of God Commentary by Swami Mukundananda: https://www.holy-bhagavad-gita.org/chapter/2/verse/31

Nair, P. (2009). *Religious Political Parties and Their Welfare Work: Relations between the RSS, the Bharatiya Janata Party and the Vidya Bharati Schools in India*. Birmingham: Religions and Development Working Paper 37.

Narada Purana (Vol. III). (1997). (G. Tagare, trans.). New Delhi: Motilala Banarsidass.

Narayanan, V. (2015). Hindu Traditions. In W. Oxtoby, R. Amore, A. Hussain, & A. Segal (Eds.), *A Concise Introduction to World Religions* (Third Edition, pp. 280–341). Ontario: Oxford University Press.

National Council of Hindu Temples. (2021). *National Council of Hindu Temples*. Retrieved from National Council of Hindu Temples: https://www.thenchtuk.org/

Nayak, S. (2022). *Mahagatha: 100 Tales from the Puranas* (Kindle Edition). Gurugram: Harper Collins.

Nesbitt, E. (2006). Locating British Hindus' Sacred Space. *Contemporary South Asia, 15*(2), 195–208.

Nicholson, A. J. (2014). *Unifying Hinduism: Philosophy and Identity in Indian Intellectual History*. New York: Columbia University Press.

Oddie, G. (2007). Was Hinduism Invented? Britons, Indians, and Colonial Construction of Religion. By Brian K. Pennington. New York: Oxford University Press, 2005. 260 pp. $47.50 (cloth). *The Journal of Asian Studies*, 66(3), 863–6.

Olivelle, P. (1999). *The Dharmasutras: The Law Codes of Ancient India*. Oxford: Oxford University Press.

Olson, C. (2007). *The Many Colors of Hinduism: A Thematic-Historical Introduction*. New Brunswick: Rutgers University Press.

Oxford Centre for Hindu Studies. (2004a). *Aum Away from Home*. Oxford: Oxford Centre for Hindu Studies.

Oxford Centre for Hindu Studies. (2004b). *Interviews*. Retrieved from British Hinduism Oral History Project: https://ochs.org.uk/interviews/

Padoux, A. (2017). *The Hindu Tantric World An Overview*. Chicago: University of Chicago Press.

Pai, A. (Ed.). (2009). *Valmiki's Ramayana: The Great Indian Epic (Amar Chitra Katha)*. Mumbai: Amar Chitra Katha.

Pai, R. (2015). *The Gita: For children*. Gurugram: Hachette.

Pai, R. (2019a). *The Gita for Children*. Gurgaon: Hachette India.

Pai, R. (2019b). *The Vedas and Upanishads for Children*. Gurugram: Hachette India.

Pallapothu, V. (2018, September 3). *Feminist Re-Tellings of the Ramayana*. Retrieved from Medium: https://medium.com/the-red-elephant-foundation/feminist-re-tellings-of-the-ramayana

Pande, M. (2018, May 26). *Angry Hanuman: This Viral Image That Won Modi's Praise Symbolises Today's Aggressive, Macho India*. Retrieved from Scroll.in: https://scroll.in/article/879108/angry-hanuman-this-viral-image-that-won-modis-praise-symbolises-todays-aggressive-macho-india

Parekh, M. (1943). *Shri Vallabhacharya: Life, Teaching and Movement*. Rajkot: M. C. Parekh.

Parrinder, E. G. (1982). *Avatar and Incarnation*. Oxford: Oxford University Press.

Patel, V. (2022). *Kaikeyi*. London: Orbit.

Pattanaik, D. (2002). *The Man Who Was a Woman and Other Queer Tales from Hindu Lore*. Abingdon: Routledge.

Pennington, B. (2022). Did Women Have to Jump into the Fire When Their Husbands Dies? In S. Ramey (Ed.), *Hinduism in 5 Minutes* (pp. 225–7). Sheffield: Equinox.

Pennington, B. K. (2005). *Was Hinduism Invented? Britons, Indians, and the Colonial Construction of Religion*. New York: Oxford University Press.

Pew Research Center. (2021). *Religion in India: Tolerance and Segregation*. Washington, DC: Pew Research Center.

Prabhupada, A. B. (1972). *Bhagavad Gita: As It Is*. New York: Collier Books.

Prabhupada, S. (2005). *On Chanting*. Retrieved from Krishna.com: https://web.archive.org/web/20050305201909/http://www.krishna.com:80/main.php?id=316

Prill, S. (2022). Is Yoga Important in Hinduism? In S. Ramey (Ed.), *Hinduism in 5 Minutes* (pp. 161–3). Sheffield: Equinox.

Prinja, N. K. (1996). *Explaining Hindu Dharma: A Guide for Teachers*. Thornton Heath: Vishwa Hundu Parishad (UK).

Prinja, N. K. (2003). *Hindu dharma. A guide for teachers* (2nd edn). Thornton Heath: Vishwa Hindu Parishad.

Puri, R. I. (Ed.). (2018). *Shakti. Tales of the Mother Goddess*. Mumbai: Amar Chitra Katha Pvt Ltd.
Radhakrishnan, S. (1968). *The principal Upanisads* (2nd impression). London: George Allen.
Raghunathan, V., & Eswaran, M. (2012). *Ganesha on the Dashboard*. Haryana: Penguin.
Rajan, R. S. (1998). Is the Hindu Gooddess a Feminist? *Economic and Political Weekly, 33*(44), 34–8.
Rajeswari, D. R. (1989). *Sakti Iconography*. New Delhi: Intellectual Publishing House.
Ramanuja. (1978). *Vedartha Sangraha of Sri Ramanujacarya* (S. Raghavachar, Trans.). Karnataka: Sri Ramakrishna Ashrama Mysore.
Rani, V. (2020, November 12). *Cardi B Apologises for Depicting Hindu Goddess Durga on Magazine Cover*. Retrieved from Vice: https://www.vice.com/en/article/akdgbb/cardib-posed-as-hindu-goddess-durga
Ranjan, A., Ahmed, B., Das, R., Gupta, M., Jain, H., Natesh, S., & Rao, R. (Eds.). (2017). *The Illustrated Mahabharata: The Definitive Guide to India's Greatest Epic*. London: Dorling Kindersley.
Raypole, C. (2020, August 18). *An Intro to Kundalini Meditation*. Retrieved from Healthline: https://www.healthline.com/health/kundalini-meditation
Rhodes, C. (2010). *Invoking Lakshmi: The Goddess of Wealth in Song and Ceremony*. Albany: State University of New York.
Rhude, K. (2018). *Hinduism Case Study – Gender: The Third Gender and Hijras*. Cambridge: Harvard Divinity School.
Rosen, S. (2006). *Essential Hinduism*. Westport: Praeger Publishers.
Rushdie, S. (1991). *Haroun and the sea of stories*. London: Granta.
Sadhguru. (2014). *Shiva – Ultimate Outlaw*. Coimbatore: Isha Foundation.
Sage Valmiki's Abdhut Ramayan (Original Text with Complete English Rendering, Explanatory Notes & Appendices). (2009). (A. K. Chhawchharia, Trans.). Faisabad: Ajai Kumar Chhawchharia.
Sand, E. R. (1990). The Legend of Puṇḍarīka: The Founder of Pandharpur. In H. Bakker (Ed.), *The History of Sacred Places in India as Reflected in Traditional Literature* (pp. 33–61). Leiden: Brill.
Satija, G. (2023, July 1). *Adipurush Case: Om Raut And Manoj Muntashir Ordered To Appear Before High Court On July 27*. Retrieved from India Times: https://www.indiatimes.com/entertainment/bollywood/adipurush-case-om-raut-and-manoj-muntashir-ordered-to-appear-before-high-court-on-july-27-607714.html
Schweig, G. M. (2012). In Quest of the "Theological" Prabhupada. In G. M. Schweig (Ed.), *A Living Theology of Krishna Bhakti: Essential Teachings of A. C. Bhaktivedanta Swami Prabhupada* (pp. 21–37). Oxford: Oxford Academic.
Sharma, A. (2000). *Classical Hindu Thought: An Introduction*. Oxford: Oxford University Press.
Sharma, A. (2008). Asramas (Stage of Life). In D. Cush, C. Robinson, & M. York (Eds.), *Encyclopedia of Hinduism* (pp. 48–9). Abingdon: Routledge.
Sharma, K. L. (2019). *Caste, social inequality and mobility in rural India: Reconceptualising the Indian village*. Delhi: SAGE Publications.
Sharma, K. N. (1990). Varna and Jati in Indian Traditional Perspective. *Sociological Bulletin, 39*(1/2), 15–31.
Sharma, S. (2003). *The Brilliance of Hinduism*. New Delhi: Diamond Pocket Books.
Sharpe, E. (1985). *The Universal Gita: Western Images of the Bhagavad Gita: A Bicentenary Survey*. La Salle: Open Court.

Shree Swaminarayan Temple - Bhuj. (n.d.). *Swaminarayana Mantra*. Retrieved from Shree Swaminarayan Temple - Bhuj: https://www.swaminarayan.faith/short-stories/swaminarayana-mantra

Shri Swaminarayan Mandir London. (2023). *School Visits*. Retrieved from BAPS Swaminarayan Sanstha: https://londonmandir.baps.org/visit-us/school-visits/

Singh, M. N. (2018). Revisiting Caste in the Philosophy of Swami Vivekananda. *Contemporary Voice of Dalit, 10*(1), 1–9.

Sivananda, S. (1945). *Lord Shiva and His Worship*. Rikhikesh: Sivanda Publication League.

Sivananda, S. (1997). *Practice of Brahmacharaya*. Uttar Pradesh: Divine Life Society.

Smith, J. Z. (2004). *Relating Religion: Essays in the Study of Religion*. Chicago: University of Chicago Press.

Sridhar, N. (2020, September 29). *Hindu View of Menstruation Part I: Menstruation as Ashaucha*. Retrieved from Indica Today: https://www.indica.today/long-reads/hindu-view-menstruation-menstruation-ashaucha/

Srinivasa Iyengar, K. (1987). *Sitayana*. Madras: Samata Books.

Srinivasan, S. (1971). *Stories of Creation from the Brahma Purana*. Mumbai: Amar Chitra Katha Pvt Ltd.

Stefon, M., & Doniger, W. (2015, March 15). *Vedanta*. Retrieved from Britannica: https://www.britannica.com/topic/Vedanta

Subramuniyaswami, S. (2001). *Dancing with Siva*. Kapaa: Himalayan Academy.

Sullivan, B. (1997). *Historical dictionary of hinduism*. London: Scarecrow Press.

Swaminarayan. (2010). *Vachanamrut*. Bhuj: Shree Swaminarayan Mandir Bhuj.

Telford and Wrekin LA. (2021). *Telford and Wrekin Agreed Syllabus*. Telford: Telford and Wrekin LA.

Thapar, R. (2005). Syndicated Hinduism. In G.-D. Sontheimer, & H. Kulke (Eds.), *Hinduism Reconsidered* (pp. 54–81). New Delhi: Manohar.

Tharoor, S. (2021). *Why I am a Hindu*. London: C Hurst & Co Publishers Ltd.

The Gospel of Sri Ramakrishna (Ninth edition). (2000). (S. Nikhilananda, Trans.). New York: Ramakrishna-Vivekananda Center.

The Song of the Goddess. The Devi Gita: Spiritual Counsel of the Great Goddess. (2002). (C. Mackenzie Brown, Trans.). New York: State University of New York Press.

Theos Think Tank. (2021). *Nobody Stands Nowhere*. Retrieved from: https://www.youtube.com/watch?v=AFRxKF-Jdos (accessed 29 January 2024).

Tirimular. (n.d.). *Tirumantiram: English Translation of the Tamil Spiritual Classic*. Retrieved from Himalayan Academy: https://www.google.com/url?client=internal-element-cse&cx=017908501278066662245:7zog_atzphi&q=https://www.himalayanacademy.com/media/books/tirumantiram/Tirumantiram.pdf&sa=U&ved=2ahUKEwjU-LrFivr_AhVzTqQEHZG7DZ4QFnoECAIQAQ&usg=AOvVaw3gfyVPlV0KFJGc-mrT4xPA

Tomalin, E., & Singh, J. (2018). *A Survey of Hindu Buildings in England Project Number 7078*. Leeds: Historic England.

Trivedi, Y. (2015). *Bhagwan Swaminarayan: The Story of His Life*. Ahmedabad: Swaminarayan Aksharpith.

Truschke, A. (2023). Hindu: A History. *Comparative Studies in Society and History*, 1–26.

Tully, M. (1992). *No Full Stops in India*. London: Penguin.

Vanamali. (2008). *Shakti. Realm of the Divine Mother*. Rochester: Inner Traditions.

Vanamali. (2010). *Hanuman: The Devotion and Power of the Monkey God*. Rochester: Inner Traditions.

Vanamali. (2012). *The Complete Life of Krishna: Based on the Earliest Oral Traditions and the Sacred Scriptures*. Rochester: Inner Traditions.

Vanamali. (2013). *Shiva: Stories and Teachings from the Shiva Mahapurana*. Rochester: Inner Traditions.

Vanamali. (2014). *The Complete Life of Rama: Based on Valmikis Ramayana and the Earliest Oral Traditions*. Rochester: Inner Traditions.

Vanita, R., & Kidwai, S. (2000). *Same-Sex Love in India: Readings from Literature and History*. New York: St. Martin's Press.

Vireswarananda. (1936). *Brahma Sutras According To Sri Sankara*. Almora: Advaita Ashrama.

Vivekananda, S. (1989). *The Complete Works of Swami Vivekananda*. Mayavata: Advaita Ashrama.

Voiels, V. (1998). *Hinduism: A New Approach*. Abingdon: Hodder and Stoughton.

Volga. (2016). *The Liberation of Sita*. London: Harper.

von Stietencron, H. (2005). Hinduism: On the Proper Use of a Deceptive Term. In G.-D. Sontheimer, & H. Kulke (Eds.), *Hinduism Reconsidered* (pp. 32–53). New Delhi: Manohar.

White, D. (2012). *Yoga in Practice*. Princeton: Princeton University Press.

Wilhelm, A. D. (2003). *Tritiya-Prakriti: People of the Third Sex: Understanding Homosexuality, Transgender Identity, and Intersex Conditions Through Hinduism*. Philadelphia: Xlibris.

Williams, R. (2019). *An Introduction to Swaminarayan Hinduism* (Third Edition). Cambridge: University of Cambridge Press.

Williamson, L. (2010). *Transcendent in America: Hindu-Inspired Meditation Movements as New Religion*. New York: New York University Press.

Winternitz, M. (1927). *A History of Indian Literature, Volume 1*. Calcutta: University of Calcutta.

Wintersgill, B. (1993). Learning About World Religions in the Basic Curriculum. In C. Erricker (Ed.), *Teaching World Religions: A Teacher's Handbook Produced by the SHAP Working Party on World Religions in Education* (pp. 42–4). Oxford: Heinemann.

Wittgenstein, L. (1968). *Philosophical Investigations*. New York: MacMillan.

Witzel, M. (1999). Substrate Languages in Old Indo-Aryan (Ṛgvedic, Middle and Late Vedic). *Electronic Journal of Vedic Studies*, 5(1), 1–68.

Witzel, M. (2005). Indocentrism. In E. Bryant, & L. Patton (Eds.), *The Indo-Aryan Controversy: Evidence and Inference in Indian History* (pp. 341–404). Abingdon: Routledge.

Wood, B. (2020). Teaching Worldviews at GCSE. In M. Chater (Ed.), *Reforming RE: Power and Knowledge in a Worldviews Curriculum* (pp. 165–8). Woodbridge: John Catt Educational Ltd.

Yeomans, R. (1978). Religious Education Through Art. In R. Jackson (Ed.), *In Perspectives on World Religions* (pp. 51–72). London: University of London, School of Oriental and African Studies.

Zeller, B. (n.d.). *Rites and Ceremonies*. Retrieved from Patheos: https://www.patheos.com/library/iskcon-hare-krishna/ritual-worship-devotion-symbolism/rites-and-ceremonies

Zelliot, E. (2003). A Medieval Encounter Between Hindu and Muslim: Eknath's Drama-Poem Hindu-Turk Samvad. In R. Eaton (Ed.), *India's Islamic Traditions, 711–1750* (pp. 64–82). New Delhi: Oxford University Press.

Index

Adipurush (film) 88, 193
Advaita 24, 26, 41, 47
Agni 11, 37, 97, 121, 123, 139
ahimsa 34, 145, 153–6, 158–61, 164
Angry Hanuman 81, 193
Antayarami 47, 50–1
aparigraha 34, 153, 164
artefacts 82–3
artha 13, 76, 107–8, 164
arti 135, 137–8, 173, 176
arts, use of in classroom 81–6
Ascetic Reform Period 12
ashramas 33, 35–7, 42, 108, 146–8, 162, 167, 175
astanga yoga 110, 175
asteya 34, 153, 161
atman 26–7, 31, 49–51, 58, 71, 100, 103, 105–6, 109, 115–16
Aum/Om 49–50, 63
avatar 17, 63–5, 73, 76, 120, 126, 143
    of Shiva 23, 73–4, 78–9
    of Vishnu 17–18, 20, 33, 63, 78, 89, 95–6, 100, 126, 143, 174

Bhagavad Gita 26, 33, 35, 38, 50, 58, 63, 90, 91, 98, 104, 111, 118, 119, 125, 127, 139–40, 158, 161
Bhagavan 47–8, 51–5, 112
bhajan 135, 137
bhakti 12, 15–19, 21, 24, 27, 32, 45, 110–12, 132–3, 138, 148, 171–3, 176
bhakti yoga/bhakti marga, see bhakti
Bhaktivedanta, A.C. Swami Prabhupada 98, 171–2
Bharita Janata Party (BJP) 159, 193–4
bhuvana-jnana, see cosmology
Bloom, Colin 194
Bochasanwasi Akshar Purushottam Swaminarayan Sanstha (BAPS) 176–7, 184–6
Brahma 52, 53, 56–66, 77, 86–7, 93–4, 98, 102, 105, 120, 123–6, 128, 145
Brahma Sutras 26, 41, 110

Brahmacharya (celibacy) 34, 161–2
Brahmacharya (ashrama) 35, 146
Brahman 12, 16, 20–4, 26–7, 41, 47–53, 61, 66, 72–4, 93–4, 104–6, 109, 112, 113, 142, 157–8, 175
brahmanda 94
brahmin 12, 21, 37, 38, 40, 42, 47, 122, 131, 147, 160, 173
British Empire 2–3, 6–8, 10, 39–43, 155, 166, 170, 181–3
Buddhism xii, 1, 12, 13, 15, 24, 26, 61, 64, 90, 110, 119, 190

Caitanya 13
Cardi B 87–8
caste 5, 7, 17, 20, 34, 36–45, 105, 111, 160, 173, 183–91
Census Data 15, 39, 41, 42, 182
Christianity 1, 14, 15, 41–3, 47, 88, 129, 132, 133, 169, 170, 190
Classical Hinduism 12–13
Colonialism, see British Empire
Commission on Religious Education xiii, xiv
cosmic egg, see brahmanda
Cosmogony 11, 93–4, 102, 104, 124
Cosmology 11, 31, 61, 93–104, 124
cultural appropriation 86–8, 143, 148–9

Dadu 13
dallit, see untouchable
darshanas 13, 24–7, 32, 118
Das, Rasamandala 19, 20, 24, 47, 50, 56, 57, 61, 119, 173
dasamarga 19
dashavataras 63–4
dharma 4, 7, 13, 14, 26, 31–45, 63, 65–6, 76, 77, 91, 93, 101–4, 107–9, 111–13, 115, 117–19, 125, 126, 131, 147, 153, 156, 159, 161, 162, 164, 167, 175, 196
dharmashastras 32–3, 118, 122
dharmasutras 32–4
Divine feminine, see Shakti
Diwali xii, 9, 76, 128, 142–4, 189

Doniger, Wendy   3, 8–12, 26, 39, 102, 120
dualism   16, 19, 25, 50, 51, 104
Dvaita Vedanta   26–7, 47, 78
Dvapara Yuga   98–101

Eck, Diana   133, 135
environmental issues   97, 156–8, 175
Epics, see Itihasa
essentialism   xiv
experiential activities   84, 149–50

feminist approaches   76–8, 90–1, 164–8
festivals   97, 129, 131–2, 136, 142–5, 183, 186
Flood, Gavin   7, 16–18, 21, 24, 107, 112

Gandhi, Mohandas   153–7, 160, 180
Ganesh   23, 79, 84–7, 112, 126, 131, 139, 144, 179
Ganga   41, 54, 71, 144, 157
Gaudiya Vaishnavas   16–17, 144, 171–3
Gautama, Siddhartha   xii, 12, 41–2, 64, 96, 129
Go Dharmic   156, 157, 159
Goddess, see Shakti
Grihastha   36, 108, 146, 162
gunas   25, 26, 95–7, 106, 107, 135, 139
Guru Nanak   3, 41, 179

Hanuman   73, 78–81, 88, 91–2, 127, 130, 144, 179, 193
Harappan Civilization   2, 9
Hare Krishna   17, 136, 171–3
hathayoga   71, 139–41
Havan   131, 136
Hindu (definition of)   xii–xiv, 2–6, 14
Hindu Council UK   170
Hindu Forum of Britain   170–1
Hinduism   xii–xv, 1–2, 6–27
Hinduism, representation of in schools   40, 189–92, 195–6
Hinduphobia   188, 192
Hindutva   193–4
Holi   143–4, 148, 195
Holt, James   xiv, 15, 41, 61, 82, 129, 132, 148, 190–2, 195
hooks, bell   xiii
humanism   xv

India   xii, 2–7, 10, 13, 18, 19, 25, 39–43, 55–6, 78, 81, 88, 90, 106, 115, 129, 131, 136, 141, 143, 148, 154–6, 158–9, 162–4, 166, 171, 174, 180–2, 184, 187–8, 191–4

Indus Valley Civilisation, see Harappan Civilization
Insight UK   10, 39, 179
International Society of Krishna Consciousness (ISKCON)   14, 17, 50, 57, 65, 118, 157, 171–4, 184
intersectionality   xiii–xv
Ishvara   23, 52, 66, 72, 174
Ishvara-pranidhana   34
Islam   xii, xv, 1, 4, 13, 15, 170
Itihasa   38, 117, 122–30

Jackson, Robert   xiii, 82, 191
jagadutpatti, see cosmogony
Jainism   6, 12, 13, 15, 24, 26, 90, 119, 150
jati   27, 38, 43
jiva, see atman
jivanmukti   109, 111, 114
jnana yoga/jnana marga   110, 112–13

Kali Yuga   98–103, 121
Kalikula   21–2
Kalki   21–2, 53, 54, 165
kalpa   98, 102, 118
kama   13, 76, 107–8, 162–3
Karma   12, 26, 31, 44, 68, 105, 106, 109–10, 115–16, 134, 153, 157, 158
karma yoga/karma marga   80, 110–11, 115
Kashmiri Shaivism   19–20
kirtan, see bhajan
Knott, Kim   9, 37, 49, 51
Krishna   17, 20, 51–2, 57–8, 64–5, 74, 78, 89, 93, 96, 101, 105, 112, 126, 136, 143–4, 160, 171–4, 176–8
kriyamana karma   110
kshatriya   37–8, 61, 62, 128
Kurma   63, 96, 123

Lakhani, Jay   42
Lakshmi   16, 20, 53, 66, 74–6, 125, 142–5, 176
language, use of   xiv, 4, 14–15, 74–5, 82
Laws of Manu   4, 32, 36, 39–41, 163
Laxmi Narayan Dev Gadi   176–7
Linga   9, 18–20, 72–3, 97, 123, 134, 145
Lingyats   20

Mahabharata   12, 38, 44, 61–3, 98–101, 103, 107, 117–19, 121, 123, 125–8, 140, 153, 158, 161, 163
Mahashivaratri   144, 145
mandir   14, 36, 61, 75, 78, 81, 86, 97–8, 122, 134–8, 172, 176–9, 183–7, 192

Index

Manu 32, 60–1, 102
Marx, Karl 44
Maslow, Abraham 114
Matsya 63, 96, 123
Maya 24, 26, 51, 53–4, 61–2, 68, 70, 104, 109, 171, 174
meditation 19, 21, 27, 50, 70–2, 110, 113–14, 132, 136, 139–42, 149, 150
menstruation 121, 145, 167
Michaels, Axel 9–13
Mimamsa 26
Mleccha 4–5
Modern Hinduism 2, 7, 9, 14, 121
Modi, Narendra xii, 9, 193–4
moksha 13, 25–7, 31, 36, 70–1, 76, 104–11, 113–16, 132, 139–42, 148, 153
moksha chitram 115–16
monism 50, 51
Mount Meru 62, 94
mukta 109
mumukshutvam 113
murti 60, 62, 67–8, 78, 83–5, 89, 133–7, 176
Muslims xii, 3–5, 13, 193, 194

Nar Narayan Dev Gadi 176
Narasimha 64, 96, 143–4
nastika 12, 15, 24, 26, 118–19
National Council of Hindu Temples 170
Navaratri 144–5
nirguna 16, 17, 23, 48, 50, 57, 61, 77, 133
Niyama 33, 34, 45, 139, 153
Northern Sant Tradition 17
Nyaya 24–6

objects, use of in classroom 83–6, 133–5

pancayatanapuja 23–4
panchamahabhutas 95–7, 135, 137
Parasurama 64, 96
Pashupatis 19
Pew Research Center 159, 160
pithas 55–6, 70, 72, 148
pluralism 56–7
Prakriti 24–5, 53–4, 72, 96, 105–7, 157
prana 91, 135
Pravachan 136
prayer 60, 74, 115, 119, 133, 136, 138, 141, 146, 149
pre-Vedic period 9–10, 18, 65
puja 24, 38, 132–3, 135–8, 142, 143, 175, 187
Puranas 13, 23, 65, 70, 89, 117–19, 122–5, 129, 136

Purusartha 107–14
Purusha 25, 37–8, 42, 50–2, 65, 104–7, 114

rajas 96, 106, 113–14, 139, 141
Raksha Bandhan 144–5
Rama 17, 20, 37–8, 57, 64–5, 74, 76–80, 89–91, 96, 100, 112, 124, 127–30, 143–4, 166, 171, 174, 188
Rama, Cult of 17
Ramakrishna 22, 57, 63, 178, 180
Ramanuja 16, 27, 51, 52
Ramayana xii, 12, 37, 38, 44–5, 64, 77–9, 86, 88–91, 117–19, 123, 127–30, 166
Rashtriya Swayamsevak Sangh (RSS) 193
Ravana 76–8, 91, 108, 127, 130, 143
religion, concept of x–xv, 1–2, 4–7
Rig Veda 3, 11, 37–8, 49, 66, 76, 95, 104, 117, 118, 120, 136, 161
rites of passage 136, 147
River Indus 3
rta 93

sadharana dharma 33–4
saguna 16, 24, 47, 61
Salt March 155
same sex relationships 162–3
samkhya 24–5, 96
samsara 26, 90, 103, 104, 107–12, 115–16
samskaras 42, 121, 145–7, 167
Sanatana Dharma 1, 7, 14, 31, 35, 117, 169, 192
sanchita karma 110
sanmarga 19
sannyasin 36, 161, 175
Sanoy Chakravorty 2, 8, 27, 41
santosha 34
Saraswati 53, 60, 112, 139, 178
sati (deity) 53–5, 70, 148
sati (practice) 166–7, 189, 190
satputramdarga 19
sattva 96, 106, 139
satya 5, 153, 161
Satya Yuga 100
satyagraha 155–6
sects of Hinduism 1, 5, 13, 22–3, 56, 134
seva 111, 134
Shaiva Asceticism 20
Shaiva Siddhanta 15, 19
Shaivism 13, 15, 18–20, 52, 60, 65, 73–4, 169
Shakti 20–3, 52–5, 61, 70, 72, 74, 124, 142, 144, 145, 165–6

Shaktism   15, 20–2, 52, 54, 74, 77, 169
Shankara   13, 22–3, 26, 40–1, 51, 73, 113
shauca   34
Shilpa Shastras   118, 134
Shiva   9–11, 13, 17–23, 52–8, 60–2, 65–74, 77, 78, 86, 93–4, 97, 104, 110, 112, 124, 128–9, 133, 136, 142–5, 148, 178
Shiva Lingum, *see* Shiva
Shiva Nataraj, *see* Shiva
Shiva Yogiraj, *see* Shiva
shudra   37, 61, 124, 160
Sikhism   xii–xiii, xv, 1, 3, 15, 41–2, 194
The Simpsons   86
Sita   20, 37, 38, 54, 74–81, 90, 108, 124, 127, 130, 143, 165, 166
Smarta   5, 15, 22–4
Smith, Jonathan Z.   xi
smrti   13, 32, 41, 117, 118
soul, *see* atman
Srikula   20–1
Sri Vaishnavas   16–17
Sriyantra   21, 22
sruti   13, 112, 117, 118
storytelling   88–91
stridharma   33, 35, 36
svadharma   34–5
svadhyaya   27, 34
Swaminarayan   52, 63, 88, 118, 120, 121, 171, 174–8, 184–7
Syndicated Hinduism   7, 8, 14

tamas   96, 106, 139
tandava   67
tantra   15, 18, 20–2, 67, 68, 71, 114, 141–2, 176
Tendulkar, Sachin   89, 196
Thapar, Romila   1, 8 15
Theos Think Tank   xiii
transgender   163–4
Treta Yuga   98–101
Trimurti   16, 53, 56–7, 60, 61, 65
Tryambaka mantra   65
Tulsidas   13, 81, 193
tupas   34

United Kingdom   2, 3, 155, 170–1, 180–96
untouchables   38, 39, 41–4, 167
Upanishads   11, 12, 23, 26, 44, 49, 113, 117–20, 136, 157

Vaikuntha   62, 101
Vaisheshika   26
Vaishnanvism   5, 13, 15–20, 52, 58, 60–2, 73, 74, 78, 118, 133, 144, 169, 171–4
vaishya   37, 61, 160
Valmiki   38, 65, 77, 123, 127, 128, 166
Vamana   64, 96, 100, 123, 143
Vanamali   20, 52–3, 65–7, 70, 72, 78–80
Vanaprastha   36, 122, 147
varna   4, 32, 35, 37–45, 61, 104
varnashramadharma   13, 37–42, 104
Veda Vyasa   120, 123, 125–6
Vedanta   16, 17, 24, 26, 57, 113, 172, 178
Vedas   11–13, 16, 24–7, 32, 35, 41, 51, 60, 66–8, 70, 87, 95, 98, 101, 105, 113, 117–22, 124, 126, 128, 129, 136, 145, 158, 162, 175, 177
Vedic period   10–12, 120
vegetarianism   20, 156, 158–60, 168, 182, 188
videhamukti   109–10, 114
Viraga   27, 113
Virashaivism   20
Vishnu   7, 11, 13, 16–18, 20, 23, 33, 38, 51–2, 55–8, 60–7, 73–9, 89, 93–4, 96, 98, 100–3, 104, 112, 120, 123, 124, 126, 135, 142, 145, 171, 174
Visistadvaita Vedanta   26–7
Vithoba, Cult of   17
Viveka   113
Vivekananda   26, 57–8, 136, 178, 181

Wittgenstein, Ludwig   8
women, role of   36, 90–1, 101, 164–8
worldviews   xi, xiii–xv, 132, 148, 149, 160, 168, 169, 179, 189, 192, 194–5

yamas   34, 139–40, 153–4
yoga   19–20, 25, 35, 45, 69–72, 80, 106, 110–11, 113–14, 127, 139–42, 148–50, 156, 175
yuga   98–103, 121, 201